Beyond Gallipoli

Beyond Gallipoli

New Perspectives on Anzac

Edited by Raelene Frances and Bruce Scates

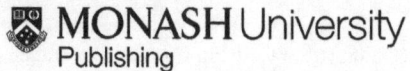

© Copyright 2016
Copyright of this collection in its entirety is held by Raelene Frances and Bruce Scates.
Copyright of the individual chapters is held by the respective chapter authors.
All rights reserved. Apart from any uses permitted by Australia's Copyright Act 1968, no part of this book may be reproduced by any process without prior written permission from the copyright owners. Inquiries should be directed to the publisher.

Monash University Publishing
Matheson Library and Information Services Building
40 Exhibition Walk
Monash University
Clayton, Victoria 3800, Australia
www.publishing.monash.edu

Monash University Publishing brings to the world publications which advance the best traditions of humane and enlightened thought.

Monash University Publishing titles pass through a rigorous process of independent peer review.

www.publishing.monash.edu/books/bg-9781925495102.html

Series: Australian History
Series Editor / Board: Sean Scalmer

Design: Les Thomas

Front cover image: Exhibition Giant, *Gallipoli: The Scale of Our War*, Private Colin Airlie Warden (1890–1915), Auckland Infantry Battalion. Photograph by Michael Hall. Courtesy of the Museum of New Zealand Te Papa Tongarewa.

Back cover image: 'Peace' ferry, with warship in the background, Anzac Cove, 2015. Photo by Bruce Scates..

> **National Library of Australia Cataloguing-in-Publication entry:**
>
> Title: Beyond Gallipoli : new perspectives on Anzac / edited by Raelene Frances, Bruce Scates.
> ISBN: 9781925495102 (paperback)
> Subjects: World War, 1914-1918--Social aspects--Australia.
> World War, 1914-1918--Social aspects--New Zealand.
> World War, 1914-1918--Social aspects--Turkey.
> War and society.
> Other Creators/Contributors:
> Frances, Raelene, editor.
> Scates, Bruce, editor.
> Dewey Number: 940.31

Printed in Australia by Griffin Press, an Accredited ISO AS/NZS 14001:2004 Environmental Management System printer.

The paper this book is printed on is certified against the Forest Stewardship Council ® Standards. Griffin Press holds FSC chain of custody certification SGS-COC-005088. FSC promotes environmentally responsible, socially beneficial and economically viable management of the world's forests.

CONTENTS

Contributors viii

Introduction: Beyond Gallipoli – New Perspectives on Anzac. 1
Raelene Frances and Bruce Scates

PART 1: CHALLENGING HISTORIES. 11

Chapter 1
The Myths of Gallipoli 13
Robin Prior

Chapter 2
Between Memory and History: Remembering Johnnies, Mehmets
and the Armenians 21
Jenny Macleod and Gizem Tongo

PART 2: MEDIAS OF REMEMBRANCE. 35

Chapter 3
What's the Story?: Journalism Ethics and the Anzac Centenary 37
Sharon Mascall-Dare and Matthew Ricketson

Chapter 4
Uncanny Valleys and Anzac Avatars: Scaling a Postdigital Gallipoli. 55
Tom Sear

Chapter 5
Commentary: The New War Ecology. 82
Andrew Hoskins

PART 3: LITERARY REPRESENTATIONS 87

Chapter 6
*Traitor/*Traitor? 89
Peter Pierce

Chapter 7
The 'Enemy' at Gallipoli: Perceptions of the Adversary in Turkish,
Australian and New Zealand Literatures 96
A. Candan Kirişci

PART 4: ART, MUSEUMS AND ARTEFACTS................... 117

Chapter 8
'A fine ideal and an imperishable memory': George Lambert's
Painting *ANZAC, the Landing 1915* 119
Janda Gooding

Chapter 9
'Filling the Void': Artistic Interpretations of the Empty Battlefield 131
Paul Gough

Chapter 10
Lest We Forget: Presentation, Commemoration and Memorialisation
of the Great War... 153
Kevin Fewster

Chapter 11
Brothers in Arms: Gordon and Robin Harper and the
Anatomy of Bravery 168
Jock Phillips

Contents

PART 5: GROUNDING MEMORY – ENCOUNTERS WITH LANDSCAPE .. 189

Chapter 12
The Caribou Trail: Commemorating the Royal Newfoundland
Regiment in the First World War................................ 191
Raynald Harvey Lemelin

Chapter 13
Archaeological Landscapes at Gallipoli: The Anzac Area at Arıburnu .. 203
Jessie Birkett-Rees

PART 6: ANZAC'S EARLY DAYS 221

Chapter 14
Anzac Day's Early Rituals 223
Bill Gammage

Chapter 15
The ABC of War: Early Children's Histories of Anzac 239
Frank Bongiorno

Index 251

CONTRIBUTORS

Jessie Birkett-Rees is a Lecturer in Ancient Cultures (Archaeology) at Monash University (Melbourne). Jessie is a landscape archaeologist who specialises in non-invasive archaeological techniques and the application of geospatial science to archaeological contexts. Her fieldwork and research have concentrated on the changing relationships between people and landscape in Anatolia, the Caucasus and Australia. Jessie worked as an archaeologist on the tri-nation Joint Historical and Archaeological Survey team investigating the northern Gallipoli battlefields (2010-2014).

Frank Bongiorno is Associate Professor in History at the Australian National University. Since 2011, he has been working with a team led by Monash University on an Australian Research Council-funded project 'Anzac Day at Home and Abroad: A Centenary History of Australia's National Day'. He is co-editor of *Labour and the Great War: The Australian Working Class and the Making of Anzac* and has contributed to several other recent or forthcoming collections on the Great War and its legacies for Australia. His most recent books are *The Sex Lives of Australians: A History* and *The Eighties: The Decade That Transformed Australia*.

Kevin Fewster, AM has been Director of Royal Museums Greenwich since 2007. Before moving to the UK he was Director of the Powerhouse Museum and Australian National Maritime Museum (both in Sydney), after starting his museum career in 1984 as inaugural Director of the South Australian Maritime Museum. In a previous life he edited for publication CEW Bean's Gallipoli diaries and co-authored the book *Gallipoli – the Turkish Story* (1985 and 2003, with a Turkish edition published in 2005).

Raelene Frances is Dean of Arts and Professor of History at Monash University. She has published widely on the history of work, women's history, Aboriginal/European contact history, religious and community history and has also co-edited several collections of essays on Australian and New Zealand history, including *Labour and the Great War*. Her prize-winning books include *The Politics of Work* and *Women and the Great War* (co-authored with Bruce Scates). Her history of prostitution, *Selling Sex*, was short-listed for the Ernest Scott Prize. She is a Fellow of the Academy of Social Sciences in Australia.

CONTRIBUTORS

Bill Gammage AM is an Emeritus Professor at the Australian National University and Fellow of the Academy of Social Sciences in Australia. He wrote *The Broken Years* on Australian soldiers in the Great War (1974+), *An Australian in the First World War* (1976), *Narrandera Shire* (1986), *The Sky Travellers on the 1938-39 Hagen-Sepik Patrol in New Guinea* (1998), and *The Biggest Estate on Earth: How Aborigines made Australia* (2011). He co-edited the *Australians 1938* volume of the Bicentennial History of Australia (1988), and three books about Australians in World War 1. He was historical adviser to Peter Weir's film *Gallipoli* and to several documentaries.

Janda Gooding was appointed Assistant Director, Collections, Content and Exhibitions at the National Museum of Australia, Canberra in 2014. Previously, she worked at the Australian War Memorial from 2005-2014 and, as a Curator at the Art Gallery of Western Australia from 1979 to 2005 where she curated many thematic, retrospective and survey exhibitions of Australian and International artists. Dr Gooding completed in 2009 a book *Gallipoli Revisited* on the importance of First World War battlefield landscapes and the intersection of landscape and historical memory in art and photography associated with Gallipoli. She is currently researching Australia's First World War official photography program.

Paul Gough is Pro Vice-Chancellor and Vice-President of RMIT University. A painter, broadcaster and writer he has exhibited globally and is represented in the permanent collections Imperial War Museum, London; Canadian War Museum, Ottawa; National War Memorial, New Zealand. Amongst his publications are a monograph on war artist Stanley Spencer: *Journey to Burghclere*, 2006; *A Terrible Beauty: British Artists in the First World War* in 2010; *Your Loving Friend*, the correspondence between Stanley Spencer and Desmond Chute, in 2011, and *Brothers in Arms*, a study of John and Paul Nash in 2014.

Andrew Hoskins is Interdisciplinary Research Professor in the College of Social Sciences at the University of Glasgow, UK. He is founding Editor-in-Chief of the Sage journal of *Memory Studies* and founding Co-Editor of the Palgrave Macmillan book series *Memory Studies*. His latest book is (with John Tulloch) *Risk and Hyperconnectvity: Media and Memories of Neoliberalism* (Oxford University Press, 2016). Project site: http://archivesofwar.com.

A. Candan Kirişci holds a Ph.D. degree from the Department of Western Languages and Literatures at Bogazici University, Istanbul, Turkey. Her dissertation topic is titled 'Nation-building and Gallipoli: Representations in Turkish, Australian and New Zealand Literatures'. Articles based on her research have been published in Turkey and New Zealand. Dr. Kirişci has been based in Washington, DC since 2013.

Raynald Harvey Lemelin is a Professor in the School of Outdoor Recreation, Parks and Tourism at Lakehead University, Canada. His research on cultural dissonance and the management of battlefields has been published in journal articles and book chapters, and conference proceedings. Dr. Lemelin has also integrated the management of cultural heritage and experiential education into various tourism field courses offered at Lakehead University.

Jenny Macleod is a Senior Lecturer in 20th Century History at the University of Hull. Her PhD was published as *Reconsidering Gallipoli* (2004), and she has now returned to the subject of Gallipoli, its commemoration and the relationship between the memory of war and national identity in her new book, *Gallipoli*, for Oxford University Press. In it she compares the way the campaign has been remembered in all the belligerent nations, including Turkey. She is the co-founder of the International Society for First World War Studies, a network of 300 academics and postgrads from 27 countries.

Sharon Mascall-Dare is an Adjunct Associate Professor of Journalism at the University of Canberra. She is also a BBC World Service documentary producer and a Military Public Affairs Officer serving in the Australian Army Reserve. Her award-winning works include the BBC documentary *Anzac* broadcast in 2012. Her academic interests focus on journalistic ethics regarding Anzac Day and the Anzac Centenary. Her publications include the *Anzac Day Media Style Guides* and *Not for Glory*, which tells the stories of women who have served in the Royal Australian Army Medical Corps from the Great War until the present day.

Jock Phillips was until recently general editor of *Te Ara – the Encyclopedia of New Zealand* (www.TeAra.govt.nz). He previously taught New Zealand and American history at Victoria University of Wellington and was the nation's Chief Historian. He has published over a dozen books of which the most relevant are a history of the New Zealand male stereotype, a study of New Zealand war memorials and a collection of letters from soldiers of the Great War. In 2014 he was given the Prime Minister's Award for Literary Achievement (non-fiction).

Peter Pierce is an Adjunct Professor in the National Centre for Australian Studies, Monash University. From 1996-2006 he was Professor of Australian Literature at James Cook University. His monographs include *Australian Melodramas: Thomas Keneally's Fiction* and *The Country of Lost Children: An Australian Anxiety*. He edited both *The Oxford Literary Guide to Australia* and *The*

Cambridge History of Australian Literature. His publications about war literature include *Clubbing of the Gunfire: 101 Australian War Poems* (co-edited); *Vietnam Days*; *Australia and the Impact of Vietnam* and *Australia's Vietnam War* (as author and co-editor); and a co-edited anthology of Australian military travel writing, *On the Warpath*.

Robin Prior is the author of six books on the first world war, most recently *Gallipoli: the End of the Myth*. He is also an editor of the *Oxford Companion to Australian Military History*. He was formerly a professor at the University of New South Wales at the Australian Defence Force Academy and is currently a Visiting Professorial Fellow at the University of Adelaide and Adjunct Professor of History at Flinders University. He was elected to the Australian Academy of the Humanities as a Fellow in 2012.

Matthew Ricketson is Professor of Journalism & Creative Writing, University of Canberra. He was previously Media and Communications editor for the *Age* newspaper and has worked on the staff of the *Australian, Time Australia* magazine and the *Sydney Morning Herald*. He is the author of three books and editor of two and is president of the Journalism Education and Research Association of Australia. He is currently a chief investigator on an Australian Research Council project examining the impact of mass redundancies on Australian newsrooms and the reinvention of journalism.

Bruce Scates is professor of History and Australian Studies at Monash University and Director of the National Centre for Australian Studies. His books include *A New Australia* (1997), *Return to Gallipoli* (2006), *A Place to Remember: A History of the Shrine of Remembrance* (2009) and *Women and the Great War* (co authored with Raelene Frances) which won the NSW Premier's History Award. He is the lead author of *Anzac Journeys* (short listed in the Ernest Scott Prize 2014), *World War One: A History in 100 Stories* (2015) and *The Last Battle: A History of Soldier Settlement in Australia* (2016). He is currently leading an international team investigating the history of Anzac Day. He is a Fellow of the Academy of Social Sciences in Australia and chaired the Military and Cultural History panel advising the Australian Anzac Centenary Board.

Tom Sear is a PhD candidate at UNSW Canberra at the Australian Defence Force Academy (ADFA.) His thesis examines the role digital and web–based technologies play in the centenary commemorations surrounding World War I. Tom completed honours in history at the University of Sydney, and has worked as a curator and historian. Tom participated in the 2015 commemoration experience on the Gallipoli peninsula.

Gizem Tongo is currently reading for a D. Phil. in Oriental Studies at St John's College, University of Oxford as Dulverton and Michael Wills Scholar. Her doctoral thesis focuses on Ottoman art during the First World War. In Oxford, she is also affiliated to the Khalili Research Centre for the Art and Material Culture of the Middle East. Her interdisciplinary research interests span history, art history, and literature with a specific focus on the visual culture of the late Ottoman Empire. Her recent publications include "Yusuf Atılgan" in *Dictionary of Literary Biography: Modern Turkish Novelists* (2013) and "Artist and Revolutionary: Panos Terlemezian as an Ottoman Armenian Painter," *Études arméniennes contemporaines* (2015).

INTRODUCTION

Beyond Gallipoli – New Perspectives on Anzac

Raelene Frances and Bruce Scates

The setting

Some one hundred years after the Gallipoli landings, a cast of the world's leading Gallipoli scholars gathered on the shores of the Dardanelles to discuss and debate that ill-fated campaign.[1] This unique collection brings together a selection chosen from around 100 papers from half a dozen countries delivered at this event. It approaches old questions in a new way, offering fresh perspectives on the Gallipoli landings and their legacy, and showcasing the work of leading and emerging scholars from the UK, USA, Canada, France, Aotearoa/New Zealand and Turkey. The conference straddled four days. It was opened in the presence of Mr Nicholas Sergi, the Australian Consul at Çanakkale, and simultaneous translation enabled a rare and much-needed dialogue between English and non-English speakers. It concluded with a voyage on a replica of the Ottoman minesweeper *Nusret* around Cape Helles, a tour of the Peninsula itself and a chance to re-trace

---

1 The conference emerged from an Australian Research Council funded project examining war and memory, LP110100264, *Anzac Day at Home and Abroad: A Centenary History of Australia's National Day*. The authors thank the other Chief Investigators, Frank Bongiorno, Keir Reeves, Tim Soutphommasane, Martin Crotty, Peter Stanley and Graham Seal, and the Partner Organisations associated with the project: the Australian Commonwealth Department of Veterans' Affairs, Victoria's Shrine of Remembrance, Legacy (Melbourne), the National Archives of Australia, the National Museum of Australia, King's College London, Çanakkale Onsekiz Mart University (COMU) and the Historial de la Grande Guerre. We also knowledge the assistance of project manager, Alice McConnell, and International Advisers, Jay Winter and Annette Becker. Thanks also to Corrie McKee, Gerhard Zelenka and Matthew O'Rourke who helped with conference organisation and/or finalising the manuscript of this book. We wish to extend our particular thanks to the Australian Consulate in Çanakkale and to two Vice Chancellors of Monash University (Professors Ed Byrne and Margaret Gardner) who provided financial support. Special thanks to Nathan Hollier for commissioning this work for Monash University Publishing, and his excellent production staff, Laura McNicol Smith and Joanne Mullins.

the story of the fighting from both sides of the trenches. Conference proceedings formally ended on 24 May, the Centenary of the Armistice between Ottoman and allied forces on Gallipoli. That symbolism was deliberately chosen – Gallipoli/Çanakkale, once a place of fierce conflict, was now a site where scholars searched for common understandings. Having said that, scholarship into war (and particularly the Gallipoli campaign) can still spark lively controversy. This was most apparent in the tense discussion (or lack thereof) that surrounded the Armenian genocide.[2] 2015 marks not just the Centenary of the Landing, but also a hundred years since the Ottoman Government's 'relocation' of its Armenian population via forced marches to the Syrian desert. There had been a tacit agreement not to address this issue at the conference. The Australian organisers were mindful of the polarised political opinion surrounding this episode, and its potential to overwhelm consideration of the Çanakkale/Gallipoli campaign itself. We were also encouraged by an assurance that a future conference would be called to consider the 'Armenian debate'. There is no sign that the Turkish government is likely to host a discussion of what many regard as a genocide any time in the immediate future. And whilst Australian delegates maintained an uneasy if diplomatic silence, several speakers invited by a Turkish Government research centre repeatedly harangued the conference participants on this very subject. In their version of events, the only genocide attempted in 1915 was a determined effort by the allies 'to exterminate the Turkish people'. The comforting language of reconciliation that now cushions the Gallipoli/Çanakkale war clearly has its limitations.[3]

This is a diverse collection but it is united by several common themes. All these papers are set in a transnational and comparative frame; they pursue cultural history rather than operational accounts of the campaign; they are, in many cases, multi-disciplinary in their approach to the past; and their sources range from textual accounts to visual narratives, war-scapes, exhibitions, material culture and postdigital imaginings.

---

2   Eugene Rogan, *The Fall of the Ottomans: The Great War in the Middle East* (New York: Basic Books, 2015) provides a good scholarly and balanced survey of this issue in the context of the 1948 UN Convention on Genocide which defined genocide as 'acts committed with the intent to destroy, in whole or in part' a distinct national or religious group. He concludes that while the evidence is by no means clear-cut, the balance falls on the side of a verdict of genocide.

3   For further discussion of this point see Peter Stanley's recollections, 'Headphones, genocide and Fanta: reflections on the Çanakkale Gallipoli Conference', *Honest History*, 4 August 2015, http://honesthistory.net.au/wp/stanley-peter-canakkale-conference-reflections-2015/ (accessed 31 March 2016).

The book

The collection begins with two essays situating the Gallipoli campaign and challenging popularly accepted narratives of its history. Robin Prior deconstructs the many myths that have grown up around Gallipoli, myths so numerous he remarks, 'that they easily exceed all the mythology of all the other campaigns of the Great War combined'. From the outset, he argues, Gallipoli was an unwinnable battle. There was very little chance of allied forces advancing beyond their narrow beachhead, let alone subduing the forts of the Dardanelles. Far from being an opportunity to relieve Russia, subdue Turkey and ultimately win the war, the harsh military reality was that the Dardanelles, from beginning to end, was something of a pathetic sideshow. Conceived as a chance to break out of the static conditions of trench warfare on the Western Front, Gallipoli simply recreated Flanders and the Somme in miniature. The campaign, he concludes, was a folly fought 'in vain', not withstanding the bravery of the men who served there.

At the close of his chapter, Prior turns to the question: did Gallipoli give birth to a nation? It is the perfect segue to the second chapter in this collection, Jenny Macleod and Gizem Tongo's inquiry into memory, history and the 'nation-building endeavors' of both Australia and Turkey. Macleod and Tongo use Mustafa Kemal Ataturk's famous 'speech' as a *'lieu de mémoire'* – or site of memory – for Turkish and Australian commemoration in order to reflect on the nature and politically-charged uses of the past. They trace the provenance of the speech and its popularisation as a major element in Turkey's 'memorial diplomacy' during the Cold War and the reconciliation narrative that has been a prominent part of Anzac Day commemorations at Gallipoli and Australia since the 1980s. The challenge they point to, though, is not so much reconciliation between Turkey and the former allied invaders but between modern Turkey and the descendants of the Ottoman Armenian population. The essay charts the ongoing attempts by the Turkish Government to silence any discussion of the events of 1915 as 'genocide'. 'The reconciliatory words of Kemal have been used to build warm relations through memorial diplomacy, but the dark underbelly of celebrating the Johnnies and the Mehmets has been the forgetting of the Armenians'. The withdrawal from this volume of three papers by Turkish academics when they learned that the word 'genocide' would be used in Macleod and Tongo's chapter is symptomatic of the ongoing sensitivity surrounding this issue.

The popular press has been one place where Gallipoli's myths have flourished; it seems appropriate that the second theme of this book deals with what we have called 'medias of remembrance'. Recognising the importance of news media in influencing public perceptions of the past, Sharon Mascall-Dare and Matthew Ricketson examine the ethics of war reporting. They ask how journalists can avoid formulaic coverage during the Anzac Centenary. How can reporters balance sensitivity with a commitment to accuracy when interviewing veterans? What storytelling approaches should they employ? Their chapter examines journalistic ethics within the context of Anzac by exploring four key themes: accuracy, subjectivity, collaborative story-telling and the reporting of trauma. In each case, the authors explore shifts in journalistic practice through recent case studies: Sharon Mascall-Dare's BBC World Service documentary, *Anzac*; Susan Neuhaus and Mascall-Dare's book, *Not for Glory* and Chris Masters' book, *Uncommon Soldier*. Two case studies from the US and the UK – the television documentary, *The Not Dead* and David Finkel's book, *Thank you for your service* – are also examined to offer further insight into ethical reporting practices. The chapter concludes by identifying resources offering guidance on ethical conduct for journalists assigned to the Anzac Centenary: *The Anzac Centenary Media Style Guide*, published in Australia and *Getting it Right*, produced by the Dart Center for Journalism and Trauma based at Columbia University.

Increasingly people create their own media, and this is the subject of Tom Sear's study of Anzac in a postdigital age: his essay explores the role the digital has played in connecting the past to the present. In 2015, sites like the Facebook page, AnzacLive, posted diary entries of long-dead historical figures. Thousands of Australians 'witnessed' the campaign through the dramatic daily testimony of individuals as diverse as Billy Hughes, Ellis Silas the soldier-artist, and John Monash, and were invited to participate in virtual conversations with these characters through Facebook posts. This fostered what Sear and others have described as an 'affective, emotional and empathetic response' to past generations' experience of war. The dangers of this avatar Anzac are readily apparent. It is not just the 'uncanny collapsing' of time and space; professional historians value a critical detachment from the past and few strive to imagine themselves a part of it. But Sear's account is as balanced as it is perceptive. It is possible, he argues, to connect with the past and at the same time critically engage with it:

> Contemporary audiences have a playful, nuanced understanding of time, history and memory that has kept pace with the accelerating conflux of the analogue, digital and postdigital eras. They know their position in time relative to historical subjects comes with privileges as well as blind

spots. They can reposition technologies that seem to disturb the social performance of commemoration or challenge connections between the past and the present as redemptive rather than disruptive.

Sear's initial essay was presented within weeks of the centenary commemorations at the Landing and engaged with the popular reimagining of Anzac at the moment of its making. It engaged with and complemented the work of Andrew Hoskins, another scholar of digital commemoration who delivered a paper at Çanakkale. Here Hoskins reflects on Sear's findings and the fate of memory in the new 'war ecology' of the postdigital era. He raises the tantalising possibility that 'the new structure of memorialisation being too close to war itself may actually undermine the future of memory, with the postdigital disabling its capacity to change, transform and dissipate, in other words a kind of ironic blockage of commemoration, by commemoration'.

Social media and the popular press are one genre of remembrance, literary representation of the campaign another. Here the collection features the work of an Australian scholar pondering the work of a New Zealand novelist and a Turkish scholar examining a range of literary forms from both Australia and Aotearoa/New Zealand. In the latter case, the engagement of Turkish scholars with cultural aspects of the conflict, and especially the cultural productions of the enemy, marks an important departure from the focus on narrowly conceived military history that has dominated Turkish historiography to date.

Peter Pierce leads this discussion with an insightful and carefully-grounded analysis of Stephen Daisley's prize-winning novel, *Traitor*. Pierce charts the various ways in which Daisley explores the themes of treachery, steadfastness, religious belief, and family allegiances. Central to Daisley's novel is the (unlikely) friendship between a New Zealand soldier, David Monroe and a wounded Turkish soldier, Mahmoud. Historians might well take exception to Daisley's incredible plot – its dramatic devices of escape from Greek islands, evasion of a firing squad and post-war persecution – but few could contest Pierce's evaluation. The *Oxford Companion to New Zealand Literature* once lamented that the Great War 'produced little literature of lasting or distinctive quality'. Something of a *tour de force*, written with 'unerring lightness of touch', and 'less concerned with the horrors of war than to the possibilities of redemption' *Traitor*, Pierce demonstrates, is a novel of (long-awaited) depth and substance.

In a bold literary sweep, A. Candan Kirişci examines the different ways in which the Dardanelles campaign has been represented in the early post-conflict literatures of Turkey, Australia and New Zealand. Her focus is on the ways in which the enemy appears in each of these national texts. Her analysis contrasts the overt propaganda orientation of the early Turkish literature with the more introspective focus of the Australian and New Zealand works, preoccupied as these were with elaborating the national type of the Anzac rather than with portraying the enemy.

From literature we move to consider the role that art, museums and artefacts have played in shaping the cultural memory of war. In his wide ranging and perceptive essay, Kevin Fewster questions the role that art and museums can and should play in commemorating war. Analysing centenary exhibitions in both Britain and Australia, this richly-illustrated discussion invites us to consider the ways in which emotions are engaged. His chapter surveys several powerful examples of how ideas are challenged and evolve in the process of exposition and dialogue. Indeed, Fewster raises the challenging question of whether war can be represented at all. Does the portrayal of combat – often now by those who have never experienced it – romanticise, sanitise or trivialise an experience well beyond the viewer's contemplation? Fewster's essay demonstrates how the Çanakkale conference gave licence to extended scholarly inquiry: his engagement with Michael McKernan on the *Love and Sorrow* exhibition (recently fielded by Museum Victoria) extending and enriching a conversation commenced on the Dardanelles. Fewster also raised the important consideration of community engagement with the Centenary via museum spaces – a rich if problematic field for historians.

From public engagement we turn to the more intimate space of the family and the way objects, photos and letters facilitate the process of remembrance. Jock Phillips' study of two brothers who went to war offers insight into the experience of a generation. Gordon and Robin Harper served with the Canterbury rifles both on Gallipoli and in an equally punishing campaign in Sinai. Both men showed extraordinary courage in the face of horrific circumstances. Both were sustained by their belief in the Empire's cause, an assertive sense of New Zealand's nascent nationalism and the less abstract bonding of soldiers under fire. A historian of masculinity, Phillips shows how the values imparted by school and family – and an intense fraternal relationship – shaped what he called 'an anatomy of bravery'. Jay Winter once remarked that courage is rather like a fine suit of clothing, handsome at first, but donned day after day, week after week, gradually worn threadbare. In this intimate microhistory, Phillips shows how courage could be resiliently reasserted through the horror of wartime.

Introduction

Janda Gooding and Paul Gough, the final contributors to this section, delve into portrayals of the battlefield itself. Gooding's chapter takes as its starting point George Lambert's oil painting *ANZAC, the Landing 1915*. It examines the sources used by the Australian artist to reconstruct the events of the Dawn landing at Gallipoli; fieldwork studies, the use of multiple perspectives, and the synthesis of memories. Using the lenses of cultural memory and history painting, the paper looks at public reactions to the painting from its first showing in 1922 to the present day. It offers suggestions for the longevity of this particular image that was described in 1924 as 'a fine ideal and an imperishable memory' of the ANZAC achievements.

Gough's paper also examines the memory-scape of the Dardanelles, exploring ways in which official and unofficial artists and photographers attempted to comprehend and visualise the new face of war. While Gooding considers the creation of a heroic narrative, Gough confronts what he calls 'the phenomena of emptiness', and how artists fathomed 'the void of war'. That last phrase is borrowed from the writer Reginald Farrer. Touring Flanders in 1916, Farrer argued it was wrong to view the 'huge, haunted solitude' of modern warscape as empty. 'It is more,' he argued, 'full of emptiness ... an emptiness that is not really empty at all'. Artists, poets and writers absorbed Farrer's line of thought, Gough argues, describing the 'Void of War' as a distinct element with its own properties and visual conditions, populating its emptinesses with latent violence, and on occasion suffusing it with a malign enchantment. Gough demonstrates that the tradition of epic narrative battle painting provided little aesthetic comfort to artists faced with radically-altered visual bearings on the front-line. Their previous training, and the monumental tendencies of war painting as a genre, had to be abandoned if meaningful and truthful visual narratives were to be created.

Warscapes were actual places as well as imagined narratives. The next section of our collection, 'Grounding Memory', examines the commemorative landscapes created in the aftermath of war. Harvey Lemelin offers a Canadian perspective on the campaign, a perspective seldom seen in a literature that has long privileged Anzac and British accounts. The Royal Newfoundland Regiment was the only North American regiment to see action at Çanakkale/Gallipoli but to date there is no on-site marker commemorating the regiment's sacrifice. This is in marked contrast to the Western Front, where a series of bronze caribou statues were erected after the war. Until this 'oversight' is addressed, Lemelin argues, the 'Trail of the Caribou' will remain incomplete, at least for many Newfoundlanders and Labradorians. Lemelin's chapter reminds us of the forgotten narratives of the campaign and how some narratives are privileged over others. It also alerts us to the ways landscapes are marked and mobilised for commemorative purposes and an ongoing contest for the spaces of remembrance. In the 1920s Australian, New Zealand and Imperial authorities claimed a presence on Gallipoli; the monuments they raised not only commemorated the dead – they also issued a retrospective claim on the battlefield. The peninsula was a contested site in 1915; Lemelin's work confirms it is contested terrain to this day.

Nor was the Dardanelles campaign Gallipoli's first encounter with war. Jessie Birkett-Rees presents an archaeological perspective on the battlefields of the Anzac/Arıburnu area, a site of conflict since well before the time of Homer and today one of the world's least disturbed First World War landscapes. She argues that archaeology, though a relative newcomer to the field of 'Great War' studies, has an important role to play in revaluating the course of campaigns. The largest archaeological artefact of the First World War is the battlefield landscape – a network of trenches, tunnels and terraces that so conspicuously changed the shape of the Gallipoli peninsula and to a large part determined the behaviour and daily life of soldiers on both sides of the trenches. Rather than examining the battlefield as a scene of victory or defeat, tactics or strategy, as do military historians, archaeologists seek to understand the development of these landscapes over time. This encompasses the formation and preservation of war-era features as well as attempting to delineate relationships between the pre-war record and the post-war commemorative landscape. Drawing on the results of the Joint Historical and Archaeological Survey (2010-15), Birkett-Rees considers the roles of archaeology on the battlefields of Gallipoli and the significance of encounters with the physical record of the past. It is important to note that that survey is confined to what is generally called the 'old Anzac area', terrain where Australian and New Zealand troops were entrenched through much of the campaign. The trail of the Caribou begins well beyond that. In commemoration, as in war then, there are winners and losers. Few visitors to this day tour that forgotten landscape of Suvla.

It seems appropriate that a collection inspired by a conference marking the centenary of the Gallipoli Landings end with a reflection on Anzac Day itself. Here we feature two new essays on the making of that landmark commemorative moment. Bill Gammage, the most senior and most distinguished of the historians featured in this volume, offers his characteristic insight into the genesis of Anzac Day. In April 1916 the anniversary of the Landing at Anzac was celebrated by what he calls 'spontaneous combustion' in Australia and New Zealand. This was a popular movement.

Introduction

Neither government proclaimed a national day, but places large and small each remembered the occasion in their own way. Such populist origins may be unique among world national days, but they also gave rise to contention and uncertainty about the rituals appropriate to Anzac Day. How should the day be commemorated? What ceremonies should be held? Should they be solemn only, or include sport and recreation? Who should lead them? When and where should each be held? Who should participate? Who should decide? Gammage takes issue with these critical questions. His preliminary findings are the precursor of a broader study of the history of Anzac Day observance both at home and abroad.

One of the preoccupations of Anzac Day is how the commemorative 'message' might be carried intact from one generation to another; an impossible task, but one that prompts Frank Bongiorno's rewarding inquiry into a child-centred view of Anzac. Bongiorno argues that children's literature (produced during and after the First World War) imparted understandings and values about war, violence, gender, empire and nation. He notes that historians have for the most part neglected this important genre, limiting our understanding of the impact and legacy of the war. Bongiorno's findings also have implications for our understanding of the continuing role of war stories in the literature read by young people – there has been an explosion of First World War-themed stories in Australian young people's literature and history in recent years, as well as continuing debate about how Anzac and war should be taught in schools. In this essay, as with all the others in this volume, there is tremendous scope for further inquiry.

Diverse and wide-ranging as this collection of essays is, we are also mindful – both as editors and as conference conveners – of its limitations. Out of a field of some 90 papers, restrictions of space meant that only 17 could be selected. We have opted for thematic coupling of papers. That meant, regrettably, that several worthy individual contributions had to be set aside. We especially regret that this particular collection does not feature the work of several PhD candidates who presented their work so ably to a demanding international audience. Withholding their contribution permits the completion of their theses, and the prospect of a subsequent book, exploring the history of Anzac Day, will offer a more appropriate platform to showcase their findings. We ended the conference with a call for further transnational scholarship into the Gallipoli campaign. This collection marks the beginning rather than the end of that endeavor.

Part 1

Challenging Histories

Chapter 1

THE MYTHS OF GALLIPOLI

Robin Prior

The myths surrounding the Gallipoli campaign in 1915 are so numerous that they easily exceed the mythology of all the other campaigns of the Great War combined. The Gallipoli myths range widely. They cover such issues as whether particular incidents in the campaign represented potentially victorious turning points, whether the campaign if successful could have shortened the war, whether inadequacies of the men and their leaders led to failure or whether it laid the foundations of two modern nations, Turkey and Australia.

It is hard to say why such a range of myths grew up around the Gallipoli campaign. But certainly, some very strong-minded individuals who wrote histories of the campaign had vested interests in the propagation of these myths. Winston Churchill, who presents himself in *The World Crisis* as the instigator of the campaign, believed that its ruination brought about the (temporary) ruination of his own career. So he sifted through the evidence to find instances of military bungling and opportunities thrown away.[1] C.E.W. Bean, the Australian Official Historian, sought out moments where the bungling of the British cost Australians victory. He was the first to see how the birth of an Australia no longer subordinate to the Mother Country could originate on the beaches of Gallipoli. C Aspinall-Oglander, the British Official historian of the campaign, and a member of General Ian Hamilton's staff at Gallipoli, sought moments where sloth and incompetence in lower order commanders brought to nothing many of the plans he had devised. The myths abound but in the limited space available I have focused on the major ones.

---

1   This was the conclusion in my book on *The World Crisis*. See Robin Prior, *'Churchill's World Crisis As History* (London: Croom Helm, 1983), 275-79.

The first involves the naval attack on the Dardanelles. This came to be the overture of the land campaign but was initially intended to make the landing of soldiers unnecessary by sending a fleet through the Narrows and forcing the surrender of Constantinople by ships alone.[2] This attack commenced on 19 February and reached its culmination in the great attack of 18 March. It failed with three allied ships sunk and three crippled.[3] But it is said that if the naval attack had been resumed, the Turkish forts would have been unable to resist the fleet because they were running so short of ammunition. There are many studies which show that the Turkish forts actually had plenty of ammunition left.[4] But to concentrate on the state of the forts is to miss a more important point – that it was not the forts that were the main obstacle to the fleet but the rows of Turkish mines that lay in the Narrows. Despite almost a month of endeavour the minesweepers had failed to clear a single mine, either because they could not make headway against the Dardanelles current or because they were deluged with shells from the concealed and mobile batteries on both sides of the Straits. With over 350 mines maintaining an impenetratable barrier to the fleet, it mattered little if the forts had sufficient ammunition or not.[5]

The second myth relates to the timing of the military campaign. Just over a month passed from the time that the navy conceded that they could not force the Straits to the time that the military landed. During this period the Turks reinforced their defences on the Peninsula. If the landings had taken place earlier, so the argument runs, they would have proved successful. This myth ignores the weather in the Eastern Mediterranean in spring. Even if troops had been immediately available to follow up the naval failure, the weather would have prohibited a landing. The seas were too rough for most of the period between operations to land sufficient troops to force their way through to the Straits or even to reinforce them and provide supplies. The last of the storms took place on 22nd April, delaying the actual landings from 23rd to 25th. An earlier landing might well have resulted in a fiasco.

---

2   Churchill to Admiral Carden (commanding Admiral at the Dardanelles) 3/1/1915, in Martin Gilbert, *Winston Churchill, vol 3, Companion Part 1, Documents, July 1914-April 1915*, 45-6.

3   Admiral de Robeck (Carden's replacement) Report 24/3/1915, de Robeck Papers, 4/4, Churchill College, Cambridge.

4   For a full discussion of this point see my '*World Crisis As History*, 97-9.

5   For the fraught question of the minesweepers see the report of a committee sent to Turkey in 1919 to investigate the failure of the naval attack, The Mitchell Committee. There is a copy in the Australian War memorial, AWM 124.

The third myth concerns the Anzac landing. It is widely believed that the Anzacs were landed in the wrong location and that this factor disrupted their operation and prevented them pushing across the Peninsula to the Narrows. Actually, the Anzac contingent was landed exactly where intended.[6] The initial landing certainly took place on a narrower front than was envisaged and this did cause some initial confusion. However, this period was short lived. The follow-up force landed in strength and on a broad front soon after the covering force and all was set fair for an advance. What then prevented the Anzacs from making ground was partly the difficulty of the country they were required to traverse but above all the timely arrival of Turkish reserves on the battlefield. First they appeared on the right flank and then on the heights to the left. There were no more thoughts of an advance after that. Indeed, late in the day thoughts turned rather to whether the entire force should be evacuated. The navy vetoed such a move and the Anzacs hung on but there were no lost opportunities on the first Anzac Day, just an insufficient force facing impenetratable country defended by an enemy in great strength.[7]

The second series of so-called lost opportunities came during the operations in August 1915. The first once more concerns the Anzacs. Their objective was the Sari Bair Ridge which dominated the entire northern position. It is widely claimed that after seizing key sections of the ridge, opportunities went begging because the navy shelled some contingents off the ridge, while others were pushed back because commanders failed to grasp the position and did not send reinforcements in a timely manner.[8]

The first of these contentions is easily dealt with. It is a fact that a small contingent of Ghurkas held a lodgment on Hill Q, one of the Sari Bair heights. However, their numbers were small, they did not hold the entire hill, they were counterattacked in strength by the Turks and they were probably subjected to friendly fire, not from the navy whose low-trajectory shells could not reach their position, but by their own artillery. This shelling, from whatever source was not the crucial factor. The Turks were too strong, the Ghurkas too weak, ever to have held the position. Even had they managed

---

6   See General Birdwood, 'Operation Order no '1 in C. Aspinall-Oglander, *Gallipoli Maps and Appendices vol 1* (London: Heinemann, 1929), 37-41. Birdwood specifies no exact landing point in these orders.

7   Robin Prior, *Gallipoli: The End of The Myth* (London/New Haven: Yale University Press, 2009), Chapter 8.

8   Extraordinarily, given his initial hostility to the entire campaign, C E W Bean claims this. See his *Official History of Australia in the War of 1914-1918: The Story of Anzac vol 2* (Sydney: Angus & Robertson, 1938), 700.

to hang on, they were enfiladed from Hill 971 to the north and Chunuk Bair to the south.[9] There was therefore never an opportunity to convert a momentary lodgment into something permanent.

The second contention was that had a group of New Zealanders who held Chunuk Bair been reinforced, their lodgment would have provided an excellent springboard for the capture of the entire ridge. This too is extremely doubtful. Firstly, the command did attempt to reinforce them but the country once more proved so baffling that few reinforcements found their way to Chunuk Bair. The other point is similar to that just made about the Ghurkas. The New Zealand force was not in strength, the men were exhausted, supplies had not reached them and the Turkish force that counterattacked them off the heights was in such strength that no conceivable reinforcing group could have secured the position.[10]

But there is an overarching factor that nullifies the whole missed opportunity argument. The fact is that the northern force, even if they had secured the heights, had no additional troops available to them to push across the Peninsula. Had the ridge been secured, nothing could have followed. However, it is difficult to see how the 17,000 men who would have been necessary to hold the ridge could have been supplied, over the treacherous intervening country, with sufficient water, food or above all ammunition to make their position secure.[11] And had they managed to do this, many more ridges lay between them and the Straits. Though these ridges were lower than Sari Bair, the experience of the Anzacs demonstrated that it was quite possible to hold a lower ridge and prevent all attempts to dislodge them. There seems little doubt that had Sari Bair fallen the Turkish forces would have been able to replicate this feat.

There is yet another myth about the August landings which focuses on the British force landed to the north of the Anzacs at Suvla Bay. Here the argument runs, had the commanders or troops of this force acted with more initiative, they would have been able to seize the Anafarta Ridge which overlooked Suvla Bay and advance down it and assist the Anzacs in driving the Turks from Sari Bair. The target for this allegation is the commander of this force, General Stopford, and the New Army troops which he commanded. The fact is that it was no part of Stopford's remit to assist the

---

9   See Colonel Allanson (who commanded the Gurkhas that day) letter to his brother 8/3/16 held by the Imperial War Museum, London, DS/Misc./69.

10 See 'Report on Operations against the Sari Bair Position: 6-10th August 1915' in NZ & A Division War Diary August 1915, AWM 4/1/53/5, Part 2.

11 Cecil Malthus, *Anzac: A Retrospect* (Auckland: Whitcombe & Tombs, 1965), 119.

Anzacs. The task that he and his force had been given was to establish a base at Suvla Bay from which all the forces in the north could be supplied over the stormy autumn season.[12]

There is no doubt that Stopford was not a great commander. He was slow to react to situations; he was often out of touch on his offshore yacht. But had he been a man of decision and imagination nothing much would have followed. His troops were struggling inland in the face of strengthening Turkish opposition. That those troops were not ably led was hardly a decisive factor. The men were short of water and had they ventured further from the landing places they may well have run short of ammunition and food as well. The fact that they were not able to capture the Anafarta Ridge had no consequences. The ridge was distant from Sari Bair and troops on it could have given little material support to the Anzac forces. Moreover, the ridge seemed to be the key in securing the Suvla Bay base. As it happened it was not. The Turkish forces which eventually forestalled the British on the ridge were never able to counterattack them back into the sea. Nor were they able to deploy sufficient artillery to threaten the base which remained intact until the end of the campaign.[13]

What of the larger purposes that the operation was supposed to serve? In short, were there any prospects that the operation at Gallipoli could have affected the war as a whole? The answer must be in the negative. The ultimate end of the campaign, it will be recalled, was to clear a way for the fleet to proceed to Constantinople to force the surrender of the Turks. Yet there is no evidence that had the fleet managed this unlikely task the Turks would have surrendered. Trenches were being dug in the capital; the city was in military hands and it is quite possible to imagine that had the capital fallen the government would have decamped to Anatolia and continued the war from there.[14]

Even if we take the next step and ask what might have happened had Constantinople fallen, we get very little further. It seems likely (the politicians were vague on this point at the time) that Britain and France envisaged that some form of Balkan coalition would immediately be formed. Churchill summed up what would have happened next most succinctly:

---

12   GHQ Order to General Stopford (commander at Suvla Bay) 13/7/1915, in WO 158/576, The National Archives, Kew.
13   Prior, Chapter 13.
14   This was the opinion of Turkish Officers in 1919 in answers given to The Mitchell Committee.

The whole of the forces of the Balkan confederation [which he estimates at just over one million men] could then have been directed against the underside of Austria in the following year [and this] must have involved the downfall of Austria and Turkey and the speedy victorious termination of the war. [15]

The problem with this is that in adding up the Serbian, Greek, Bulgarian and Rumanian armies, observers such as Churchill took no account of how armies with no common language and equipment could have been combined in an efficient way. Moreover, the internecine hatreds of the Balkan states for each other would not have made the traverse of, say, Bulgarian armies across Serbia, an easy matter to arrange. There were formidable difficulties with communications as well. There were only two railway lines linking the Balkans with Austria in 1915 and it is certain that these narrow-gauge links would have proved insufficient to supply armies of the size suggested by Churchill.

Then there is the state of these armies to consider. The Rumanian army may be taken as an example. In 1914 this army had little modern artillery and was particularly deficient in heavy pieces. What they had was pulled by oxen because of the shortage of tractors and horses. Machine guns were in very short supply, eight divisions of the Rumanian army having none at all. The Rumanians had only ammunition for two months of heavy fighting and one shell factory, which delivered two shells per day. They had no gas, virtually no aircraft and no equipment such as trench mortars.[16]

There is no reason to believe that other Balkan armies were in any better condition. The Greek army was in the process of changing much of its equipment in 1914 and was not in a fit state to take the field. The Greeks had no armament industry and were looking to the major powers to re-equip them. This prospect vanished at the outbreak of war when these powers found that they had insufficient equipment for their own forces.

These then were the armies that Churchill and others expected to take on and defeat the armies of Austria-Hungary and Germany. It seems certain that the Austrians would have had the capacity to deal with this motley array alone. If by mischance they had been forced back, the Germans would have rushed to their aid. The issue would then have been beyond doubt.

---

15 Winston Churchill, *The World Crisis* (London: Odhams, 1951), 849.
16 See for example Charles Petrie, 'The Roumanian Campaign 1916', *Army Quarterly*, 14 (1927), 341 and P. Seicaru, *La Roumanie dans la Grande Guerre* (Paris: Minard, 1968), 346.

Any Balkan alliance then was probably chimerical, but even if one had been formed and their armies placed in the field, their prospects were dismal. More likely is that no such alliance would ever have been formed even if Constantinople had fallen.

Indeed this investigation lays bare the fallacy behind the entire Gallipoli adventure. Turkey and the Balkan states were but minor players in the Great War. Rather than prove an accretion of strength to either side, they would have become a burden or rapidly exited the war as Rumania did when it was attacked by Germany in 1916. The great engine of the war from the point of view of the Central Powers was the German army, and it happened to be on the Eastern and Western fronts. As far as Britain was concerned, they had to defeat Germany in the west or lose the war. In this sense there was no way around. The defeat of Turkey in 1915 would have saved temporarily the lives that were lost in the Palestinian and Mesopotamian campaigns from 1916 to 1918. But had Turkey fallen in 1915, those troops would have been transferred to the killing fields of the Western Front. How many would have survived this ordeal is speculative, but it seems certain that the overall death toll would have been higher.

All this leads to an unwelcome conclusion about Gallipoli and the Dardanelles. Despite the bravery of the allied troops who fought there, the campaign was fought in vain. It did not shorten the war by a single day, nor in reality did it ever have that prospect. As Churchill said (and then promptly forgot), 'Germany is the foe & it is bad war to seek cheaper victories'.[17] Gallipoli was certainly bad war. As it happened, it did not even offer a cheaper victory or in the end any kind of victory. But even if it had, the downfall of Turkey was of no relevance to the deadly contest being played out in France and Flanders.

What of the fact that two modern nations were borne at Gallipoli? In the case of Turkey there is some merit in the proposition. Certainly, Mustapha Kemal, the founder of the modern Turkish state first came to prominence at Gallipoli. However, a decade elapsed before the state was established and there were many other factors involved in the making of modern Turkey. Some of them are the harsh terms imposed on Turkey by the peace, the invasion and expulsion of Greek forces (followed by the Greek population) in the early 1920s, the exhaustion of the allies after the war and the discrediting of the Young Turk government by entering the war on the German side.

---

17   Churchill to Lord Fisher (First Lord of the Admiralty) 4/1/1915 in Martin Gilbert, *Churchill Companion Documents, vol 3*, 71.

As for Australia, it became a nation in 1900 and by 1915 had established a series of unique parliamentary, industrial and commercial arrangements which clearly proclaimed its nationhood. It in fact provides the perfect example of how a nation can be created without the blood test of war. Some Australians have insisted that unless such a test is applied the country is something less than a nation. Such notions should be dismissed for the bloodthirsty hankerings of insecurity that they are. Those who know the true cost of war will be content with Australia's peaceful path to independence.

Chapter 2

BETWEEN MEMORY AND HISTORY

Remembering Johnnies, Mehmets and the Armenians

Jenny Macleod and Gizem Tongo

> Those heroes that shed their blood, and lost their lives ... You are now lying in the soil of a friendly country. Therefore, rest in peace. There is no difference between the Johnnies and the Mehmets to us where they lie side by side, here in this country of ours. You, the mothers, who sent their sons from far away countries ... wipe away your tears. Your sons are now lying in our bosom and are in peace. After having lost their lives on this land, they have become our sons as well.[1]

This magnanimous and heart-rending elegy, attributed to the founder of the Turkish Republic Mustafa Kemal Atatürk, is probably the most well-known quotation to commemorate the Gallipoli Campaign. It has been carved on many war memorials, quoted in various commemoration events, and, more than any other, it has 'spoken' for the post-war political relationship between Turkey and Australia. This essay uses this 'speech' as a window on to the changing relations among the belligerent countries involved in Gallipoli, and hence the intersection between commemoration, national identity, and international relations.

From George Mosse's war memorials as 'shrines of national worship' to Benedict Anderson's deliberately absurd Tomb of the Unknown Marxist, the

---

1   Inscription on the Kabatepe Ari Burnu Beach Memorial which was unveiled on 25 April 1985 on the occasion of the official renaming of Ari Burnu as Anzac Cove.

link between the commemoration of death in war and nation building is well established.[2] Yet the role of commemoration in diplomacy has received less attention.[3] Australia has used the commemoration of Gallipoli on Anzac Day as a means to develop its own distinct national identity, whilst the memory of the campaign has played a lesser but still significant role in the forging of the Republic of Turkey's new identity. Nor was it the only example of a new identity being forged through memory of the campaign. Over time, these two separate nation-building endeavours have interacted such that a new powerful meaning for the campaign has emerged which has significant implications for the two countries' international relations.

This transnational approach mirrors developments in the historiography of the First World War which has seen a shift from a national framework of analysis to a transnational one.[4] A crucial precursor to this has been a broadening and deepening of scholarship, such that the history of nations, empires and peoples beyond those of Britain, France and Germany has thus developed. Thus in military history, the work of Edward Erickson, Mesut Uyar and others have brought the possibility of not only dissecting the defeat at Gallipoli in terms of Allied errors, but of understanding the victory at Gallipoli in terms of Ottoman skill and efficiency.[5] Similarly, in the realms of the cultural history of the campaign, a field long dominated by the examination of Australia's passionate commitment to remembering the Anzacs,[6] there are now the first analogous works which examine Turkish

---

2   George L. Mosse, 'National Cemeteries and National Revival: The Cult of the Fallen Soldiers in Germany', *Journal of Contemporary History* 14:1 (1979): 16; Benedict Anderson, *Imagined Communities: Reflections on the Origin and Spread of Nationalism*, 3rd ed. (London: Verso, 1983), 9–10.

3   For example, Matthew Graves, 'Memorial Diplomacy in Franco-Australian Relations', in *Nation, Memory and Great War Commemoration* eds. Shanti Sumartojo and Ben Wellings (Oxford: Peter Lang, 2014), 169–88.

4   Jay Winter and Antoine Prost, *The Great War in History: Debates and Controversies, 1914 to the Present, Studies in the Social and Cultural History of Modern Warfare* (Cambridge: Cambridge University Press, 2005), 193–198.

5   Edward J. Erickson, *Ordered to Die: A History of the Ottoman Army in the First World War* (Westport, Connecticut: Greenwood Press, 2001); Edward J. Erickson, *Gallipoli: The Ottoman Campaign* (Barnsley: Pen & Sword Military, 2010); Stanford J. Shaw, *The Ottoman Empire in World War I, Volume I: Prelude to War* (Ankara: Turkish Historical Society, 2006); Stanford J. Shaw, *The Ottoman Empire in World War I, Volume II: Triumph and Tragedy, November 1914-July 1916* (Ankara: Turkish Historical Society, 2008); Mesut Uyar, *The Ottoman Defence against the Anzac Landing: 25 April 1915* (Sydney: Big Sky Publishing, 2015); Harvey Broadbent, *Gallipoli: The Turkish Defence* (Carlton, Vic: Melbourne University Publishing, 2015).

6   Amongst a vast literature these works stand out: Alistair Thomson, *Anzac Memories: Living with the Legend* (Melbourne: Oxford University Press, 1994); Kenneth Stanley

memory in a scholarly fashion.[7] Building on these works it is now possible to trace the transnational flow of ideas between countries.[8] It will be seen that in the commemoration of war, this can be a powerful tool for reconciliation, but can also lead to tensions and occlusions.

This essay uses Kemal's 'speech' as a '*lieu de mémoire*' for Turkish and Australian commemoration in order to explore this phenomenon.[9] It has become the single most important interpretation of the campaign where an international audience gathers to remember Gallipoli. It is a repository of sacred meaning, an 'ode', and thus a 'secular prayer'.[10] Three particular aspects of Pierre Nora's observations on lieux de mémoire will be explored. (1) Nora suggested that 'Memory is always suspect in the eyes of history, whose true mission is to demolish it, to repress it.'[11] The clash of these approaches to the past became apparent when historians began to query the provenance of the speech. (2) Memory 'is subject to the dialectic of remembering and forgetting, unconscious of the distortions to which it is subject, vulnerable

---

Inglis, *Sacred Places: War Memorials in the Australian Landscape* (Carlton South, Victoria: Melbourne University Press, 1998); Bruce Scates, *Return to Gallipoli: Walking the Battlefields of the Great War* (Cambridge: Cambridge University Press, 2006); Marilyn Lake et al., *What's Wrong With Anzac? The Militarisation of Australian History* (Sydney: University of New South Wales Press, 2010); Carolyn Holbrook, *Anzac: The Unauthorised Biography* (Sydney: New South Publishing, 2014).

7   Pheroze Unwalla, 'Re-Imagining Gallipoli: Imperial Pasts and Foreign Presence in a History of Turkish National Remembrance, 1923-2013', (PhD, SOAS, University of London, 2014); Vedica Kant, 'Çanakkale's Children: The Politics of Remembering the Gallipoli Campaign in Contemporary Turkey', in *Remembering the First World War*, ed. Bart Ziino (London: Routledge, 2015), 146-165; Jenny Macleod, *Gallipoli, Great Battles Series* (Oxford: Oxford University Press, 2015). Macleod's chapter on Turkish memory was written with Gizem Tongo.

8   George Frederick Davis, 'Anzac Day Meanings and Memories: New Zealand, Australian and Turkish Perspectives on a Day of Commemoration in the Twentieth Century', (PhD, University of Otago, 2008); George Davis, 'Turkey's Engagement with Anzac Day, 1948-2000', *War & Society* 28:2 (2009): 133–61; Roger Hillman, 'A Transnational Gallipoli?', *Australian Humanities Review*, 51 (2011): 25–42.For a transnational history of the war, see J. M. Winter, ed., *The Cambridge History of the First World War*, 3 vols (Cambridge: Cambridge University Press, 2014).

9   Pierre Nora, 'From Lieux de Mémoire to Realms of Memory', in *Realms of Memory: Rethinking the French Past Vol. 1 Conflicts and Divisions*, ed. Pierre Nora (New York: Columbia University Press, 1996), xvii.

10 Catherine Simpson, 'From Ruthless Foe to National Friend: Turkey, Gallipoli and Australian Nationalism', *Media International Australia*, no. 137 (2010): 58–66; Bronwyn Lea, 'Lest We Forget: Binyon's Ode of Remembrance', *The Conversation*, 26 April 2013, https://theconversation.com/lest-we-forget-binyons-ode-of-remembrance-13642.

11 Pierre Nora, 'General Introduction: Between Memory and History', in *Realms of Memory*, ed. Pierre Nora, 3.

in various ways to appropriation and manipulation, and capable of lying dormant for long periods only to be suddenly reawakened.'[12] It will be seen that Kemal's speech has not always had the prominence it currently enjoys, mysteriously having been forgotten for decades. (3) Following on from this is the theme of silence. Memory 'accommodates only those facts that suit it.' [13] A conscious choice has been made to exclude the Armenian genocide from the remembrance of events. And both Australian and Turkish states have been complicit in this process, as have historians, who actively and consciously chose to give voice to a story of honourable fighting in Gallipoli, and to silence the shameful history of mass deportations and killings of the Armenians. Robert Manne noted this disjunction in Gallipoli's historiography in 2007.[14] How has this come about? It is rooted both in the practice of history – we historians tend to work within distinct and discrete fields – and in the way that silence, as Jay Winter explains, 'is socially regulated, socially constructed, socially preserved, and socially destroyed. All societies have spaces of silence.'[15] An early version of this essay was presented as the keynote lecture at an international congress at Çanakkale Onsekiz Mart University, in November 2014, and the occasion and its aftermath illustrates Winter's point. Facing a grand lecture hall filled with local officials, military officers, academics and students, and preceded by speeches in Turkish, the political stance of which, in the absence of a translator, she could not discern, Jenny Macleod made a last minute decision to omit the section of the lecture which referred to the genocide. Social anxiety had prompted silence. Later the organiser of the conference declined to include the full text of the keynote in the conference proceedings because of 'domestic politics.'[16] Now, reconfigured and updated here, this essay offers an exploration of Kemal's speech placed in the context of the broader commemorative arrangements of the two countries as a richly suggestive lieu de memoire that will enable reflections on the nature of history, memory, and the uses of the past.

---

12 Nora, 'General Introduction: Between Memory and History', 3.
13 Nora, 'General Introduction: Between Memory and History', 3.
14 Robert Manne, 'A Turkish Tale: Gallipoli and the Armenian Genocide', *The Monthly*, February 2007, http://www.themonthly.com.au/monthly-essays-robert-manne-turkish-tale-gallipoli-and-armenian-genocide-459 http://www.armeniandiaspora.com/showthread.php?177086-A-Turkish-Tale-Gallipoli-And-The-Armenian-Genocide [Accessed 5 February 2014].
15 Suzan Meryem Kalaycı, 'Interview with Jay Winter', *Tarih: Graduate History Journal of Boğaziçi University*, Issue: 1 (2009), 34. See also, Michel-Rolph Trouillot, *Silencing the Past: Power and the Production of History* (Boston: Beacon Press, 1995), 48.
16 Private email to Jenny Macleod, 28 May 2015.

History, memory and Kemal's 'speech'

In his Dawn Service address at Anzac Cove in 2015, Australia's Prime Minister Tony Abbott remarked, 'Gallipoli shaped modern Turkey as much as it forged modern Australia and New Zealand'.[17] This is not quite true, although all these nations emerged from the demise of empires, the Ottoman and British respectively. In the case of Australia, as a Dominion, it was already on the peaceful path towards self-government expected of Britain's white settler colonies in 1915. But in emotional terms, it is fair to say that the memory of Gallipoli has provided a means to break the bonds of Britishness. A new national identity was forged through the Anzac legend, which ascribed distinctive national qualities to Australian soldiers, and over time 'Anzac' has acquired the status of what Ken Inglis has identified as a 'civil religion'.[18] By contrast, the Republic of Turkey emerged from the War of Independence (1919-22) that overturned the punitive Treaty of Sèvres imposed upon the defeated Ottoman Empire at the end of the First World War. Mustafa Kemal became the country's first President and adopted the name, Atatürk (Father of the Turks). Kemal had been a senior officer at Gallipoli, playing a decisive role at two key moments, but it was the War of Independence that made his name. Until his death in 1938, Atatürk led his country in an ambitious modernisation programme which imposed a homogenous, secular and mono-lingual Turkish identity in place of the formerly multi-ethnic, multi-religious and multi-lingual Ottoman culture.

There was, however, a dark aspect to this programme. In 1919, Enver, Talat, and Cemal Paşas had been sentenced to death in absentia by the Ottoman Special Military Tribunal for several war crimes, including the massacres of Armenians and Greeks.[19] But with the foundation of the Turkish Republic, there was no longer any such willingness to face up to what had happened in 1915. Indeed, a significant part of the republican project was to monopolise the authority to write the new nation's history through the Turkish Historical Society. Its work obliterated the history of

---

17 Davis, 'Anzac Day Meanings and Memories', 190–8. The Hon Tony Abbott MP, Prime Minister of Australia, '2015 Dawn Service, Gallipoli', 25 April 2015. Available online: https://www.pm.gov.au/media/2015-04-25/2015-dawn-service-gallipoli [Accessed 6 May 2015].

18 Kenneth Stanley Inglis, 'Anzac, the Substitute Religion', in *Observing Australia 1959 to 1999*, ed. Craig Wilcox (Carlton South, Vic: Melbourne University Press, 1999), 61–70; Inglis, *Sacred Places*, 458–63.

19 For the most comprehensive study on the subject, see, Vahakn N. Dadrian and Taner Akçam, *Judgement at Istanbul: The Armenian Genocide Trials* (New York: Berghahn Books, 2011).

non-Muslims, including Ottoman Armenians, and failed to acknowledge the Armenian genocide. Meanwhile, Gallipoli was remembered for the stoicism of the ordinary Turkish soldier Mehmetçik, and for the heroic role of Kemal.[20] Thus, denialism and a close attention to the uses of the past have played a key role in the formation of the Turkish Republic. As Vedica Kant has noted, 'Atatürk's role in the victory at Canakkale has been so successfully established as a foundational cornerstone of the republic that it simply cannot be removed from the historical narrative'.[21] Thus despite the advent of the Justice and Development Party (Adalet ve Kalkınma Partisi, AKP), a socially conservative party of the Right with Islamic roots which has worked to roll back some elements of Kemalism, Kemal's 'speech' has continued to be used in the commemoration of Gallipoli. In 2010, for instance, the then Prime Minister Recep Tayyip Erdoğan quoted it and then continued in a more belligerent tone, 'this noble nation and the noble army of this noble nation showed their affection, generosity, hospitality, and friendship to the soldiers who had come from distant lands to kill them, hence this nation is a great nation and its army is a great army.'[22]

Perhaps as a result of its ubiquity, this vital lieu de memoire for Gallipoli has been subject to exacting questions from historians about its provenance.[23] From the tortuous web of evidence it seems clear that Atatürk did not deliver this speech himself. Attention then turns to whether or not his

---

20 For the belated development of the idea of Kemal as the heroic 'Man of Destiny' in response to initiatives in London and Sydney, see Ayhan Aktar, 'Mustafa Kemal at Gallipoli: The Making of a Saga, 1921-1932' in *Australia and the Great War: Identity, Memory and Mythology*, Michael JK Walsh and Andrekos Varnava eds. (Melbourne University Press, 2016), 149-171.

21 Kant, 'Çanakkale's Children', 159.

22 'Erdoğan'ın, Çanakkale Zaferi'nin Yıldönümü Konuşması', *Cumhuriyet*, 18 March 2010, available online: http://www.cumhuriyet.com.tr/haber/diger/128186/Erdogan_in__Canakkale_Zaferi_nin_yildonumu_konusmasi.html

23 Adrian Jones, 'A Note on Ataturk's Words About Gallipoli', *History Australia* 2, no. 1 (2004), doi:10.2104/ha040010; Davis, 'Anzac Day Meanings and Memories'; David Stephens, 'Gold, Rum but No Sign of Ataturk's Minister at Anzac, April-May 1934', *Honest History*, 1 December 2015, http://honesthistory.net.au/wp/no-sign-of-ataturks-minister-at-anzac-april-may-1934/. Cengiz Özakıncı, '1915 Çanakkale Savaşı Anıtlarına Kazınan 'Conilerle, Mehmetçikler Arasında Fark Yoktur' Sözleri Atatürk'e Ait Değil', *Bütün Dünya*, March-April 2015. Translated into English as 'The words 'There is no difference between the Mehmets and the Johnnies' engraved on the 1915 Gallipoli monuments do not belong to Atatürk', *Honest History* (available online: http://honesthistory.net.au/wp/tracking-ataturk-honest-history-research-note/); Anthony Pym, 'On the passage of transcendent messages: Johnnies and Mehmets' (version 2.3, September 28 2015), an unpublished essay, available as a link within 'Gold, Rum', *Honest History*.

Interior Minister, Şükrü Kaya, delivered the speech on Atatürk's behalf in 1934. The main source for this was a 1953 interview with Kaya conducted by the Turkish journalist Yekta Ragıp Önen.[24] There are no other sources to corroborate this story. This message to the former invaders was not mentioned in an otherwise closely detailed account of 1934's only pilgrimage by foreigners, the Duchess of Richmond cruise.[25] Nor did the newspapers of 1934 report the speech, although they did relay a briefer message with similar sentiments. 'The Ghazi's Message' was reported as:

> The Gallipoli landing and fighting on the Peninsula showed to the world the heroism of all who shed their blood there, and how heart-rending for their nations were the losses this struggle caused.[26]

He had issued a similar, lengthier message in 1931 to the 'Worthy Foemen' of the Anzacs.[27] The sentiment of the 'speech' is thus in keeping with other messages issued by Kemal about the Anzacs. Nonetheless, the text of the 'speech' can only be reliably traced as far back as 1953. A translation of it was relayed to an RSL delegation in 1960 – note the absence of any 'Johnnies':

> Oh heroes, those who spilt their blood on this land, you are sleeping side-by-side in close embrace with our Mehmets.
>
> Oh mothers of distant lands, who sent their sons to battle here, stop your tears. Your sons are in our bosoms.
>
> They are serenely in peace. Having fallen here now, they have become our own sons.[28]

At neither point did it gain much attention. Thereafter, the 'speech' surfaces once more in the late 1970s.

A 1978 Turkish pamphlet relates the story of how it became the subject of correspondence between Uluğ İğdemir, General Director of the Turkish

---

24   Şükrü Kaya, interview by Yekta Rakıp Ören, *Dünya*, 10 November 1953, 5.
25   Stanton Hope, 'Gallipoli Revisited: An Account of the Duchess of Richmond Pilgrimage-Cruise', n.d..
26   *The Times*, 26 April 1934, 13; 'Former Enemy', *Sydney Morning Herald*, 26 April 1934. See also George Davis, 'Turkey's Engagement', 136–7, which notes a similar message to a Brisbane newspaper in 1931, and the obscurity of the 1934 speech.
27   'Worthy Foemen', *Daily Mail*, Brisbane, 25 April 1931, cited in Davis, 211–12.
28   Davis, 'Anzac Day Meanings', 215, fn 99. No specific source is cited for this quotation. Pym, 'On the passage of transcendent messages', 16.

Historical Society and Alan J. Campbell, Chairman of the Gallipoli Fountains of Honour Committee in Brisbane.[29] The words that were ultimately engraved on the plaque at the memorial are the now familiar text, including the phrase about 'Johnnies and Mehmets'. Controversy rages as to whether this phrase was 'concocted in 1977-8' by İğdemir and Campbell,[30] or whether it is merely a reasonable translation of the sense and sentiment of the 1953 text.[31] In many ways this is a classic example of the difference between the simplicity of a reconciliatory memory versus the dogged insistence on fact and evidence of history. Why did it not become popular sooner? It could have been taken up in 1960, but instead struck a chord in 1977–8. Since its use in Brisbane, Kemal's speech has been inscribed on memorials in Anzac Cove, Wellington, Albany and Canberra (all 1985), Adelaide (2008), Melbourne (2015), and Sydney (2015). It has been quoted in four Prime Ministerial speeches (1990, 2008, 2010, 2013), in museums and websites, and has inspired an orchestral composition.[32] As such, it maps perfectly on to the idea of the second memory boom from the late 1970s,[33] and more specifically on to the contours of the Anzac revival.[34]

Memorial diplomacy and Kemal's speech

It seems more than coincidental that Kaya's interview was published at the same moment that memorial diplomacy got under way. During the Korean War when Turkey, having aligned with the West, fought alongside British, French, Australian and New Zealand soldiers in the United Nations forces, a variety of warm words and gestures were made. In 1953, *Milliyet* newspaper wrote in its Çanakkale week coverage (ie commemoration of 18 March) about 'our present very valuable allies and beloved friends the English and French naval and army forces ... we laid the foundations of our today's friendship and alliance 38 years ago in the Çanakkale and Gallipoli battles.'[35] From 1953, Turkish representatives started to attend Anzac Day

---

29   Uluğ İğdemir, 'Atatürk ve Anzaklar/Atatürk and the Anzacs', *Türk Tarih Kurumu yayınları*. XX. dizi (Ankara: Türk Tarih Kurumu Basımevi, 1978).
30   Stephens, 'Gold, Rum but No Sign of Ataturk's Minister at Anzac'.
31   Pym, 'On the passage of transcendent messages', 19.
32   'Tracking Ataturk', *Honest History*, available online: http://honesthistory.net.au/wp/tracking-ataturk-honest-history-research-note/ [Accessed 3 March 2016].
33   Winter, *Remembering War*, 26.
34   Jenny Macleod, 'The Fall & Rise of Anzac Day: 1965 & 1990 Compared', *War & Society* 20:1 (2001): 149–168.
35   *Milliyet*, 18 March 1953, 2.

overseas, and there were low key demonstrations of friendship in connection with Anzac Day that were used as soft diplomacy to cement the new NATO alliance.[36] Turkey's small scale commemorations of Gallipoli were attended by larger crowds than previously,[37] and nationalist students initiated a bid to build a monument for the Çanakkale martyrs in 1952.[38] This 41 metre-tall memorial overlooks the narrows. Amongst the donors were New Zealand veterans and in the accompanying letter, the New Zealand Prime Minister wrote to his Turkish counterpart, Adnan Menderes, saying that 'In Korea Turkish soldiers displayed the same heroism and solidity as they had done in Gallipoli'.[39] In return, the Turkish government acquiesced to a request from veterans in Ashburn, New Zealand for some stones from Gallipoli with which to build a memorial of their own.[40] During the fundraising process, there was a keen appreciation of the mismatch in the memorials on the peninsula. As the *Milliyet* newspaper commented in 1958, 'Çanakkale is full of memorials, yet these memorials have been erected for British and French soldiers who were defeated by the heroic Mehmetçik'.[41]

The Martyrs' Memorial was completed in 1960, nonetheless, it belatedly makes an important point. Henceforth, the dominant memorial on Turkish soil marked Turkish victory.[42] This 'dialogical memorialization'[43] – memorials that are built in a dialogue with each other became particularly apparent from the mid 1980s. In 1985, the Turkish government unveiled the Kabatepe Ari Burnu Beach memorial with Kemal's words and officially renamed the part of their territory known as Ari Burnu as Anzac Cove, a name that had been in unofficial usage in Turkey since at least 1957.[44] This memorial was one of 20 Turkish monuments built in a spate of activity during the

---

36   Davis, 'Turkey's Engagement', 139.
37   *Milliyet* states that around 500 university students came to the city for the commemoration ceremony. '18 Mart Çanakkale Zaferinin Yıldönümü,' *Milliyet*, 18 March 1952, 7.
38   'Çanakkale'de Bir Mehmetçik Abidesi Yaptırılıyor,' *Milliyet*, 5 May 1952, 2.
39   'Yeni Zelandalı Eski Muhariplerin Çanakkale Abidesi İçin Teberuu,' *Milliyet*, 20 September 1958, 3.
40   'Çanakkale'den Yeni Zelanda'ya Taş Götürülecek,' *Milliyet*, 9 January 1959, 2.
41   'Çanakkale'de Türk Şehitlği: Yok,' *Milliyet*, 9 February 1958, 1.
42   John McQuilton, 'Gallipoli as Contested Commemorative Space', in *Gallipoli: Making History*, ed. Jenny Macleod (London: Frank Cass, 2004), 150–4.
43   Brad West, 'Dialogical Memorialization, International Travel and the Public Sphere: A Cultural Sociology of Commemoration and Tourism at the First World War Gallipoli Battlefields', *Tourist Studies* 10:3 (1 December 2010): 209–25.
44   Server Rıfat İskit, *Resimli-Haritalı Mufassal Osmanlı Tarihi*, 6 (1957), 35.

1980s.[45] Then, in 1990, the 75th anniversary of Anzac day was attended by international political leaders, and at substantial cost to the Australian government, a delegation of Australian veterans. The commemorations were an opportunity for high-level political meetings and the friendship between Turkey and her 'old enemies' was a repeated theme. Thereafter, the memory of Gallipoli became increasingly prominent in Turkish public life. To give but two examples: the foundation in 1992 of Çanakkale Onsekiz Mart University – that is a university named after the victory, and the launch of a new 500,000 Turkish Lira note on 18 March 1993 which featured the image of the Çanakkale Memorial on its reverse.

This is the other side of the story of the Anzac revival. In 1990, Anzac, Australia's civil religion, was born again and since then Australia has demonstrated a strongly-felt possessiveness about Gallipoli which has required ever greater cooperation with Turkey to facilitate access to the peninsula. The Kemal 'speech' has no doubt been useful in smoothing this path, even whilst it also provided a meaning for the campaign that allies, enemies, militarists and pacifists could all appreciate. Thus Australia's Prime Minister, Bob Hawke, in an eve of Anzac Day speech at a dinner hosted by the Turkish Prime Minister Yıldırım Akbulut in Ankara used Kemal's words and the memorial developments to turn on the diplomatic charm. Later at Anzac Cove, however, he up-ended Kemal's sentiments (that the fallen 'have become our sons as well') to effectively assert that the sacred ground had become our land as well: 'this place is in one sense a part of Australia'.[46]

Since Hawke's visit in 1990, three other Australian Prime Ministers have addressed the Dawn Service at Anzac Cove: John Howard in 2005, Julia Gillard in 2012 and Tony Abbott in 2015. Gillard used her speech to praise the honourable generosity shown to their former foes:

> The Turkish honoured our fallen and embraced them as their own sons.
>
> And later they did something rare in the pages of history – they named this place in honour of the vanquished as Anzac Cove.
>
> We therefore owe the Republic of Turkey a profound debt.[47]

45　İskit, 143, fn 47.
46　Robert Hawke, 'Speech by the Prime Minister at Official Dinner Given by Prime Minister Akbulut, Ankara, 23 April 1990', (https://pmtranscripts.dpmc.gov.au/release/transcript-8008); 'Speech by the Prime Minister Dawn Service, Gallipoli, 25 April 1990', (https://pmtranscripts.dpmc.gov.au/release/transcript-8013)
47　Julia Gillard, 'Dawn Service, Gallipoli', (Pmtranscripts.dpmc.gov.au/release/transcript-18532).

From 1996 onwards, Turkish-Australians unofficially joined in the Melbourne parade, a development officially endorsed by the RSL in 2006. The involvement of other former enemies, notably German and Japanese ex-soldiers remained unthinkable.[48] Gillard went on to announce that the centenary year of 2015 would be named 'the Year of Turkey' in Australia and 'the Year of Australia' in Turkey.[49] The President of the ACT, RSL branch, John King, invited the Turkish military attaché to march on his right and co-lead the march on Anzac Day 2015.[50] At Lone Pine on Anzac Day, Abbott remarked, 'The care taken of this place, reflects the foe that is now a friend. So today I salute a noble adversary and I thank the Republic of Turkey for accepting our sons with theirs.'[51]

It is important to acknowledge, however, that these close relations also placed constraints upon what can be said about Turkey. In May 2012, the New South Wales Parliament passed a motion recognising the Armenian genocide. As a result, politicians from New South Wales were told that they would not be given visas to attend the centenary commemorations at Gallipoli. A statement from the Turkish Foreign Ministry echoed the language of Kemal's speech to explain their response:

> These persons who try to damage the spirit of Çanakkale /Gallipoli will also not have their place in the Çanakkale ceremonies where we commemorate our sons lying side by side in our soil.[52]

This was in keeping with a broader plan to use memorial diplomacy to enforce silence about the genocide. In 2011, the then Turkish Foreign Minister Ahmet Davutoğlu outlined his ambition for the centenary of the Gallipoli landings:

---

48   Daniel Hoare, 'Turks Allowed to Join Anzac March', in *The World Today* (2006). By 2004, Turks, Vietnamese, Koreans and Serbs had all joined in Sydney's Anzac Day march. Tony Stephens, 'Time Marches Past', *Sydney Morning Herald*, 26 April 2004. The inclusion of campaigners seeking recognition of Aboriginal service and the Frontier Wars has proved more problematic, although an Aboriginal smoking ceremony was included in the commemoration at Lone Pine in August 2015.

49   Phillip Coorey, 'Day Embodies the Nation's Values, Says Gillard', *Sydney Morning Herald* (NSW), 26 April 2012.

50   AAP, 'Anzac Day Centenary: 2015 Year of Turkey in Australia,' *Australian Times*, 27 April 2012.

51   ABC News, 'Anzac Day 2015: PM Abbott delivers speech in Lone Pine'. 25 April 2015 [Video]. Available online: https://www.youtube.com/watch?v=uauxn8gSkJw [Accessed 30 April 2015]. See also, https://pmtranscripts.dpmc.gov.au/release/transcript-24398

52   Hamish Boland-Rudder, 'Canberra to Commemorate 'Anzac Week' in 2015', *Canberra Times* (ACT), 8 June 2012.

We are going to introduce the year of 2015 to the whole world. We will do so not as the anniversary of a genocide as some people have claimed and slandered, but as the anniversary of the glorious resistance of a nation, the anniversary of the resistance at Çanakkale.[53]

Thus when the centenary came around Turkey organised an expanded programme of Gallipoli commemorations, including an event scheduled on 24 April – a date without meaning in regard to the campaign. Invitations were sent to 102 countries, including the Armenian President, Serzh Sargsyan, who angrily noted the attempt to overshadow his own country's commemoration of the start of the genocide:

> Alas, Turkey continues its traditional policy of denialism. Year by year, 'improving' its tools of history distortion, this time Turkey marks the anniversary of the Battle of Gallipoli on April 24 for the first time, while it began on March 18, 1915 and lasted till late January, 1916. Furthermore, allies' land-campaign – Gallipoli land battle – took place on April 25, 1915. What purpose does it serve if not a simple-minded goal to distract attention of the international community from the events dedicated to the centennial of the Armenian Genocide?[54]

In some regards the plan worked. The Turkish President, Erdoğan, was reported as saying 'Thank God, 20 heads of state came to ours, while two went to theirs'. In fact 17 heads of state attended the Gallipoli commemorations in Turkey, while four went to Yerevan. As journalist Cengiz Çandar put it, 'in the contest of the "G-words," Gallipoli won over the Genocide'.[55] In particular, the plan to enforce silence had worked in the country most susceptible to pressure. In advance of the centenaries, Australia's Minister for Foreign Affairs, Julie Bishop confirmed that the Australian government does not recognise the events in the Ottoman Empire as 'genocide'.[56] There could be no chance of jeopardising its ability to hold its commemorations at Gallipoli.

---

53   'Davutoğlu: 12 Yıl Sonra Cihan Devletiyiz', *Takvim*, 25 April 2011.
54   'President Serzh Sargsyan responds to Turkish President's letter-invitation', *Armenpress*, 16 January 2015. Available online: http://armenpress.am/eng/news/790596/nakhagah-serzh-sargsyany-pataskhanel-e-turqiayi-nakhagahi.html [Accessed 16 April 2015].
55   Cengiz Çandar, 'In Turkey's Battle of the G-words, Gallipoli Wins', *Al-Monitor*, 27 April 2015. Available online: http://www.al-monitor.com/pulse/originals/2015/04/turkey-armenia-international-standing-after-two-centennials.html# [Accessed 28 April 2015].
56   The Hon Julie Bishop MP, Minister for Foreign Affairs, to Mr Ertund Ozen, Australian Turkish Advocacy Alliance, 4 June 2014 [letter] Available online: http://

And yet, despite Turkey's efforts to distract attention away from it, the Armenian genocide was more prominently remembered and discussed around the world in April 2015 than ever before following Pope Francis' use of the word 'genocide', a vote on the subject by the European Parliament,[57] and Kim Kardashian's visit to the capital of Armenia.[58] Memorial diplomacy as a tool to enforce silence thus has its limits. It has less effect on individuals or organisations who have no stake in the diplomatic relationship. Thus in Sydney the Armenian Genocide Centenary National Commemoration Evening on 24 April 2015 was held, but Australia's Treasurer, Joe Hockey, who is of Armenian descent withdrew from his plan to speak on the occasion.[59] Earlier in his career he had spoken passionately about the genocide in the Australian Parliament, but now as a government minister it seems diplomatic considerations had come into play.

In Turkey itself, the state's power to control collective memory and enforce the denialist position has been challenged in recent years. A growing number of Turkish intellectuals and scholars, including Taner Akçam, Uğur Üngör, Fatma Müge Göçek, and the Nobel laureate Orhan Pamuk, have opened the debate on this once taboo topic. This has fed into and in turn been empowered by growing support from individuals and human rights groups who have organised conferences and commemorations every 24 April. In 2015, the centenary commemoration in Istanbul, organised by various international and Turkish human rights organisations such as the Turkish Human Rights Association IHD and DurDe (Say Stop to Racism and Nationalism), was attended by thousands of Turkish people as well as thousands of people coming from various parts of the diaspora.

In her essay 'The History Question: Who Owns the Past?' the Australian historian Inga Clendinnen writes, 'The Turks, we were told, were honourable

---

www.ata-a.org.au/press-release-fa-minister-julie-bishop-events-of-1915-are-not-genocide/ [Accessed 12 March 2015].

57   Richard Spencer, 'Turkey accuses EU of 'enmity' over 1915 Armenian genocide recognition', *Daily Telegraph*, 17 April 2015. Available online: http://www.telegraph.co.uk/news/worldnews/europe/turkey/11546643/Turkey-accuses-EU-of-enmity-over-1915-Armenian-genocide-recognition.html [Accessed 25 June 2015].

58   Ian Black, 'Kim mania as Armenia catches up with the Kardashians', *The Guardian*, 12 April 2015. Available online: http://www.theguardian.com/world/2015/apr/12/kim-kardashian-kanye-west-armenia-catches-up-with-kardashians [Accessed 16 April 2015].

59   Jared Owens, 'Hockey abandons plans to speak at Armenian 'genocide' centenary ceremony', *The Australian*, 24 April 2015. Available online: http://www.theaustralian.com.au/national-affairs/hockey-abandons-plans-to-speak-at-armenian-genocide-centenary-ceremony/story-fn59niix-1227318708211 [Accessed 25 June 2015].

enemies,' but she continues, 'remembering the Armenians, we flinch.'⁶⁰ In this Clendinnen is right but incomplete. During the war, Australians were well informed about the massacres. The newspaper coverage included a report from Charles Bean where he wrote, 'The Turks, as the world knows, are at the present moment engaged-in an endeavour to wipe out the Armenian nation before they are stopped.'⁶¹ But subsequently Australia (as elsewhere) chose to forget the Armenians just as Bean did in the poem he inserted in *The Anzac Book* about 'Abdul': 'though your name be black as ink. / For murder and rapine / [here at Gallipoli] / You've played the gentleman'.⁶² In the Ottoman Empire, there was a brief window after the ending of military censorship and particularly following the escape of the CUP leaders from the country, when the Ottoman press became fiercely critical of the CUP and its Armenian policies. But with the founding of the Republic, the memory of the Armenians was silenced. One hundred years later, the Gallipoli campaign still is one of the most important collective memories for Turkey and the most important one for Australia, but this history is neither a single nor a simple one. Like every society, both Australia and Turkey have spaces of silences from their history. The reconciliatory words of Kemal have been used to build warm relations through memorial diplomacy, but the dark underbelly of celebrating the Johnnies and the Mehmets has been the forgetting of the Armenians.

---

60 Inga Clendinnen, 'The History Question: Who Owns the Past?', *Quarterly Essay*, 23 (Melbourne, Vic: Black Inc, 2006), 13.

61 Captain Bean, 'An Armenian's Simple Talk: Horrible Story of Massacres,' *West Australian*, 2 December 1915, 8.

62 *The Anzac Book: Written and Illustrated in Gallipoli by the Men of Anzac* (London; New York; Melbourne: Cassell, 1916).

Part 2

Medias of Remembrance

Chapter 3

WHAT'S THE STORY?

Journalism Ethics and the Anzac Centenary

Sharon Mascall-Dare and Matthew Ricketson

In 2002, on the death of Alec Campbell, Australia's 'last living Anzac', the Australian author and journalist Tony Stephens composed a feature article for the *Sydney Morning Herald*.[1] It was a thought-provoking piece, highlighting the fallibility of memory and the burden of celebrity: as an Anzac, Campbell had become 'national property', carrying a responsibility that his wife described as 'quite dreadful' on occasion. In an interview with Stephens, author of *The Last Anzacs*,[2] Campbell had rejected the mythology imagined by others: 'I joined for adventure,' he had said matter-of-factly, 'There was not a great feeling of defending the Empire. I lived through it, somehow. I enjoyed some of it. I am not a philosopher. Gallipoli was Gallipoli.'[3]

Stephens' journalism acknowledged the complexity – and questioned the mythology – inherent in the Anzac experience, but his work was not typical. In 2010, Sharon Mascall-Dare – co-author of this chapter –

---

1   Tony Stephens, 'Last Anzac is Dead', *Sydney Morning Herald* (17 May 2002) available at: http://www.smh.com.au/articles/2002/05/16/1021544052449.html (accessed 12 March 2015).
2   Tony Stephens, *The last Anzacs : lest we forget* (Fremantle: Fremantle Arts Centre Press, 2003).
3   See John Shaw, 'Alec Campbell, Last Anzac at Gallipoli, Dies at 103', *New York Times* (20 May 2002) available at: http://www.nytimes.com/2002/05/20/world/alec-campbell-last-anzac-at-gallipoli-dies-at-103.html (accessed 12 March 2015).

interviewed thirty journalists, commentators and broadcasters who had been assigned to Anzac Day media coverage in the previous decade: their responses raised concerns about formulaic coverage and the prevalence of cliché.[4] Anzac Day had become a media ritual, a 'season' in its own right, but despite more air-time and column centimetres the quality of reporting was inconsistent at best and clichéd at worst. As the veteran journalist John Hamilton described, there was a need for reporters to 'get their boots dirty' and seek a deeper, richer understanding of the Anzac story.[5] Alternative journalistic approaches were necessary to prevent coverage from becoming stale; accuracy was needed, but so too was fresh reporting, original lines of journalistic inquiry and an ethical approach grounded in greater awareness of the number of war veterans, of conflicts present as well as past, who suffer from Post-Traumatic Stress.

From 2014 until 2019 – the Anzac Centenary commemoration period – the need for ethically responsible, original journalism on the Anzac story has become even more important. A national focus on a 'Century of Service' has put the spotlight on veterans old and new; the story extends well beyond Gallipoli. The return of a new generation of servicemen and women from the wars in Afghanistan and Iraq has posed a new set of challenges for reporters. As James Brown argues in *Anzac's Long Shadow*, many younger veterans reject Anzac mythology and feel burdened by its legacy; the conflating of historical and contemporary experience is highly problematic.[6] For journalists there is also the issue of ethical responsibility, particularly when interviewing those who have experienced Post-Traumatic Stress.

The purpose of this chapter is to set out and to discuss alternative approaches available to journalists that will enrich and deepen media coverage during the Anzac Centenary years. As a working journalist, Mascall-Dare has taken a particular interest in the development of alternative journalistic models: her BBC World Service radio documentary *Anzac*[7] tested a prototype framework for reporters assigned to Anzac Day and the Anzac Centenary;

---

4   Sharon Mascall-Dare, 'An Australian Story: Anzac Day coverage investigated ', in *The Information Battlefield*, ed. Kevin Foster (Melbourne: Australian Scholarly Publishing, 2011), 162-80.

5   Mascall-Dare, *An Australian Story*, 170.

6   Brown, J., *Anzac's Long Shadow: The Cost of Our National Obsession* (Melbourne: Black Ink Incorporated, 2014).

7   *Anzac* is available via the BBC at http://www.bbc.co.uk/programmes/p011cfw3 (accessed 12 March 2015).

her *Anzac Day Media Style Guide*[8] has incorporated that framework into a handbook that offers guidance, background information and story ideas to Australian journalists. This paper explores the making of *Anzac* alongside four other case studies that show how alternative journalistic approaches can be taken in writing and broadcasting about veterans' experiences: Susan Neuhaus's book, *Not for Glory*,[9] Chris Masters's book, *Uncommon Soldier*,[10] the UK television documentary, *The Not Dead*[11] and David Finkel's book, *Thank You for Your Service*.[12] In each case, we will discuss the repercussions of each work for journalism practice and ethics; we close by reviewing the resources available to journalists seeking to reflect Australians' experiences of war with originality, accuracy and ethical responsibility.

Anzac

On Saturday 8 December 2012, at 2205 GMT, the BBC World Service broadcast a radio documentary publicised as an exploration of 'tension and interplay between myth, memory and multiculturalism in the fraught process of creating a modern Australian identity.'[13] Entitled *Anzac*, the documentary aimed to tell the stories of Australians 'trying to understand themselves and their past'. As the documentary maker, Mascall-Dare also sought to question prevailing interpretations of the Anzac legend. By exploring forgotten narratives, the broadcast aimed to contribute alternative perspectives on the commemoration of war and remembrance in contemporary Australia.

Anzac was more than an attempt at original storytelling. Its production processes challenged journalistic convention by testing a new framework for Anzac Day reporting: it explicitly drew on debate among historians regarding interactions between history and memory[14] to develop a customised

---

8   For the 2015 edition see, Sharon Mascall-Dare, *2015 Anzac Day Media Style Guide – Centenary Edition*, available at: http://monkeydostudio.com.au/books/anzac-media-style-guide/ (accessed 12 March 2015).

9   Susan Neuhaus and Sharon Mascall-Dare, *Not for Glory – a century of service by medical women to the Australian Army and its allies* (Brisbane: Boolarong Press, 2014).

10 Chris Masters, *Uncommon Soldier*, (Sydney: Allen & Unwin, 2012).

11 At the time of writing, *The Not Dead* is available via youtube: https://www.youtube.com/watch?v=MvA3K-tC6t8 (accessed 12 March 2015).

12 David Finkel, *Thank You for Your Service*, (Melbourne: Scribe Books, 2013).

13 See http://www.bbc.co.uk/mediacentre/proginfo/2012/50/ws-anzac (accessed 12 March 2015).

14 Sharon Mascall-Dare, 'Interactions between history and memory: a new approach to Anzac Day coverage', *An Australian Story: Media and Memory in the Making of Anzac Day* (PhD thesis, University of South Australia 2013), 93-122, available at:

methodology that combined journalism theory with the practice of ethnography. It was both a work of journalism and a doctoral artefact, drawing on Mascall-Dare's background as a working journalist. Once tested and refined, the framework was also incorporated into the *Anzac Day Media Style Guide* as a practical tool for story generation.

The foundation of the methodology lay in Janet Cramer and Michael McDevitt's framework for ethnographic journalism (see fig. 3.1). Their framework advocated immersive reporting and participant-observation; it also accommodated subjectivity and collaborative story-telling. Ethical treatment of interviewees was integrated into its methods: a commitment to pursue authenticity through collaboration offered interviewees greater influence, and agency, over how their stories were portrayed. Rather than speak on behalf of interviewees, the reporter 'becomes a medium, through which the group's story is told'. This contrasts with conventional news reporting where a journalist's perspective dominates because it is the journalist (or their editor) who determines which news event is reported and who is included – and excluded – from the news report.

	Conventional In-depth Features	Ethnographic Portraits
Newsworthiness	Conceptualization	
	• Change • The unusual • Celebrities and elites	• Adaptation • Hidden meanings • Rituals and practices
Relationship with sources	Reporting	
	Autonomous professional	Socially acceptable incompetent
Observation	Deductive	Inductive
Interviewer	The miner	The traveller
Narrator Epistemology	Writing	
	Journalist Balance	Group Authenticity

Fig. 3.1. Cramer and McDevitt's framework for ethnographic journalism[15]

Cramer and McDevitt's framework was aimed at all journalists, but it was not designed for a specific context or assignment. In order to customise the framework for Anzac Day reporters, and test it through the production

---

http://arrow.unisa.edu.au:8081/1959.8/152321 [accessed 12 March 2015].

15 Janet Cramer and Michael McDevitt, 'Ethnographic Journalism' in: *Taking it to the Streets: Qualitative Research in Journalism*, ed. Sharon Iorio (Mahwah: LEA, 2004).

of *Anzac*, Mascall-Dare sought to reflect academic debate about the intersection of history and memory. Six key characteristics of the framework's methodology were prioritised for analysis and discussion:

- immersion through participant observation;
- an inductive approach;
- the acknowledgement of subjectivity;
- narration by the group, not just the journalist;
- shared editorial control; and
- the pursuit of authenticity over balance.

All six characteristics challenged newsroom practice as well as ethical guidelines: objectivity and editorial independence continue to be advocated as intrinsic to ethical journalistic conduct.[16]

In her analysis of immersive journalism and participant observation, Mascall-Dare drew on the work of Jay Winter and Emmanuel Sivan, positioning Anzac Day at 'the intersection of private memories, family memories, and collective memories.'[17] This was contested territory, requiring a reporter to apply a 'lens' that distinguished history from memory and recognised that memories are socially framed. Through a series of questions, the framework applied this lens in order to identify original story angles: Does the dawn service draw on historical fact or invoke individuals' memories? What interaction is there between history and memory? Whose memories are chosen and why? In what ways are those memories socially framed? What appears to be the view/agenda of the organising committee (as an elite influence within 'the collective')? What is the reaction/view/memory of attendees (as individuals and as part of 'the collective')?

Mascall-Dare identified that journalists, as participant observers, could also apply the lens to their own experiences and interactions. Reporters bring their own memories to Anzac Day services that are socially framed: they may be personal; they may be family memories; they may be narratives learned in school that conflate history, as constructed in textbooks, with the memories of a teacher. The work of the journalist is, therefore, both a product and producer of memory, carrying an ethical responsibility for

---

16 For example, see *Media Entertainment & Arts Alliance – Journalists' Code of Ethics*, available at: http://www.alliance.org.au/code-of-ethics.html (accessed 12 March 2015).

17 Jay Winter and Emmanuel Sivan, 'Setting the framework', *War and Remembrance in the Twentieth Century*, eds. Winter and Sivan (Cambridge: Cambridge University Press, 1999), 9.

reporters to 'remember' accurately, conscious of the risk of distortion and the repercussions of forgetting.

Awareness of this responsibility prompted further questions that were also integrated into the methodological framework. What are the memories and/or experiences that a reporter brings to an assignment? Are they helpful, in adding colour or human interest, or do they compromise his/her ability to portray history, memory and their interactions accurately? What can be done to record and remember facts, observations and an interviewee's memories/ views accurately?

A similar process of inquiry was also applied to the acknowledgment of subjectivity. Although Cramer and McDevitt identified subjectivity as a key characteristic of ethnographic journalism, they did not offer guidance about ways it might be expressed or how often. Similarly, their notion of 'traveling' rather than 'mining' to obtain information required further exploration. Mascall-Dare identified that as 'travellers' journalists have 'baggage', carried as subjectivity.

When reporting on Anzac Day, a reporter's 'baggage' can take a number of forms: psychological, emotional or intellectual. When viewed through a lens that distinguishes memory from history, such baggage takes on new significance. How open is a reporter to 'new' memories that challenge 'old' historical narratives? How ready are reporters to 'abandon' their baggage, and report memories that may challenge their audiences to reconsider assumptions and preconceptions? In order to discover new territory, construct alternative narratives and incorporate memories that challenge official histories, there must be a willingness to accept that 'new' territory exists. Discovery requires imagination; it also requires an acknowledgement of silences and a readiness to remember the forgotten.

Mascall-Dare's next stage of analysis focussed on group narration and shared editorial control. While journalists may be comfortable with the former, the latter continues to be excluded by many newsroom practices. The reasons why are closely linked to ideas of the importance for journalists of retaining editorial independence, free from hegemonic or other influences, especially when dealing with politicians and those well versed in the dark arts of public persuasion. Allowing interviewees to 'push' a particular agenda is considered a form of manipulation.

When viewed through the lens applied previously during the customisation process, the decision-making process for shared control was clarified. What is the motivation behind an interviewee's request to make edits to a narrative? Does the request relate to upholding the truth of an individual memory, as remembered and held personally, or does it relate to the memory of someone else (another individual, or a group)? Does the request concern the accuracy in recording of history, and if so, whose history?

Acknowledging the fallibility of memory, and its shifts and distortions within the context of Anzac, was also integrated into the framework. Interviewees do not always remember accurately: checking information with three independent sources (a common newsroom practice known as triple sourcing) was confirmed as a viable method to mitigate the risk of memory shifts and distortions. There was also acknowledgement that journalists, too, must be aware of their fallibility. Reporters do not, necessarily, recall facts and experiences accurately: they may confuse and forget information, as do their interviewees. Their 'baggage', and their exposure to others', may influence how they frame and process content. In the same way that interviewees are influenced by the process of interviewing, interviewers are also affected.

Finally, the customisation process turned to the pursuit of authenticity. In Anzac Day reporting, interactions between memory and history are intrinsic to the telling of the story: the exploration of individual memories confirm, deny and at times confuse any official narrative. The story of Anzac Day was continuing to evolve: it could not be told through one single narrative. This was accommodated by the framework and became a key theme in the documentary.

Once developed, the customised framework was tested as a 'prototype' through the production of *Anzac*. Mascall-Dare evaluated its application through reflective practice and this led to further modifications. The final iteration (see fig. 3.2) was incorporated into a reporters' 'crib-sheet' published in the *Anzac Day Media Style Guide* which was first released in 2012 and has been updated in 2014, 2015 and 2016.

Anzac was well-received by industry and the public:[18] it met its objectives in using alternative journalistic methods to produce a documentary that aimed to be both accurate and original. In particular, *Anzac* explored alternative and forgotten narratives, including multicultural themes, acknowledging the tensions raised by a commemorative tradition that has been conflated with nationalism. It told the story of Billy Sing, an Anzac of Chinese ancestry;

---

18   *Anzac* received positive previews in *The Independent* on 8th December 2012; *The Daily Mail* on 8th December 2012; and was Gillian Reynolds' 'Pick of the Week' in *The Daily Telegraph*, on 6th December 2012. It won two awards at the 2013 New York Festivals International Radio Awards: silver for 'Best Writing' and a bronze for 'Best History Program'. It was a finalist in the 2013 United Nations of Australia Association Peace Awards (Multicultural Affairs category) and Highly Commended at the 2013 SA Media Awards.

Fig. 3.2 Anzac Day reporting: a customised framework[19]

	Conventional in-depth features	Ethnographic portraits	Anzac Day reporting
	\multicolumn{3}{c}{Conceptualisation}	
Newsworthiness	• Change • The unusual • Celebrities and elites	• Adaptation • Hidden meanings • Rituals and practices	• At first, an angle is chosen that makes sense to the outsider; interviewees are then asked to clarify/respond to this angle. Assumptions and beliefs are challenged through immersion, from an insider's perspective. • The story of the story • Adaptation of Anzac Day commemoration to new or forgotten memories/histories • The 'why' of ritual and practices • A new concept of currency: Anzac Day remembrance conflates the past with the present.
	\multicolumn{3}{c}{Reporting}	
Relationship with Sources	Autonomous professional	Socially acceptable incompetent	Acknowledgment of interactivity and interplay of roles: the journalist is both an individual and part of a collective; the interviewer is both influence and audience; sources express views that are both personal and socially framed. Differentiating roles is helpful. By identifying with the audience initially, the journalist creates engagement. By identifying with interviewees (as a participant observer) the journalist uses an insider's perspective to challenge the audience's assumptions. Throughout, journalists are not objective: they identify with their news organisation; with their audience; with their interviewees; and they hold their own views. Some form of collaborative editorial control is important to mediate between newsrooms, audiences and interviewees.
Observation Interviewer	Deductive The miner	Inductive The traveller	Inductive and self-aware; subjective The traveller with 'baggage' Initially etic, then emic

---

19   Sharon Mascall-Dare, 'An Australian story: the making of 'Anzac'', *An Australian Story: Media and Memory in the Making of Anzac Day* (PhD thesis, University of South Australia 2013), 168-9, available at: http://arrow.unisa.edu.au:8081/1959.8/152321 [accessed 22 March 2016].

	Conventional in-depth features	Ethnographic portraits	Anzac Day reporting
		Writing	
Narrator Epistemology	Journalist Balance	Group Authenticity	Group, mediated by the journalist. Narratives are discussed collaboratively to ensure accuracy. Hegemonic influences are managed and identified collaboratively. Authenticity is sought through the telling of individual stories, not a 'grand narrative' Risk analysis is required before a reporter commits to ethnographic journalism as their approach to an assignment. Ethnographic journalism requires trust between interviewees and their sources. Without trust, immersion is difficult and authenticity is likely to be compromised (unless tension, mistrust and suspicion are integral to the story). Once trust has been established, the need to exert editorial control becomes redundant. Collaboration becomes a natural consequence. Interviewees trust the journalist to portray them fairly and the journalist trusts his/her sources to collaborate fairly, providing feedback that meets the project's objectives. A pragmatic approach is required. If interviewees cannot be trusted to collaborate fairly – in pursuit of accuracy and authenticity – then journalists require editorial control to prevent censorship and/or misrepresentation. In this case, ethnographic journalism is not the best approach and the method chosen requires reconsideration. Moves from the etic to the emic. Navigates between the two to provide 'signposts' for the audience.

it also included Arthur Walker, a Ramindjeri man who fought at Gallipoli. Subjectivity was expressed and acknowledged; authenticity was pursued through collaboration with interviewees. But while the documentary received positive feedback, and was recognised for its high ethical standards, the drawbacks of its production process should also be acknowledged.

The customisation process delivered a viable framework for ethical journalistic practice in the context of Anzac Day reporting, but it required a long time-frame. The length of time spent immersed in the subject matter was atypical of a journalistic assignment – the background research phase (for the accompanying PhD exegesis) took four years to complete which is a long time, even for long-form journalism. Once production of *Anzac* was underway, however, the pressure of deadlines and limited resources were no different from any other assignment – the framework was found to be viable in a feature-making context. To make the framework more accessible and user-friendly for newsroom reporters, the 'crib-sheet' was developed for the style guide.

By pursuing ethnographic methods and signposting the expression of personal views throughout the documentary, *Anzac* was able to challenge audiences' assumptions and beliefs through the representation of a range of perspectives (including those of the producer/presenter). Care was also taken to avoid sentimentality or the glorification of war. There was recognition of its horror and its legacy, as the Adelaide-based reporter Andrew Faulkner told Mascall-Dare during an interview in 2010: 'If there is an over-arching story it is that we should remember the people that died… it is that war is bloody terrible.'[20]

Not for Glory

Not for Glory – a century of service by Australian medical women to the Australian Army and its allies explores women's contributions to the Royal Australian Army Medical Corps, noting that such stories were worthy of recognition as part of Anzac Centenary commemorations. Almost all the women featured in the book had not received publicity previously: the book's originator and co-author, Susan Neuhaus, is a doctor and academic who set out to find stories that had not been previously told, undertaking more than five years' research in libraries and research facilities in Europe and New Zealand, as well as Australia. Her collaboration with Mascall-Dare – who worked on

---

20   See Mascall-Dare, *An Australian Story*, 177.

the project as a journalist – gave a voice to women whose narratives had been previously forgotten or overlooked. It also provided an opportunity to tell her own story, featured in the book's *Epilogue*. In doing so, the book demonstrated collaborative story-telling in a long-form journalistic context.

While earlier chapters of the book focussed on women who were no longer living, later chapters drew on interviews with women who were either still serving in the Australian Army or had retired, including Neuhaus herself. Rather than 'mine' for quotes and pursue her own interpretation, Mascall-Dare drew on the collaborative story-telling methods developed during her Anzac documentary, combining ethnographic interviewing with oral history methods, offering interviewees the opportunity to set the terms of their interview and review the data presented before publication.

The outcome, in the second half of the book, was interviewees' memories told as stories. *Not for Glory* did not claim to be an official history, although some historical sections were included and extensive historical research was undertaken in order to contribute context, drawing on Neuhaus's expertise as a surgeon and former Army Medical Officer. In setting the terms of their interviews, and retaining editorial control over their portrayal, a number of the women reported a sense of ownership and empowerment; the book gave them a voice through both its production processes and its content.

The contrast between *Not for Glory*'s collaborative methods and conventional newsroom practice became clear during publicity surrounding the book's launch in November 2014. One woman featured in the book was contacted by a journalist in her local area seeking an interview about her story. While she had experienced challenges during her Army career, she saw her military service as positive: in the book, the recounting of her story recognised the multi-faceted nature of her experiences. When contacted by the local journalist, however, she was disappointed to discover that the reporter was only interested in her negative experiences: repeatedly, she was asked whether she had experienced gender discrimination and harassment in the Australian Army. When she explained that she had not, the local journalist refused to go ahead with the interview, even though the media outlet had been planning to cover the launch of the book for some weeks. The message to her was clear: either the interviewee adhered to the storyline determined in advance by the journalist, or the interview did not go ahead.[21]

---

21   Mascall-Dare was involved in the negotiations regarding this media contact; the interviewee's name has been withheld to protect her privacy.

In this context, accuracy is a necessary but not sufficient element of newsworthiness. It was evident that a more sensational narrative may have secured publicity in local media, but it was only a part of the whole story. Neuhaus encountered similar questioning in some of her media interviews about the book. While multi-faceted narratives can be accommodated in long-form journalism, what Neuhaus and the woman interviewed by a local media outlet found was that daily news reporting still prefers a single angle that highlights conflict which is included in almost every definition of news values but is an outcome that is ethically problematic, when as a result important voices and perspectives are excluded or silenced.

Thank You for Your Service

David Finkel, an American journalist and author, makes it his mission to find and recover voices that have been excluded or silenced. The title of his 2013 book, *Thank You for Your Service*, comes from the phrase routinely uttered by Americans to their countrymen and women returning from the current wars in Afghanistan and Iraq but many veterans loathe it. One of them, Adam Schumann, suffering from post-traumatic stress disorder and having come close to committing suicide, is invited by a well-meaning Veterans Affairs officer to an all-expenses-paid pheasant hunt promoted as a weekend for 'Healing Heroes, Healing Families!' He hates the 'We Support the Troops' bumper stickers on cars driven by people who have never been to war, never will go, and who say to soldiers, 'Thank you for your service,' with their 'gooey eyes and orthodontist smiles'.[22] They fawn over the soldiers with gunshot scars and missing limbs but they miss Schumann's invisible scars; that makes him feel even more worthless.

Yet Schumann was an exceptionally brave soldier who hoisted on his back a wounded comrade whose blood ran into Schumann's mouth as he carried him to safety, and remained stained into his tastebuds years afterward. Schumann was also brave enough to ask for a 'mental health evacuation' when he could no longer go on fighting. Life after three tours of duty is as hard, if not harder, for him, for his wife Saskia and their young children. He can't work for any sustained period, he and Saskia fight bitterly and continuously. The book opens with a scene of him cradling his four-day old baby in their bed and as he falls asleep loosening his grip and waking only when he hears a crack followed by a thud as the baby hit the floor.

---

22   Finkel, *Thank You for Your Service*, 127.

Thank You for Your Service, which was made into a film in 2016, is an almost unbearably sad book; it is also an important book for those who have not experienced war as it is almost impossible to read without beginning to appreciate the appalling toll war takes on combat troops. It is a sequel of sorts to Finkel's 2009 book, *The Good Soldiers*,[23] which chronicled the eight months he spent with a battalion of 800 US Army soldiers from Fort Riley, Kansas, that was known as the 2-16 (Second Battalion, 16th Infantry Regiment of the Fourth Infantry Brigade Combat Team, First Infantry Division). Where *The Good Soldiers*, which won several prestigious awards, showed how the Bush administration's 'surge' policy in 2007 actually affected troops on the ground, *Thank You for Your Service* follows them home to report on what Finkel calls 'the after-war' which turns out to be disturbingly bleak. By 2010, he writes, the number of former troops who commit suicide exceeds the number of combat deaths and averages almost one a day.

A long-serving *Washington Post* journalist who now devotes much of his time to book-length journalism, Finkel is an extraordinarily compassionate writer. He almost never inserts himself into the narrative yet through painstaking research, saturation interviewing and first-hand observation, he takes the reader deep into the desperate struggles, the daily setbacks and the small victories of the returned soldiers and their families. The book is rendered in a series of scenes with half a dozen or so returned soldiers and a widow who talks to her husband's ashes because she can't bring herself to deal with them. Finkel also shows the quietly heroic efforts of those who seek to help the veterans; most of them are either veterans or are married to one.

Two of the veterans commit suicide, one after subjecting his wife to sickening verbal abuse and violence, the other after feeling both desolate guilt and dumb defiance over his role in the deaths of nine men including two journalists in Iraq. This event later became notorious as the 'Collateral Murder' video on the WikiLeaks website. Finkel has been criticised, with some weight, for failing to condemn the soldiers over the event, which he first wrote about in *The Good Soldiers*. In that book he was primarily concerned with 'documenting their corner of the war, without agenda';[24] in this one Finkel does not shy away from describing the impact of the killings but he allows himself this editorial comment about the millions of viewers who commented on the 'Collateral Murder' video 'in absolutes and certainties,

---

23   David Finkel, *The Good Soldiers* (Melbourne: Scribe, 2009).
24   Finkel, *The Good Soldiers*, 285.

as if war could be comprehended fully by a high-speed connection to the Internet and a carefully edited video clip'.[25] But it is not necessary to reduce the matter to an either/or choice; we need both WikiLeaks' disclosing of important information that had been kept secret and Finkel's quest to understand rather than judge.

Uncommon Soldier

David Finkel's book is part of a sizeable, rich US literature of long-form journalistic accounts of the wars in Afghanistan and Iraq.[26] The comparable literature in Australia is smaller. There have been several notable books but the premise of Chris Masters' *Uncommon Soldier*, published in 2012, is that despite Australia's involvement in the wars in both Afghanistan and Iraq, the public has been told little about the soldiers' experiences either good or bad.

In the mid-2000s, as a long time reporter with ABC television's prestigious current affairs program, *Four Corners*, Masters lobbied for access to the Australian soldiers deployed in Afghanistan. He was met with resistance, he writes, because the military's reason for being is to fight wars not publicity campaigns. Eventually, the military hierarchy began to see how little of the lived reality of the Australians' efforts overseas was being reported. The public generally understood the courage needed to put your life in danger for your country but little beyond that.

Masters did gain access, initially to training camps for soldiers, at Kapooka in rural New South Wales, and for officers, at Duntroon in Canberra, then to Afghanistan where he was embedded with troops. He witnessed fierce fighting as well as the satisfactions – and the frustrations – of working to build relationships with local Afghans to help them re-build their country. The only way to build trust with the military, he writes, is to earn it and eventually he is invited to attend the 2nd Commando Regiment's Anzac Day dawn service.

The first noteworthy point about *Uncommon Soldier* is the amount of useful and relevant information it provides, whether context about the history and politics of Afghanistan or the cost to taxpayers of deploying soldiers – about

---

25　Finkel, *Thank You For Your Service*, 227.
26　Steve Weinberg, 'The book as an investigative vehicle for news', *Nieman Reports* (Spring 2007), available at: www.nieman.harvard.edu/reports/07-1NRspring/p104-0701-weinberg.html (accessed 12 March 2015), and Matthew Ricketson, *Telling True Stories* (Sydney: Allen & Unwin, 2014), 12-14.

$1 million a year – or the barracks-room wit where soldiers coin nicknames for officers such as Blister – 'pops up after hard work'. The second is that the book gradually unfolds a rounded portrait of the Australian military that is by turns sympathetic, tough-minded and clear-eyed. Masters shows us the uglier side of military life – the alpha males, the misogyny, the hazing rituals, the uneasiness about homosexuality, the army's institutional inflexibility – but he also reveals the psychological benefits of submitting your individuality to the service of a unit, and the camaraderie flowing from it. 'Loners tend not to survive because the engine of the corps of cadets is fuelled by the internal combustion of co-operation, with sole operators a mistrusted contaminant.'[27] He also allows us to see the truly extraordinary courage shown by many troops including Victoria Cross winners Mark Donaldson and Ben Roberts-Smith.

Masters immersed himself in military life but he does not immerse the reader by presenting soldiers in the narrative from their own perspective as Finkel does in *Thank You for Your Service*, which may have something to do with his approach to long form journalism but also to the difference between American and Australian soldiers. Where the former 'can seem like contestants in a talent quest,' the latter do not perform on cue. Indeed, when Masters and his film crew walk into a recreation room saying they want to gather footage, the soldiers flee: 'A consequence of the intense group bonding is the individual's aversion to attention.'[28] They have what is called a 'carton rule', whereby anyone appearing in the media is obliged to buy a carton of beer for their mates. Masters understands the Australian wariness of 'big-noting' but comments 'it does not help when trying to tell their story, a story they universally conceded was not getting through to the broad public.'[29]

The Not Dead

Where Masters tells the stories of many Australian soldiers for the first time, and Finkel's extraordinarily empathic reporting and writing enables readers to begin to understand the impact of combat on soldiers, *The Not Dead* uses a particularly innovative method of story-telling to explore the lives and experiences of former servicemen who have post-traumatic stress. A documentary first aired on Channel Four in the United Kingdom in 2007,

---

27 See Masters, 58-9.
28 Masters, 115.
29 Masters, 115.

The Not Dead's story-telling method blends poetry with testimony in its portrayal of traumatic memory.

The documentary film incorporates the stories of three men from three generations: Cliff, who returned from Malaysia in 1951; Rob who served in Iraq and Eddie who served in Bosnia. In a break with conventional journalistic practice, the film does not rely solely on interviews, script or footage: it incorporates poetry to convey the men's experiences through metaphor and description. According to publicity material released by the International Documentary Film Festival – Amsterdam:

> Director Brian Hill films the men in an unembellished manner, intentionally placing them against the backdrop of archive footage and their current everyday reality, which they still seem isolated from. Poet Simon Armitage wrote a series of poems based on their deeply emotional accounts, and the men recite them as they look straight into the camera. In the process, these revisited nightmarish experiences intensify their history, rendering it universal.[30]

Reviews of the film called it 'deft and moving', 'bleak, beautiful, blistering' and 'incredibly moving'.[31] The incorporation of war poetry was seen as highly original, offering new avenues for audience empathy and engagement. *The Not Dead* was the result of continuing collaboration between Armitage and documentary film director Brian Hill that used similar production methods in previous works: *Feltham Sings* (2002) told the stories of inmates in a young offenders' institution though rap and music; *Pornography – The Musical* (2003) gave an insider's perspective on Britain's pornography industry through interview and song. While the pair's collaboration had previously dealt with confrontational content, *The Not Dead* raised questions about ethical practice in media interviews, particularly when interviewees are asked to recall experiences of trauma.

As Armitage acknowledged: 'Most of the poems I wrote revolved around a key 'flashback' scene, requiring each soldier to re-visit the very incident he was desperately hoping to forget.'[32] This contrasted with his other poems, which were less direct in their portrayal of troubling experiences – production of *The Not Dead* required interviewees to confront their

---

30   See http://www.idfa.nl/industry/tags/project.aspx?id=54239848-7caf-4e61-a909-d8a641aa72c3 (accessed 12 March 2015).

31   See http://www.centuryfilmsltd.com/thenotdead.htm (accessed 12 March 2015).

32   Simon Armitage, *The Not Dead* (Pomona: Hebden Bridge, 2008).

traumatic memories directly, as part of an interview process that had both creative and therapeutic consequences.[33] It is not known what steps were taken to ensure that the interviews were carried out in accordance with recommended ethical practice. It appears from the documentary that the veterans participated willingly and there has been no negative reaction from them about their experience – at least not publicly; what is evident is that the style of representation on screen offered an alternative approach to the representation of traumatic memory in a media context.

While the use of poetry was described as 'intensifying', for the interviewees it might also have been experienced as distancing: enabling them to refer to their experiences in the words of an 'other' – namely Armitage. This approach provided an opportunity, potentially, for simultaneous engagement and disengagement – an outcome discouraged by conventional documentary-making that encourages interviewees to describe memories in detail, reliving through recalling, in order to maximise the impact of content.

It is notable that the inclusion of poetry in Armitage and Hill's work has not been widely adopted by other documentary-makers; it remains a hallmark of their collaboration. In Australia, the blending of poetry and testimony to tell veterans' stories has taken place on stage – notably in the Sydney Theatre Company's production *The Long Way Home*[34] – but is yet to be explored in a journalistic format.

Conclusion

The case studies in this paper demonstrate a willingness, on the part of some journalists and writers, to pursue a more immersive style of reporting that pursues authenticity as well as ethical responsibility. Still, such examples remain the exception rather than the rule in Australia: as Mascall-Dare identified in her analysis of interviews with Anzac Day reporters, journalists need guidance, support and increased resources in order to achieve the standards they have set for themselves.

The Anzac Centenary offers an opportunity to diversify coverage of veterans' affairs in Australia; it also offers an opportunity to review and expand the resources available to journalists for the task. The Dart Center for

---

33 J. Gutorow, "Damaged beyond help'? Simon Armitage's *The Not Dead* and the paradoxes of trauma', *Trauma: Theory and Practice* (Prague: Czech Republic, 2011).

34 See Jason Blake, 'The Long Way Home: Soldiers' stories have real impact', *Sydney Morning Herald* (9 February 2014) available at: http://www.smh.com.au/entertainment/theatre/the-long-way-home-soldiers-stories-have-real-impact-20140209-329sp.html (accessed 12 march 2015).

Journalism and Trauma offers practical advice on ethical conduct and self-care to journalists assigned to stories involving war, violence, conflict and trauma; it is actively engaged in journalism education in Australia through its website (www.dartcenter.org) and Dart Centre Asia Pacific, based in Melbourne. The *Anzac Day Media Style Guide* also offers independent guidance to journalists, including advice on ethical conduct and protocol, backed by an editorial advisory board that includes representatives from academia, the media, Ex-Service Organisations and the wider defence community. Journalists also have access to briefing material from the Department of Veterans' Affairs, the federal government's Anzac Centenary website and state government agencies.

Despite the availability of such resources, material support for ethically responsible, original journalism is still lacking. Immersive reporting is time-consuming and expensive; as a business, long-form journalism is not economically viable for newsrooms under financial pressure. While the conventional paradigm of journalism is changing – with audiences becoming reporters, particularly through social media – there is still a place for immersive reporting that demonstrates a deeper, richer understanding of matters of public interest. As Australia revisits its national narrative through the Anzac Centenary years there is an opportunity to ask how that story should be told, and how its reporters can be supported – ensuring that authenticity, integrity and ethical standards are upheld.

Chapter 4

UNCANNY VALLEYS AND ANZAC AVATARS

Scaling a Postdigital Gallipoli

Tom Sear

To mark the centenary of the Gallipoli campaign in 2015, news organisations and image libraries created 'then and now' montages of the Gallipoli battlefields by digitally combining photographs taken nearly a century apart. Getty Images used photo editing software to generate composite digital images that merged fragments of black and white scenes, showing troop arrivals and advances, with modern colour digital footage of these places today. *Guardian Australia* photographer Mike Bowers created the *Anzac Cove and Gallipoli: Then and Now* interactive. It allowed viewers to transition between historical photographs and contemporary images taken at precisely the same location with the click of a mouse.[1] Bowers said, 'I spent 10 days at the end of January 2015 producing this material, I wanted to bring the battlefield pictures left to us by the soldier photographers to life' (Plate 4.1).[2]

---

1   Mike Bowers, 'Anzac Cove and Gallipoli: Then and Now – Interactive', *The Guardian*, Retrieved from http://www.theguardian.com/news/ng-interactive/2015/apr/22/anzac-cove-and-gallipoli-then-and-now-interactive (accessed March 23, 2016). Gallup, Fairfax & Getty Images, 'This Digital Composite Image Shows Australian Soldiers, Including…', Getty Images, Retrieved from http://www.gettyimages.com.au/detail/news-photo/waves-from-the-aegean-sea-lap-onto-the-shores-of-anzac-cove-news-photo/469684318 (accessed March 23, 2016). Australian Broadcasting Corporation, 'Interactive Photos: See Gallipoli Today and 100 Years Ago', Retrieved from http://www.abc.net.au/news/2015-04-21/gallipoli-photos-then-and-now/6408400 (accessed March 23, 2016).

2   Amanda Meade, 'Guardian Australia's Mike Bowers Wins Kennedy Award for Gallipoli Photo Essay', (2015). Retrieved from http://www.theguardian.com/

It is hard not to feel unsettled by these images. The fixed camera position and enduring clifftops and tidelines appear to signal timelessness, just as they bridge a particular past and a particular present in each place. The historical figures appear and disappear like ghosts, while the kinetic urgency of their bodies dissolving and emerging into lapping waves and blowing bushes make them seem solid, alive. The stillness and loss of colour in the older images amplifies the sensation of their momentousness, just as their fading away suggests that they have also been absorbed into longer narratives of conflict and occupation in that place. The pace of the transitions evokes both the distance between the then and the now, and the closeness of these events in our memories. As the crowded landing scenes give way to the emptiness of the modern beach, and then change again in the reverse, under our command they evoke eerie and disquieting sensations. It is this uncanny quality, also evoked by other digitally-generated commemorations, which will be explored in this chapter.

The lead up to April 2015 saw the jagged cliffs and valleys of Turkey's Gallipoli Peninsula scanned, digitised and colourised, buzzed by drones, rendered into digital topography, captured in selfies, moulded in miniature, and peopled by commemorative crowds, hyper-real model soldiers and historical avatars with social media profiles. The centenary of the Gallipoli campaign produced a vast assemblage of commemorative activity, generated in an era that is beginning to be called the 'postdigital'. As David M. Berry describes it, the postdigital represents a world where 'computation has become spatial in its implementation, embedded within the environment, in the body and in society, it becomes part of the texture of life itself which can be walked around, touched, manipulated and interacted with in a number of ways'. '"Being online" and "being offline"', he argues, 'is now anachronistic' as is 'the notion that we have "digital" or "analogue" worlds that are disconnected and discreet'.[3]

This chapter explores the changing character of war commemoration in the postdigital[4] age by focusing on the centenary of the Gallipoli campaign

---

    world/2015/aug/08/guardian-australias-mike-bowers-wins-kennedy-award-for-gallipoli-photo-essay?CMP=Share_iOSApp_Other (accessed March 23, 2016).

3   David M. Berry, 'The Postdigital Constellation', in *Postdigital Aesthetics*, eds. David M. Berry and Michael Dieter (Basingstoke: Palgrave Macmillan, 2015), 50.

4   The use of the term 'postdigital' in this chapter is a temporal viewing platform, rather than strict periodising concept, to suggest an epistemology of the historical present after the computational turn in which the distinction between 'the digital and non-digital becomes increasingly blurred'. The term postdigital is an evolving neologism to 'grapple with the immersive and disorientating experiences of computational infra-

in Australia, New Zealand and Turkey in 2015. In particular, it reflects on the turn towards commemorative activities that seek to generate empathy and connection between contemporary audiences and historical subjects by collapsing space and time and rendering the 'past' as a new kind of 'present'.

These popular forms have disquieted some historians, who lament their apparent lack of distance, awareness of cultural context and complex understandings of agency and perspective. However their proliferation and popularity suggests they deserve scholarly attention not only within history and memory studies, but also – given the increasing entanglement between digital and analogue, past and present – in relation to a range of insights drawn from philosophy, media studies, and digital aesthetics.

Media, memory and history in the postdigital world

The experience of Gallipoli in 2015 existed in the confluence and diffusion of media, memory and history-production in the postdigital era. Jay Winter has argued that there were two key memory booms in the twentieth century. The first generation occurred from the 1890s to the 1920s, when the memorialisation of the dead of the First World War was associated with national identity, while the second arose from memories of the Second World War.[5] The mediatisation of oral history, witnessed accounts, the museum as a site of storytelling and recreated experience, and the dominance of the visual on television characterised the second boom, and the Holocaust figured large as a trope for comprehension of social memory.[6]

Andrew Hoskins, reflecting on the digital era – after the 'connective turn' and in the midst of the emergence of informational infrastructure – has observed a convergence and reflexivity between the memory of nodal conflicts from the twentieth century, contemporary war and media ecologies. The immediacy and media-saturated nature of contemporary war, diffuse

---

structures as they scale up and intensify'. (Berry and Dieter, 2-3., 4., Footnote 2. Geoff Cox, 'Postscript on the Post-digital and the Problem of Temporality', in *Postdigital Aesthetics*, 151-162). The term serves as a marker to place historical 'nationalist' and 'hyperconnective commemoration' (Sear, Routledge, forthcoming) within an emergent 'historical trajectory of planetary scale computation' from this 'blur', where 'The Stack we have becomes The Stack-to-come'. Benjamin Bratton,*The Stack: On Software and Sovereignty*, (Cambridge: The MIT Press, 2015), xx., 16., 293., 352.

5 Jay Winter, *Remembering War: The Great War between Memory and History in the 20th Century* (London: Yale University Press, 2008); Andrew Hoskins and Ben O'Loughlin, *War and Media: The Emergence of Diffused War* (Cambridge, UK; Malden, MA: Polity Press, 2010).

6 Winter.

in cause and effect, is connected with a media culture engaging in constant, revisionistic memorialisation of nodal events of the past. Just as today's wars are viewed through the lenses of the past, so the database/archive of the internet releases and stores a constant flow of images and memories of past wars, while current conflicts taking place in our digital culture are instantly memorialised, escalating or escaping the arcs familiar with twentieth-century conflict. Obsessive accumulation of information about the past in a post-scarcity world paradoxically creates a new kind of forgetting – there is no real need to 'remember' when past data is stored externally, and constantly pushed into the present. Memory and history, Hoskins argues, live within media ecologies, each integrated but parts of larger systems of perception. Hoskins also suggests that in our contemporary era there is a blurring of history and memory. History looks more like memory after the connective turn.[7]

Just as the meaning of memory and memorialisation changed in the twenty-first century, so too the way in which western society consumes and produces 'history' has become more diverse and diffuse[8]. As the past becomes digitised and uploaded into the vast database of the web, the ecology of history has changed to embrace participation and hybrid forms. The experience of Gallipoli for Australian audiences in the period surrounding the centenary in 2015 typified the maturity of this consumption. Local history boomed with the creation of new honour rolls and restoration of existing memorials, extending the significance of 'places' (both within Australia and beyond it) as a prime focus for commemoration. Family history too offered an intimate and particular way to connect with the history of World War I. Online genealogy resources such as digitised archives, search engines, Wikipedia and corporate providers facilitated the discovery or renewal of family links to Gallipoli. Historical reenactors were involved from the capture of German New Guinea, to Turkish reenactor troops mingling with commemorators and the current Turkish Special Forces on the Gallipoli peninsula. Mainstream television in Australia created numerous war-themed documentaries,

---

7   Andrew Hoskins, 'Media, Memory, Metaphor: Remembering and the Connective Turn', *Parallax* 17, no. 4 (2011); Andrew Hoskins and Ben O'Loughlin, 'Arrested War: The Third Phase of Mediatization', *Information, Communication & Society* (2015); Andrew Hoskins, 'The War Vector and the New Structure of Memorialization', Chapter from *21st Century War: Media, Memory, History*, (Forthcoming), also presented at Çanakkale/ Gallipoli Wars International Conference, Çanakkale Onsekiz Mart University, Turkey, May 22, 2015; Hoskins and O'Loughlin, *War and Media*; Andrew Hoskins, 'A New Memory of War', in *Journalism and Memory*, eds. Barbie Zelizer and Keren Tenenboim-Weinblatt, (Basingstoke: Palgrave Macmillan, 2014), 179–91.

8   Jerome De Groot, *Consuming History: Historians and Heritage in Contemporary Popular Culture* (London; New York: Routledge, 2009).

adaptations and drama shows. Major Gallipoli films like Russell Crowe's *The Water Diviner* were released internationally; plays and performance artwork from dance to original music compositions were staged. Museums updated exhibitions and toured travelling shows throughout Australia. Popular and public historians frequently appeared on TV, and sales of popular histories of Gallipoli in print exploded.[9]

In *Private Lives Public History*, Anna Clark writes compellingly about the merits of responding thoughtfully and openly to the diverse ways in which people connect with the past. She argues 'we need an idea of history which accommodates not only "what happened" but the many ways we "think" about the past'.[10] She usefully adopts Jörn Rüsen's view of historical consciousness as 'making sense' of the past 'for the sake of understanding the present'.[11] Clark notes how the 'peopling' of history over the last four decades has led not only to a growing inclusiveness in historical practice, but also a strong emphasis on personal links to the past (whether through genealogy, place associations or shared experience) as a conduit to intimate, empathetic connection.[12] It is also worth exploring, as I do below, how the diverse publics who are increasingly active in history-making also possess a sophisticated – and frequently critical – appreciation of history's production and consumption, as well as of the complex, dynamic ways in which the 'past' and 'present' might shape each other.

As the experience of Anzac Day 2015 shows, the digital has played a key role in reconnecting the past with the present, both in relation to conflict and commemoration, and to the enfranchisement of wider communities of history makers. The Australian community has rapidly developed a large appetite for digital media, internet-based interactivity and networked technologies like smartphones, and they increasingly access historical information via these platforms. In April 2015 there were 2, 318, 078 searches for the term Anzac in Google, compared to 810,390 in the same month a year earlier. In addition, in April 2015 there were 1,023,770 searches for the term Gallipoli in Google, compared to 354,380 in the April 2014.[13] But in a postdigital

---

[9] Tom Sear, 'Dawn Servers: Anzac Day 2015 and Hyperconnective Commemoration', in *War Memory and Commemoration*, ed. Brad West (Forthcoming, Routledge, 2016).

[10] Anna Clark, *Private Lives, Public History* (Melbourne: Melbourne University Publishing, 2016), 4.

[11] Clark. 4.

[12] Clark, 142.

[13] Sear, 'Dawn Servers'. Tom Sear Account, Google, Campaign Management – Google Adwords, Retrieved from https://adwords.google.com/ (accessed June 27, 2015).

world, the digital's influence on how Gallipoli is understood extends beyond the number of hits on a site, or likes for a Facebook post. Digital technologies and ways of seeing, connecting and imagining are shaping new representations of Gallipoli as a place and as an historical event.

Recreating Gallipoli 1915: Models, avatars and making the past present

One of the most striking characteristics of some of the new forms of commemorative activity surrounding Gallipoli 2015 was their impulse to recreate the events of 1915 so that audiences engaged with them as if they were happening now, not in the past. Three distinctive perceptions were critical to their success: historical accuracy, emotional authenticity, and a strange, compelling disturbance of time.

Sarah Kenderdine observes that the digital enables an opportunity to animate and reimagine the archive. Kenderdine draws upon archaeologist Michael Shanks' notions of 'prosthetic architectures,' of archives which emphasise 'personal affective engagement' and Latour's 'migration of the aura' to indicate how the digital affords new strategies for inhabiting places, re-embodying and performing the archive[14].

In New Zealand, multidisciplinary creative design and effects teams, normally associated with big budget cinema and gaming, supersized and miniaturised historical characters. The Museum of New Zealand Te Papa Tongarewa, working closely with Weta Workshop, developed *Gallipoli: The Scale of Our War*.[15] Utilising 3D printing and silicone, Weta Workshop created Ron Mueck-style hyper sculptures of real characters from Gallipoli, two and a half times life-size, as the central focus of the exhibition (Plate 4.2).[16] In

---

14 Michael Shanks, 'Michael Shanks: Animating the Archive', Retrieved from http://documents.stanford.edu/michaelshanks/186,http://documents.stanford.edu/michaelshanks/186; (accessed March 23, 2016). Bruno Latour, 'The Migration of the Aura or How to Explore the Original through Its Fac Similies', Retrieved from http://www.bruno-latour.fr/sites/default/files/108-ADAM-FACSIMILES-GB.pdf (accessed March 23, 2016). Sarah Kenderdine, "Sarah Kenderdine Keynote, EVAA 2016," See http://evaa.com.au/2016/01/sarah-kenderdine-to-keynote-at-evaa/; (accessed March 23, 2016)

15 Museum of New Zealand Te Papa Tongarewa, 'Gallipoli: The Scale of Our War', Retrieved from http://gallipoli.tepapa.govt.nz (accessed March 23, 2016).

16 Weta Workshop, 'Gallipoli: The Scale of Our War (2015)'. Retrieved from http://wetaworkshop.com/projects/gallipoli-the-scale-of-our-war/ (accessed March 23, 2016); Alan Taylor, 'The Hyperrealistic Sculptures of Ron Mueck'(2013). Retrieved from http://www.theatlantic.com/infocus/2013/10/the-hyperrealistic-sculptures-of-ron-mueck/100606/ (accessed March 23, 2016).

the 'making of' video, entitled 'Building Gallipoli', Weta workshop creative director Sir Richard Taylor explained how the project was personality and character driven. Taylor described how he considered that the soldiers and nurses were just like 'kids of today'. 'Characters' were selected who had written Gallipoli diaries. Actors and staff members then re-enacted moments from the real life personalities' experiences on Gallipoli, while motion capture digitally scanned their bodies. These scans were then 3D printed, silicone sculpted, and had painted features, hair and clothes added.[17] The accompanying website featured an array of elements from the exhibition reconfigured as a digital assemblage, including collection objects, often photographed in HD digital close up, the characters' stories and sound recording of their 'voices' tiled together. Details of images, models and quotes – a close-up of a tear about to roll down a stubbly cheek, or poignant words in handwriting – when clicked on, open new pages that reveal more detailed content. Each object and personal story is given a time scale and location to fix and locate it. The exhibition and the website convey an intense intimacy, combined with multiple layers of detail, and stark juxtapositions of perspectives, both past and present.[18]

While the Te Papa/Weta exhibition emphasised large-scale hyper-realistic modelling to generate empathetic connection, the Dominion Museum used crowdsourced miniatures to create an incredibly detailed scale model of Gallipoli. *The Great War Exhibition* features a year by year description of New Zealand's involvement in World War I.[19] Gallipoli was, from the outset, a key focus for the exhibition. Filmmaker Sir Peter Jackson created, in collaboration with Weta Workshop, Perry Miniatures, and New Zealand amateur model makers (who individually hand-painted each figure), a diorama of the Kiwi actions on Chunuk Bair.[20] Jackson requested grubby realism in the scale figure painting and the resulting display presents a panoptic view of the battlefield one might see from a drone: the scale and scope of the engagement is captured at the same time as the frozen poses of each figure offer the possibility of viewing the attitude and even the facial expression of each soldier. In this, the scene offers a similar audience experience to the simultaneity of mass and

---

17 Weta.
18 Te Papa.
19 Dominion, 'The Great War Exhibition, Wellington, New Zealand', Retrieved from http://www.greatwarexhibition.nz/(accessed March 23, 2016). Michael Forbes, 'Jackson Unveils War Exhibition', Retrieved from http://www.stuff.co.nz/national/last-post-first-light/67843693/sir-peter-jackson-shows-off-his-great-war-exhibition-in-wellington (accessed March 23, 2016).
20 Andy Palmer, 'Mustering the Troops: Photos'. Retrieved from http://anzacdiorama.blogspot.com.au/p/these-are-first-public-photos-of.html (accessed March 23, 2016).

individual sacrifice present in both data visualisations and poppy displays of World War I casualties.[21]

Jackson also expressly forbade the use of any black and white photographs in the exhibition. All images including, controversially, those from the Australian War Memorial, were coloured,[22] to give the impression of the experiences being lived 'in the present'. In an era of digital image manipulation, where Photoshop image colourisation of historical photographs is accessible to professionals and hobbyists, there has been a proliferation of these kinds of images distributed online. The result is an eerie hybrid, with the lighting, tones and contrasts derived from the original camera, photographer and developer blended with colours made by the particular pixels, screens, programs, and historical and technical knowledge of the colouriser.[23]

Other New Zealand recreations of Gallipoli were also told through the lens of creative and cinematic industries working in a material, post-screen world.[24] Also based upon war diaries of soldiers and a nurse, Leanne Pooley's *25 April* animated the stories of six diarists with digital animation and motion capture.[25] New Zealand's commemorations co-opted all the dynamics of their cinematic industry, but inverted them into the creation of hyper-real 'Gallipolis' in the present. Exhibition and websites used the language of cinematography, of shot construction, POV and zoom to focus attention on the 'reality' of the past experienced in the present.

The Presidency of the Republic of Turkey also utilised cinematic devices to deliver a centenary tribute. Urban Turkey has one of the world's highest consumptions of news via social media.[26] Equally, Twitter consistently

---

21 Tom Sear, '"We Are the Dead": Poppies & Postdigital Visualisations in Centenary Commemorations of the First World War', (Forthcoming, publication arising from http://evaa.com.au/).

22 Forbes. John McDonald, 'The Great War Exhibition and Gallipoli: The Scale of Our War Reviewed', Retrieved from http://www.smh.com.au/entertainment/art-and-design/the-great-war-exhibition-and-gallipoli-the-scale-of-our-war-reviewed-20150429-1mv4o4.html (accessed March 23, 2016).

23 'WW1 Colourised Photos', Retrieved from https://www.facebook.com/WW1-Colourised-Photos-450822585061599/?fref=ts (accessed March 23, 2016). Doug Banks, 'Colourise History ', Retrieved from http://www.colourisehistory.com/ (accessed March 23, 2016).

24 McDonald.

25 Leanne Pooley, '25 April Trailer'. Retrieved from https://www.youtube.com/watch?v=gfeKrG74_uQ (accessed March 23, 2016). IMDb, '25 April (2015)'. Retrieved from http://www.imdb.com/title/tt3728746 (accessed March 23, 2016)

26 Reuters Institute, 'How Turkey Uses Social Media', Retrieved from http://www.digitalnewsreport.org/essays/2015/how-turkey-uses-social-media/ (accessed March

reports the world's highest requests for tweet removals from the Turkish government. Between January and June 2015 Twitter received more than 310 requests, dwarfing the nearest highest, Russia, with 68.[27] During April 2015 the Turkish Government temporarily blocked social platforms YouTube, Twitter and Facebook.[28] President Recep Tayyip Erdoğan had previously commented, 'Twitter schmitter, we'll close them all (social platforms)'.[29] Nonetheless, President Erdoğan made his first tweet in February 2015.[30] As Hoskins and O'Loughlin have noted, the response of international governments, the military and mainstream media to the disruption of social media has been mixed. However the strategic necessity of these forces to respond is undoubted.[31]

With the centenary of the landings approaching, the Presidency produced a video re-enactment which conjured up Gallipoli as an intergenerational version of Anderson's imagined community, combined with a sense of the sacred ascendant.[32] On 20 April 20 2015 President Erdogan tweeted a link to a Government produced YouTube video commemorating the battle of Çanakkale to his 6.25 million followers. The tweet received 21,000 retweets and 8000 likes, ranking highly in the context of Gallipoli-related tweets over the Anzac Day 2015 period.[33] The video featured President Erdoğan reciting the Arif Nihat Asya poem, 'Dua' (Prayer).[34] It intercuts contemporary images of Erdoğan paying respects to a grave at the Çanakkale Martyrs' Memorial

---

23, 2016).
27 Twitter, 'Removal Requests Worldwide Jan-Jun2015', Retrieved from https://transparency.twitter.com/removal-requests/2015/jan-jun (accessed March 23, 2016)
28 Reuters Institute.
29 Reuters Institute.
30 Reuters Institute.
31 Hoskins and O'Loughlin, *Arrested War.*
32 Benedict Anderson, *Imagined Communities: Reflections on the Origin and Spread of Nationalism* (Verso, London, 2006).
33 @RT_Erdogan, 'Çanakkale Zaferi'nin 100.Yıldönümünde Tüm Şehit Ve Gazilerimizi Saygı Ve Minnetle Anıyoruz' (accessed March 23, 2016). Retrieved from https://twitter.com/RT_Erdogan/status/590213821609934848 (accessed March 23, 2016) Erik Borra and Bernhard Rieder, 'Programmed Method: Developing a Toolset for Capturing and Analyzing Tweets', *Aslib Journal of Information Management* 66, no. 3 (2014). Tom Sear, The Digital Methods Initiative Twitter Capture and Analysis Toolset (DMI-TCAT API), Anzac Tweet Capture 25 April 2015, UNSW CBR @ ADFA (2015).
34 hurriyetdailynews.com, 'Turkish President Erdoğan's Gallipoli 'Prayer' Stirs Debate', Retrieved from http://www.hurriyetdailynews.com/turkish-president-erdogans-gallipoli-prayer-stirs-debate.aspx?pageID=238&nID=81350&NewsCatID=338 (accessed March 23, 2016). hurriyetdailynews.com 'Poetic Prayer Makes Erdoğan

(*Çanakkale Şehitleri Anıtı*) on the peninsula, and dramatised contemporary Turkish citizens 'remembering' their ancestral connections to the Çanakkale battles. These citizens are shown literally hearing ancestral invocations of martyrdom made on the battlefield, and this footage is further intercut with re-enactments in the style of the 2012 Turkish film *Çanakkale 1915*.[35] The video, 'viewed' almost 150,000 times[36] was widely debated on Turkish social media.[37] The hashtag #100YıllıkDestanÇanakkale trended briefly between April 20 and 25 when President Erdoğan made regular Çanakkale/Gallipoli tweets in English and Turkish. Like most successful tweets, those with multimedia, such as the video, received the most likes and shares. Blended visualisations, shared on social media, continue through 2016 to have on-going impact in official Turkish Çanakkale commemoration online.[38]

Hoskins and O'Loughlin argue that the 2010s marks a third phase of mediatisation, of arrested war. They argue that while Western government and elites struggle with phase two, militaries have embraced the 'social media logics of personalization and spreadability'. However it is news organisations who have adapted most effectively: mainstream live historical retellings reflect some of this capacity to capture user generated content.[39]

The drive for mainstream outlets to present Gallipoli narratives and thereby occupy the media assemblage during 2015 was transnational. Online sources had by 2015 become a main focus of Australian news consumption.[40] The more subtle message of the Reuter's Institute report was that platform-centric social media feeds were now a key focus, competing

---

Couple Shed Tears in Albania', Retrieved from http://www.hurriyetdailynews.com/video-poetic-prayer-makes-erdogan-couple-shed-tears-in-albania.aspx?pageID=238&nID=82390&NewsCatID=510 (accessed March 23, 2016).

35   IMDb, 'Çanakkale 1915 (2012)', Retrieved from http://www.imdb.com/title/tt2415964/ (accessed March 23, 2016).

36   @RT_Erdogan, 'Çanakkale Zaferi'nin 100.Yıldönümünde Tüm Şehit Ve Gazilerimizi Saygı Ve Minnetle Anıyoruz' ; Türkiye Cumhuriyeti Cumhurbaşkanlığı, '100 Yıllık Destan Çanakkale', Retrieved from https://www.youtube.com/watch?v=OzpgpKBzSMw (accessed March 23, 2016). Presidency of the Republic of Turkey, 'A Centennial Epic: Çanakkale [Gallipoli], with English Subtitles', Retrieved from https://www.youtube.com/watch?v=pTp900r8CGQ (accessed March 23, 2016).

37   hurriyetdailynews.com, 'Turkish President Erdoğan's Gallipoli 'Prayer' Stirs Debate'.

38   @RT_Erdogan, Tweet, 18 March 2016. Retrieved from https://twitter.com/RT_Erdogan/status/710901924489510913?lang=en (accessed March 26, 2016).

39   Hoskins and O'Loughlin, *Arrested War*.

40   Reuters Institute, 'Australia', Retrieved from http://www.digitalnewsreport.org/survey/2015/australia-2015/ (accessed March 23, 2016). See also ABC, *Media Watch*, 13 June 2016. Retrieved from http://iview.abc.net.au/programs/media-watch/FA1535H020S00 (accessed June 24, 2016).

with the traditional web and broadcast mediums for media consumers', and advertisers', attention. This meant that by early 2015 media entities had to begin to infiltrate platforms, in particular, Facebook and Twitter, to maintain market presence. The Gallipoli centenary was an ideal event to explore this engagement presence. As the centenary of World War I commenced in Australia, news outlets positioned digital Gallipoli recreations at the centre of their presence on social media platforms Facebook and Twitter.

Major media organisations used multi-platform social media technologies, and the storytelling skills of creative industries and their staff journalists, to recreate the events of Gallipoli of 1915 in contemporary formats and timescales. Both News Corp and the Australian Broadcasting Corporation (ABC) reassembled the diary material of real historical personalities to compose a 'real time' narrative of Gallipoli 1915 on social media.

The ABC collaborated with Twitter, the Museum of Australian Democracy, the National Library of Australia and the Australian War Memorial to live tweet @ABCNews1915. The project drew upon 60 individual historical characters' accounts to recreate the events of Gallipoli in parallel time 100 years hence. Prominent Gallipoli event figures including @AlbJacka_1915, @Bridges1915, @BillyHughes1915 and @MKAtaturk1915, @CaptFaik, and @KingOMalley1915 tweeted 'status updates' from their own 'twitterbot' accounts (Fig. 4.1). On April 24, 2015 @ABCNews1915 was trending on Australian twitter. The project received 1,177,899 impressions in Australia.[41] @ABCNews1915 animated Anzacs into a Twitter operating as a 'platform supporting networked structures of feeling' in what Zizi Papacharissis terms 'the present affect'.[42] Twitter followers experienced the Gallipoli landings in a simulacrum of real time. Long dead historical figures appeared in a personal feed and the online civil space of twitter with bots and contemporaneous tweeps. The detached robotic quality of the interaction ironically created a true dread, fuelling the imminence of dramatic irony and fear. Historical Gallipoli Twitterbots appearing in a person's feed within a 'normal' temporal perception created a weird sensation of time distortion and historical hyper-reality. Most people knew the arc of the story, but the tweets invited engagement as if the events were unfolding, and what was to come was not inevitable.

---

41 Eric Napper, @ABCnews1915, Retrieved from https://twitter.com/ABCNews1915?lang=en. Eric Napper interview with Tom Sear, 9 July 2015, 5:38PM. Canberra. Audio.

42 Zizi Papacharissi, *Affective Publics: Sentiment, Technology, and Politics*, (New York: Oxford University Press, 2014).

Fig. 4.1. @TomDrane1915, Tweet, 24 April 2015.
Courtesy, ABC. Screenshot

2015 also saw the emergence of a new form: the historical avatar. Digital technology has enabled the reanimation of historical figures into online 'presences'. Social media further enables the active 'participation' of animated avatars into a 'live' recreation of narrative and temporal experience. News Corp Australia's *AnzacLive* embraced this opportunity. The project took the diaries of nine prominent Australian Gallipoli diarists, and with the augmentation of Facebook profiles, reanimated these characters. Historical Gallipoli 'diary' entries from 1915 were posted by the character's Facebook profiles (Fig. 4.2) on their timelines on the same dates and times 100 years hence. The 'timeline' nature of a Facebook feed provided the temporal space for these characters to intersect on a followers' 'feed' in parallel time to their experience on Gallipoli in 1915. *AnzacLive* delivered integrated content on social media platforms Facebook, Twitter, and Instagram, an explanatory website, a live blog on 25 April, and the news.com.au web page to tell the story of the Anzac landing.[43] In collaboration with the cultural institutions who house the diaries, the State Library of NSW and the Australian War Memorial, News Corp told the story of the Anzac landing from the diarists' entries 'as if they are alive and posting right now'.[44]

The storytelling harnessed both the 24-hour news cycle and an era of social media-rich journalism. Up to 30 journalist 'custodians' managed each diarist's Facebook profile from 6am to 10:30 pm each day posting up to 14-18 times a week throughout 2015. Custodians inhabited their diarist character,

---

43 News Corp Australia, 'Anzac Day 2015 | Anzac Live Post | Anzac Stories', Retrieved from http://www.anzaclive.com.au/ Retrieved from https://www.facebook.com/anzaclive Retrieved from https://twitter.com/AnzacLive Retrieved from https://www.instagram.com/anzaclive/ (accessed March 23, 2016) (2015); Aurelie (Lily) Perthuis, 'Anzac Live – Case Study', Retrieved from http://www.anzaclive.com.au/casestudy.html (accessed March 23, 2016). Justin Lees, 'Anzaclive: Facebook from the Frontline [Internal Briefing Document]', (Sydney: News Corp Australia, 2015).

44 Lees. Anzaclive: Facebook from the Frontline [Internal Briefing Document].

selecting posts, learning life stories, period diction and syntax to approach authenticity when answering follower's questions live.[45] The project's visual designer emphasised connectivity between the past and present for contemporary audiences. Faced with sepia tones, limited images and word-heavy diary entries the designer colourised pictures, used 'then and now' images, memes, new studio portraits of images related to characters, data visualisations and video clips to enliven the project's interface. The design brief extended into brand and profile identities across integrated platforms.[46]

The project achieved significant reach in an extremely competitive marketplace for Gallipoli content. News Corp claimed the Facebook pages, Twitter and Instagram accounts had a combined 49,406 dedicated Page Likes/account Followers. The hashtag #anzaclive was attached to every post and was seen 51.5 million times, with a top post reaching 1.7 million people with shares.[47] The project continued the entire length of the 'real' Gallipoli campaign with final Gallipoli posts being those of the diarists during the December evacuation. While the diarist ostensibly 'left' Gallipoli in December 2015, the project continues. As at March 2016, the *AnzacLive* lead 'narrator profile' continued to post daily to 18,102 followers on World War I History, the live retelling of Australian involvement in 'real time' and military commemoration more generally. In early 2016, narrator page likes continue to increase. Characters are set to return, briefly as a 'tribute' for Anzac Day 2016. *AnzacLive* will tell the stories of Australian involvement in the battles of Fromelles and Pozieres in Mid-2016.[48]

Project Lead Justin Lees designed the project to ask 'what would it be like to talk to these people, and live through their experience with them.'[49] Lees suggested 'they were young people just like us, and if alive in 2015 would be communicating in the same way, as today's 20somethings ... on social media.'[50] The collapsing of temporal, subjective and historio-ethnographic distance was key to the phenomenological experience of 2015 Gallipoli commemorative immersion. The *AnzacLive* online video entitled 'The Faces of War' begins: 'They were just like us. These men lived and fought

---

45   Lees. Anzaclive: Facebook from the Frontline [Internal Briefing Document].
46   Aurelie (Lily) Perthuis, email correspondence with Tom Sear, 21 December 2015.
47   Lees, "Anzaclive: Facebook from the Frontline [Internal Briefing Document]. Perthuis, 'Anzac Live – Case Study'.
48   News Corp Australia, Retrieved from https://www.facebook.com/anzaclive (accessed March 23, 2016). Justin Lees interviewed by Tom Sear, 21 March, 2016.
49   Lees. Anzaclive: Facebook from the Frontline [Internal Briefing Document].
50   Lees. Anzaclive: Facebook from the Frontline [Internal Briefing Document].

100 years ago. Today they'd be our brothers, fathers, sons, friends'. This is followed by sepia photographs of World War I soldiers gradually 'photo shopped' and fading into coloured contemporary images of a businessman, school boy, soldier, chef, and finally, instead of a slouch hat we see a young man wearing an archetypal grey 'hoody'.[51] This video extends Paul Keating's eulogy for the Unknown Soldier ('He is all of them. And he is one of us')[52] into the postdigital realm, and demonstrates *AnzacLive*'s intention to collapse the time and space between contemporary online publics and create an empathetic connection with the audience. These correlations were also media-rich ways to bridge the risk of audiences experiencing the 'uncanny valley' of disturbing sensations when the recreation's flaws, silences, blank spots or unreality threatened to break the illusion.

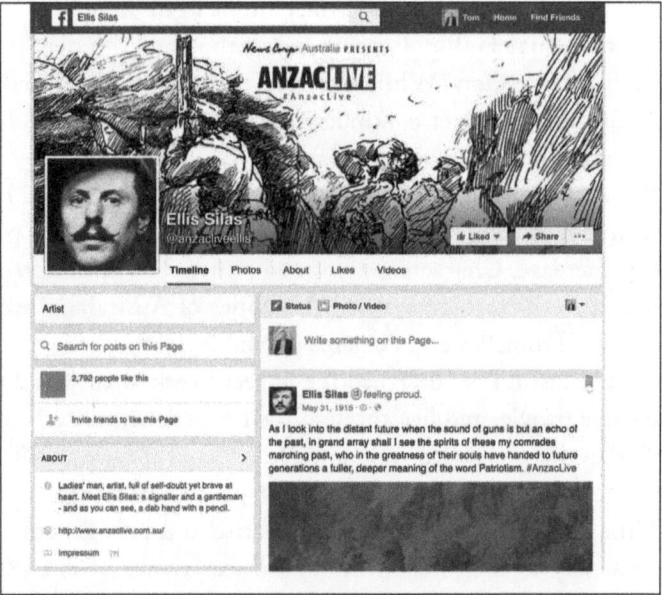

Fig. 4.2. Ellis Silas Facebook Profile, AnzacLive, Screenshot.

Followers of *AnzacLive* who commented on posts, actively and consistently suspended disbelief when responding to Gallipoli diarist Facebook avatars. When on 16 May 2015, the Ellis Silas profile posted from his diary 'In

---

51 News Corp Australia, 'The Faces of War', Retrieved from https://www.facebook.com/anzaclive/videos (accessed March 23, 2016).

52 Paul Keating, 'Remembrance Day 1993, Australian War Memorial', Retrieved from https://www.awm.gov.au/talks-speeches/keating-remembrance-day-1993/ (accessed March 23, 2016).

my heart I know I am done', his followers demonstrated a response pattern which was illustrative of a trend across all profiles. Empathy predominated: Jen Featherstone wrote 'Oh Ellis. I know there are no words that can help with how you are feeling. Keep safe.' Kristen Nielson 'tagged' Ellis and stated 'keep strong, you can do keep going. Our prayers are with you.' Ironic reflection, a temporal suspension of belief which incorporated the Facebook audience, was also common. For example, Marjorie Earl, in a post with five likes, reached out, posting, 'Thank you for your honesty, Ellis – I only pray that someone, somewhere, sometime learns of what you and so many others are going through and says "No, I am not sending anyone else to war".' Other comments also reflected upon historical change. Bev Davies alluded to contemporary psychological analysis of warfare in her comment: 'Now recognised as Post Traumatic Stress Cisorder (sic) & not treated as a weakness of mind! Our diggers & in fact all soldiers faced the prospect of "shell shock" & being disrespected if it developed! Hopefully, with recognition of PTSD we treat them better than they were back then!'[53]

Understanding Gallipoli through the personal perspective was the product of Gallipoli's return to popular consciousness during the second memory boom of the 1970s. Bill Gammage's work, published in 1974, focussed upon diaries to turn a personal lens on writings that had been scoured purely for tactical information in the 1920s. Gammage's framework informed the film *Gallipoli*, which placed experience and embodiment as the medium for engaging with the conflict.[54] Equally, the medical and psychological objectification of the soldier after the Vietnam conflict enhanced the 'personalisation' of Gallipoli. The emergence of the soldier as 'victim' and the construction of the category PTSD in the aftermath of Vietnam after 1980 fuelled the affective, emotional and empathetic response to military history more widely.[55] *AnzacLive* demonstrates how normalised this view had become. Australian consumers of *AnzacLive* who made comments have internalised the commemorative drive of the 1970s. However, the epistemological perspective for knowing Gallipoli through personalisation has undergone a major change in the postdigital era.

The live retellings of Gallipoli seen in 2015 enabled those engaged in remembrance to 'speak' to the dead and acknowledge their suffering.

---

53   News Corp Australia. Ellis Silas, Facebook post, May 16, 2015.
54   Bill Gammage, *The Broken Years: Australian Soldiers in the Great War* (Canberra: Australian National University Press, 1974). David Williamson and Peter Weir eds., *The Story of Gallipoli*, (Melbourne: Penguin Australia, 1981).
55   Christina Twomey, 'Trauma and the Reinvigoration of Anzac: An Argument', *History Australia* 10, No. 3 (December 2013): 85-105.

Now empathy could be recursively directed back at those in the past. Inga Clendinnen has questioned the emergence of empathy's utility as seemingly redemptive in historical, particularly fictional understanding. With hindsight everyone follows the plot, lacking the prescience of their doom or success. 'By contrast,' Clendinnen writes, 'the real past is surrounded by prickle bushes of what I have to call epistemological difficulties' because 'my imagination like my emotions and assumptions, has grown organically out of my own experiences within my cultural milieu.'[56]

Appreciating the complexities of empathy is at the heart of many stories from Monash University's online video-based Anzac Centenary 100 Stories project. In Frank Wilkinson's story, 'understanding' lies at the historical core of the story's location in the present. In 1927 a 'Shellshocked' Wilkinson battered his wife and child to death with a hammer before slashing his own throat. In the online video depicting Wilkinson's story on the Monash University website, his wife Elizabeth's final words, read at out at the inquest, appear hauntingly on the black screen: 'He couldn't help it', and repeated, 'He couldn't help it'.[57] The effect is one of horror. Shock. The video depicts the retelling of events where a victim speaks to a new 'public' as a witness. As Kelly Jean Butler argues, a culture of witnessing in the exposition of Australian history developed in response to the testimony of indigenous people and asylum seekers in the 1990s.[58] To quote Miller and Tougaw, the process of witnessing 'records a movement from individual experience to the collective archive, from personal trauma to public memory'.[59] The Monash Stories team reanimated Elizabeth's testimony into this contemporary 'witnessing' discourse.[60]

The Monash Stories team have revealed that the Anzac Centenary Advisory Board were uncomfortable with the proposed inclusion of the Wilkinson story in official national commemoration. They were advised that if 'Canberra was to adopt the 100 Stories in the project in its commemorative

---

56   Inga Clendinnen, 'The History Question: Who Owns the Past?,' *Quarterly Essay*, no. 23 (2006): 22-23.

57   Monash University, 'At Breaking Point', Retrieved from http://future.arts.monash.edu/onehundredstories/at-breaking-point/ (accessed March 23, 2016).

58   Kelly Jean Butler, *Witnessing Australian Stories: History, Testimony, and Memory in Contemporary Culture* (New Brunswick, NJ: Transaction Publishers, 2013), 5.

59   Nancy K. Miller and Jason Tougaw, *Extremities: Trauma, Testimony, and Community* (Urbana: University of Illinois Press, 2002), 13; Butler, *Witnessing*, 5.

60   For discussion of the broader context of contemporary collaborative on-site and online memorial commemorative cultures see, Penelope Papailias, 'Witnessing in the age of the database: Viral memorials, affective publics, and the assemblage of mourning', *Memory Studies* 1750698015622058, first published on January 6, 2016. doi:10.1177/1750698015622058.

program, Frank Wilkinson's story would have to go'.[61] The affective authenticity of this story, and the visceral reaction of the Board is what De Groot identifies via Kristeva as 'a massive and sudden emergence of uncanniness' evoking the past as crisis of self-hood where the contemporary world must 'strive to control it through organizing principles that obviate its horror'.[62] This is an allegory, then, of 'how a nation finds memory problematic and challenging'.[63] Indeed, in response, the Monash team created materiality in the place of Wilkinson's destruction – placing flowers at a grave, dedicating a physical book. The uncanniness of this experience of the Wilkinsons' story and redemption in physical qualities in the present reveals the paradox of the past's role in the phenomenology and epistemology of the present. The uncanniness is in the strangeness of the contradictory 'Otherness' of the history, where abjection stands in for emptiness, a want, a past that indubitably happened but is also absent, creating 'contemporary identity while demonstrating its lack of solidity'.[64]

The anxiety of the unknowability of the past, simultaneous with the haunting ghostly in the revenants of the Gallipoli dead returning as the historical social media avatars of *AnzacLive* and @ABCNews1915, disrupts the present. Drawing upon Derrida's notions of spectrality, where 'mourning consists always in attempting to ontologize remains to make them present',[65] De Groot argues that these ghosts complete a knowledge, by pointing to the insubstantially of the present's epistemology, composed as it is of an emptiness of the past. These Gallipoli hauntings, then, point to an emptiness of the past/present dynamic as a way to comprehend the melancholia of the present.[66]

Connecting to Gallipoli 2015: Agency, participation and postdigital historical consciousness

The participation of the audience within the new media assemblage illustrates the process of 'knowing' central to popular digital historiography. De Groot

---

61 Bruce Scates, Rebecca Wheatley, and Laura James, *World War One: A History in 100 Stories*, ed. Bruce Scates, Rebecca Wheatley and Laura James, World War I (Melbourne: Viking, an imprint of Penguin Books, 2015), vii-ix.
62 Jerome De Groot, *Remaking History: The Past in Contemporary Historical Fictions* (London: Routledge, 2016), 216.
63 De Groot, *Remaking History*, 118.
64 De Groot, *Remaking History*, 118. Julia Kristeva, *Powers of Horror: An Essay on Abjection*, (New York: Columbia University Press, 1982).
65 Jacques Derrida, 'Specters of Marx', *New Left Review*, no. 205 (1994). Jacques Derrida, 'Specters of Marx', (New York: Routledge, 1994). De Groot, *Remaking History*, 113.
66 De Groot, *Remaking History*, 112.

suggests audiences in the new phase of historical consumption 'are complicit in their rendering of another, unreal world,' and in their collusion he argues, arises 'an understanding…of what is at stake ethically, and ideologically in ignoring 'reality' for escapism'.[67] At the same time, that 'escapist' moment might create 'comprehension' for a more 'active' reading of text.[68]

The participatory audience may be using the past to understand a contemporary subjectivity. The contemporary online subject exists in a world where 'authenticity' is at once constructed and paradoxically has its own value.[69] The past has an aura of authenticity which social media migrates to the present. *AnzacLive* is understood by its audience through the televisual trope it draws on: Reality TV and the power of celebrity. It is built around a list of nine diverse real characters stuck in a situation, and defined by a set of rules.[70] All could potentially be thrown off the Gallipoli 'show' at any time – although in *AnzacLive* this would be through violence or disease rather than online voting. Reality TV is surveillance mediated as interactive entertainment. This interactivity is as a form of productive surveillance allowing for the commodification of the products generated, which Mark Andrejevic describes as the 'work of being watched'.[71] Audiences' engagement however, involves a 'tacit understanding' even a complicit, participative agreement that can be described as 'the authenticity contract'.[72]

The social media 'authenticity contract' intersected in 2015 with other longstanding Anzac social contracts. The intermeshing of these contracts revealed the complexity of these contractual exchanges in online realities. Anzac has always operated in a nexus of government and the market.[73] Indeed, while the centenary has offered numerous opportunities for business

---

67 De Groot, *Remaking History*, 151.
68 De Groot, *Remaking History*, 152.
69 Gunn Enli, *Mediated Authenticity: How the Media Constructs Reality* (New York: Peter Lang, 2015). Gunn Enli, '"Trust Me, I Am Authentic!": Authenticity Illusions in Social Media Politics', in, *The Routledge Companion to Social Media and Politics*, ed. Axel Bruns, et al. (New York: Routledge, Taylor & Francis Group, 2016), 121-137.
70 Jo Hawkins, 'Anzaclive and @Abcnews1915 Exploiting Anzac Day Legend', *Crikey*, Retrieved from http://www.crikey.com.au/2015/04/07/dead-men-talking-can-%E2%80%98zombie%E2%80%99-anzacs-enrich-our-understanding-of-war/?wpmp_switcher=mobile (accessed March 23, 2016).
71 Mark Andrejevic, *Reality TV : The Work of Being Watched* (Lanham, Md.: Rowman & Littlefield Publishers, 2003). De Groot, *Consuming History*, 166-7.
72 Enli, *Mediated Authenticity*. Enli, '"Trust Me, I Am Authentic!"', 123.
73 Jo Hawkins, 'Anzac for Sale: Consumer Culture, Regulation and the Shaping of a Legend, 1915-21', *Australian Historical Studies* 46, no. 1 (2015).

to exploit commemoration, it also demonstrated their lack of flexibility in social media economics. Consumers of commemoration online revealed their capacity to consciously understand the functions of memory, and intervene with content of their own that powerfully demonstrated their agency.

In April 2015 the Australian based supermarket chain Woolworths was forced to withdraw a digital campaign following a social media backlash and Government threats. The campaign featured an online meme generator, which enabled people to upload a profile picture of a familial serviceman or woman, which was then superimposed with the corporate tagline 'Fresh in our Memories' and the Woolworths logo on the image before reposting.[74] The intention was to enable Australians to create personalised memes to add to a larger, collective remembering – conveniently co-branded with Woolworths itself, presumably with the capacity to 'go viral'.

The meme generator was soon co-opted and trolled. The site was shut down within hours as the parody memes went viral and the Department of Veterans' Affairs and the Australian War Memorial took action against Woolworths. Spoof memes clustered around the hashtag #freshinourmemories.[75] The online public produced thousands of memes within days.[76] Some memes used historical images of death from Gallipoli, the 24 May 1915 truce in particular, to illustrate the irony of Woolworths' tagline. Many referenced the horrors of the first and other nodal wars of the twentieth century. The campaign might be criticised as an example of commercialisation and 'brandzackery'.[77] However, what the consumers of memorialisation – with the unexpected memes they generated around the hashtag – most criticised the company for was their lack of digital literacy. Rather than predominately using words, meme creators used the collectively understood

---

74 Australian Broadcasting Commission, 'Woolworths under Fire for Anzac 'Fresh in Our Memories' Campaign', Retrieved from http://www.abc.net.au/news/2015-04-14/woolworths-under-fire-for-anzac-promotion/6392848 (accessed March 23, 2016). Melissa Davey, 'Hashtag Backlash: Marketing Campaigns That Turned into Social Media Disasters', *The Guardian*, Retrieved from http://www.theguardian.com/media/2015/dec/27/hashtag-backlash-marketing-campaigns-that-turned-into-social-media-disasters (accessed March 23, 2016).

75 Twitter, #freshinourmemories, Retrieved from https://twitter.com/search?q=freshinourmemories&src=typd&lang=en (accessed March 23, 2016).

76 'Anzac Marketing – Best We Forget', Retrieved from http://bestweforget.net/ (accessed March 23, 2016). See also authorship claim, for website curation @rpy, https://twitter.com/rpy retrieved from https://twitter.com/NewtonMark/status/594091655675785216 (accessed March 23, 2016).

77 Jo Hawkins, 'Why Limit Anzac Marketing Outrage to Woolworths?,' Retrieved from http://www.historypunk.com/2015/04/why-limit-anzac-marketing-outrage-to.html. (accessed March 23, 2016).

visual language of the internet to lambast, simultaneously demonstrating their control over online territory. Woolworths' online 'epic fail' was as much about misunderstanding social media users as it was about misjudging the public view around the centenary – and of course, how these two things were tied together. Far from simply reacting to 'brandzac,' the online public revealed an agency and sophisticated understanding of a new form of online memory that social media and the internet as a database has created out of the visual nature of second memory boom. A comprehensive examination of the examples hackers created shows nearly all depict recent cultural events, particularly online phenomena like Melbourne teen and social media star 'Corey,' or the ocular centric online public phenomena of the 'white-gold / blue-black dress'.[78] This demonstrated a public with high visual literacy ironically playing with the notion of contemporary memory.

These 'produsers'[79] were knowingly making a joke about the new, accelerated trajectory of online events and the irony of endless referencing the nodal wars of the twentieth century as tropes of cultural memory itself. These irreverent responses suggested that the 'audience' for the marketing was making a clear point about the artificiality and opportunism of Woolworths' initiative, while offering yet another form of corrective to those who transgress the code of conduct that is culturally expected around Anzac commemoration. In March 2016 as Anzac Day approaches again, the hashtag remains active with posts daily using 'FreshInOurMemories' to reflect upon a culture of instant online memorialisation itself.[80] Even failed social media campaigns are now memorialised. In February 2016 @NewtonMark tweeted: 'Anzac Day isn't far away. That time for us to remember #FreshInOurMemories'.[81]

Connecting Gallipoli 1915 and 2015: Selfies and social remembering

Personal digital devices connected to the internet have enabled a period of intense personalisation of experience and documentation of individual

---

78 See http://bestweforget.net/. Wikipedia, 'The Dress (Viral Phenomenon) – Wikipedia, the Free Encyclopedia', Retrieved from https://en.wikipedia.org/wiki/The_dress_(viral_phenomenon) (accessed March 23, 2016).

79 Axel Bruns, 'Produsage: Towards a Broader Framework for User-Led Content Creation', *Creativity and Cognition 2007*, CC2007 – Seeding Creativity: Tools, Media, and Environments, (New York: 2007), 99-106.

80 Hoskins, 'The War Vector'.

81 @NewtonMark, Retrieved from https://twitter.com/NewtonMark/status/703191107677474816?lang=en (accessed March 23, 2016).

memory, in combination with the creation of a vast super public online. The selfie epitomises those forces. A selfie is a self-portrait taken with a camera phone, usually at arms-length, and shared on social media. The word is an Australian invention. The etymology follows the Australian linguistic tradition of abbreviating and adding a suffix to produce words like tinnie, ciggie, firie, barbie, sickie, Westie, soapie.[82]

The emergence of the selfie as cultural form is due primarily to their enabler, the smartphone. Smartphones are now embedded in contemporary life. Smartphones have quickly become connective interfaces between an individual and a ubiquitous, computational version of the social, performed in digital spaces such as Facebook, Twitter and Instagram.[83] They are networked digital tools that have become our prosthetic memories, storing images, text and video meticulously – and effortlessly – tethered to time, place and social connections. As a result, mobile devices are part of a contemporary process of 'mutually shaping media, place and memory.' At the same time, they are locative technologies that capture and communicate complex notions of self.[84]

Selfies express the complex presence of the self within a dynamic digital assemblage. A selfie is a statement of human agency. Equally, because selfies are created and distributed via an array of nonhuman agents they are instantly located within an infrastructure of a digital superpublic.[85] Taken with mobile phones, selfies illustrate the hybrid environment between being 'online' and 'offline' that users now inhabit.[86] The 'selfie assemblage', Hess argues, expresses four elements: 'the self, physical space, the

---

[82] @OxfordWords, 'The Oxford Dictionaries Word of the Year 2013 is "selfie"', OxfordWords blog. Retrieved from http://blog.oxforddictionaries.com/2013/11/word-of-the-year-2013-winner/ (accessed March 24, 2016) Josh Hawkins and Rhys Keir, 'How to Speak Australian: Abbreviate Everything', Retrieved from https://www.youtube.com/watch?v=yDb_WsAt_Z0 (accessed March 23, 2016).

[83] Gerard Goggin and Larissa Hjorth, eds., *The Routledge Companion to Mobile Media*, (New York: Routledge, 2014). Jason Farman ed., *The Mobile Story: Narrative Practices with Locative Technologies*', (New York: Routledge, 2013). Jordan Frith, 'Smartphones as Locative Media', *European Journal of Communication* 30, no. 4 (2015).

[84] Didem Özkul and Lee Humphreys, 'Record and Remember: Memory and Meaning-Making Practices through Mobile Media', *Mobile Media & Communication* 3, no. 3 (2015).

[85] Theresa M. Senft and Nancy K. Baym, 'What Does the Selfie Say? Investigating a Global Phenomenon', Introduction, *International Journal Of Communication* 9 (2015): 1588-1606.

[86] Adriana De Souza E Silva, 'From Cyber to Hybrid: Mobile Technologies as Interfaces of Hybrid Spaces', *Space and Culture* 9, no. 3 (2006).

device and the network.'[87] The selfie simultaneously emplaces the user in a material physical place while 'embedded into social networks'.[88] Simultaneity becomes further entangled with memory cultures when selfies are taken at commemorative sites. The Tumblr page 'Selfies At Serious Places' has positioned the appropriateness of placing the self as the focus of an experience of a commemorative site.[89] Funeral selfies have also been academically interrogated. Funeral selfies illustrate how increasingly visual images produce and circulate the affect associated with place. Moreover, they upload to the network the 'ambient intimacy' of maintaining presence in both a social network and place simultaneously.[90]

Gallipoli and Anzac Day selfies exist within this dynamic. Melbourne programmer David Johnson has for several years curated a tumblr called *Anzac Day Selfies*.[91] In these selfies, and the related follower comments, the casual vernacular forms of online platform expression jostle, sometimes uncomfortably, with the traditions of Anzac mourning or Gallipoli commemoration. Young people wink with tongues out, or declare 'Have a good day guys #anzacday'. Bikini clad Instagram stars tag #lestweforget with multiple emoji. Anzac selfies can be read as problematic even more clearly when extracted from the online flow, and aggregated together as a way to police the austere, respectful traditions of Gallipoli commemoration within the 'slacktivism' of online media. Equally, Anzac Selfies can draw social dynamism into a ritual space with other vernacular online platform practices which are part of a 'live communication' demonstrating participation in an event or shared social practice.[92]

---

87   Aaron Hess, 'The Selfie Assemblage', *International Journal Of Communication* 9 (2015): 1632.

88   Hess.

89   @heyfeifer, 'Selfies at Serious Places,' tumblr, Retrieved from http://selfiesatseriousplaces.tumblr.com/?og=1 (accessed March 24, 2016).

90   James Meese, Martin Gibbs, Marcus Carter, Michael Arnold, Bjorn Nansen, Tamara Kohn, 'Selfies at Funerals: Mourning and Presencing on Social Media Platforms', *International Journal Of Communication* 9 (2015); Martin Gibbs, James Meese, Michael Arnold, Bjorn Nansen, Marcus Carter, '#Funeral and Instagram: Death, Social Media, and Platform Vernacular', *Information Communication & Society* 18, no. 3 (2015): 1818-1831. Ingrid Richardson and Rowan Wilken, 'Parerga of the Third Screen: Mobile Media, Place and Presence', Chapter 11, in Rowan Wilken and Gerard Goggin (eds.), *Mobile Technology and Place*, (New York: Routledge, 2012), 181-198. Larissa Hjorth and Kay Gu, 'The Place of Emplaced Visualities: A Case Study of Smartphone Visuality and Location- Based Social Media in Shanghai, China', *Continuum* 26, no. 5 (2012): 699-713.

91   David Johnson, 'Anzac Day Selfies', tumblr, Retrieved from http://anzacdayselfies.tumblr.com/?og=1. (accessed March 24, 2016).

92   Meese et al., 'Selfies at Funerals'.

The selfie is part of a wider pathologisation of young people and social media.[93] A generational lack of 'connection' of millennials to an Australian past is often represented as a 'Baby Boomer' fear. In the Australian soap *Home and Away*'s April 2015 Anzac Special, the selfie signifies an uncaring, narcissistic youth out of touch with the generations before them.[94] The smartphone and the selfie are initially represented as the device which augments their alienation, digitally disconnecting them from the past, and from broader collective understandings of Australia's history. But it is ultimately perceived as a potential redemptive vehicle for resolving perceived cultural breaches between past and present.

The *Home and Away* Anzac Centenary Special depicted teenagers making the common Australian school pilgrimage to Canberra. The teenagers take a selfie on the steps overlooking the parade ground at the Australian War Memorial as a signification of their alienation from the Anzac myth. The teens collectively intone 'bored' at the moment of digital capture. Enraged, the female 'Baby Boomer' teacher snatches the smartphone and dispatches them inside. Once they enter the Memorial the selfie becomes redemptive. With soundtrack accompaniment of Trip Hop DJ Dirty South's song '*Unknown*' we watch as the image of the selfie taken on the steps fuses into the identical composition of an image of the men of the 5th Division taking a smoko on Montauban road in December 1916.[95] These transformations occur on a collective and individual level. A singular young man's face is compared with the image of the centenary's ubiquitous 'handsome man',[96]

---

93   Kath Albury, 'Selfies, Sexts, and Sneaky Hats: Young People's Understandings of Gendered Practices of Self-Representation', *International Journal Of Communication* 9, (2015): 1734-1745.

94   @backtothebay, 'H&A Marks Anzac Centenary – News – Home and Away', Retrieved from http://www.backtothebay.net/news/2015/03/26/alf-anzac-storyline/ (accessed March 24, 2016).

95   Jazz Twemlow, 'Selfies at the Australian War Memorial? Shame on You, Summer Bay High', Retrieved from http://www.theguardian.com/tv-and-radio/2015/apr/20/selfies-at-australian-war-memorial-anzac-summer-bay-high (accessed March 24, 2016). Australian War Memorial, 'Unidentified Men of the 5th Division Partaking in Cigarettes and Resting by the Side of the Montauban Road, near Mametz, While Enroute to the Trenches. Most of the Men Are Wearing Sheepskin ...' @AWMemorial, Retrieved from https://www.awm.gov.au/collection/E00019/ (accessed March 24, 2016). Dragan Roganović, Dirty South+FMLYBND, *The Unknown Feat Fmlybnd New Official*; Dirty South, 'Dirty South | Official Website', Retrieved from http://dirtysouth.com (accessed March 24, 2016). See also, Retrieved from https://en.wikipedia.org/wiki/Dirty_South_(musician) (accessed March 24, 2016).

96   Australian War Memorial AWMP06003.001, 'Studio Portrait of an Unidentified First World War Soldier in Australian Service Uniform, Including Greatcoat

Peter Corlett's *Man in the Mud* is transposed to a flashback of teen angst,[97] a young man confronted with the faces of men lost in the Sandakan Death Marches evokes the assemblage of an online Instagram wall.[98]

The fusion of contemporary Australian youth with the young people of World War 1 invokes Kristevan and Lacanian concepts of the return of the specular 'uncanny stranger' of the past within the self.[99] The selfie is a digital trope which can both alienate and connect the past and present. While 'Anzac Selfies' can highlight a possible disconnect with the values of Australian military sacrifice, equally the 'ambient intimacy' of the selfie form can enable the representation, or a perception of, an actual fusion with the identities and 'spirit' of people from the past. Where the avatars of hyperreal social media and supersized physical recreations of soldiers and nurses of the past facilitates an active, potentially two-way, engagement between past and present lives, the selfie affords a new kind of synthesis and integration.

Conclusion

In 1970 robotics professor Masahiro Mori sought to envisage people's reactions to a robot which acted or looked human. He postulated that the reaction would shift from 'empathy to revulsion' as it approached, but did not fully obtain, human qualities. This descent into 'eeriness' has become known as 'the uncanny valley'.[100]

Experimentation since then has suggested that this is a real human effect in digital or robotic human recreations, but the theories for why, and

---

and Slouch Hat.', @AWMemorial, Retrieved from https://www.awm.gov.au/collection/P06003.001/ (accessed March 24, 2016). Sarah Michael, 'Woolworths Face $50,000 Fine for Unauthorised Use of the Word 'Anzac',' Retrieved from, http://www.dailymail.co.uk/news/article-3039212/Woolworths-face-50-000-fine-unauthorised-use-word-Anzac-s-revealed-solider-used-plug-disrespectful-campaign-unidentified-digger-no-copyright-image.html (accessed March 24, 2016).

97 Wikipedia, 'Man in the Mud', Retrived from https://en.wikipedia.org/wiki/Man_in_the_mud (accessed March 24, 2016).

98 team home and away, 'Home and Away backstage Anzac Special', Retrieved from https://www.youtube.com/watch?v=df2Ie67n_d8 (accessed March 24, 2016).

99 Julia Kristeva, *Strangers to Ourselves* (New York: Columbia University Press, 1991), 182-92. Sara Beardsworth, *Julia Kristeva: Psychoanalysis and Modernity* (Albany: State University of New York Press, 2004), 189-92. Sadeq Rahimi, 'The Ego, the Ocular, and the Uncanny: Why Are Metaphors of Vision Central in Accounts of the Uncanny?', *International Journal of Psychoanalysis* 94, no. 3 (2013).

100 Karl F. MacDorman, Norri Kageki, and Masahiro Mori, 'The Uncanny Valley', *IEEE Robotics and Automation Magazine* 19, no. 2 (2012).

what is the trigger in humans, vary. Whether the origin is biological or cultural remains unclear. Some suggest that the feeling may arise from an unconscious reminder of mortality and death.[101] Others focus attention on what the 'uncanny valley' reveals about perceptions of human likeability and trustworthiness.[102] Much empirical research on the uncanny valley examines how humans infer 'trustworthiness', for example, from the affective cues (such as subtle facial expressions) of human-human interaction.[103] Gray and Wagner suggest that while typical explanations of the uncanny valley focus upon robotic appearance, what may actually be unnerving is the presence of 'mind' in a robot or bot.[104] One recent experimental study suggested that a machine that lacked a humanlike appearance but gave signs of having 'experience' is unnerving. This research suggests that a perception of mind, and perception of intuitive, implicit essence of mind, is located in feelings and emotions. It emphasises that the perception of experience (capacity to feel and sense) rather than agency (act and do) is what is perceived as fundamentally human.[105]

It is along the thin ridge of this uncanny valley that so many of these new postdigital commemorations must walk, under sniper fire both from academic historians and their own publics. Their effectiveness derives from the accuracy with which they depict 'experience' – drawing as they do on meticulous visual renderings, careful historical research or the authenticity of first-person accounts. They rely on connections forming between contemporary minds and past minds (and contemporary audiences with each other) through the medium of emotions and shared social interaction. The empathy that flows as a result is genuine, and while to a considerable degree disbelief is suspended, at the same time, their success also stems from the audience's historical awareness that this interaction is strange and impossible. Contemporary audiences have a playful, nuanced understanding of time, history and memory that has kept pace with the accelerating conflux of the

---

101 Nathan Pensky, 'Twitter Bots and the Uncanny Valley', *The Daily Dot*, Retrieved from http://www.dailydot.com/technology/twitter-bots-uncanny-valley/ (accessed March 24, 2016).

102 Kevin Hoff and Masooda Bashir, 'Trust in Automation: Integrating Empirical Evidence on Factors That Influence Trust', *Human Factors* 57, no. 3 (2015). Maya B. Mathur and David B. Reichling, 'Navigating a Social World with Robot Partners: A Quantitative Cartography of the Uncanny Valley', *Cognition* 146 (2016): 22-32.

103 Mathur and Reichling, 31.

104 Kurt Gray and David M. Wegner, 'Feeling Robots and Human Zombies: Mind Perception and the Uncanny Valley', *Cognition* 125, no. 1 (2012): 129.

105 Gray and Wegner, 129.

analogue, digital and postdigital eras. They know their position in time relative to historical subjects comes with privileges as well as blind spots. They can reposition technologies that seem to disturb the social performance of commemoration or challenge connections between the past and the present as redemptive rather than disruptive.

Mark McKenna has expressed concern that 'in popular memory, the *distance* from the past prized by professional historians takes second place to being *present* in the past'.[106] Anna Clark has asked in reply, 'Is it not possible to connect *and* critically engage with the past?'[107] The evidence from Anzac Day 2015 suggests it is – if we appreciate the complex meanings and makings of history in the present with the same attentiveness that we promise, as historians, to bring to the past. Our expanding contribution may be to connect and engage with people around their already quite complex understandings of how the past is a part of 'my cultural milieu'.[108]

It is essential for historians seeking to facilitate and examine this connection and engagement to consider the larger, rapidly evolving dynamics at play in the postdigital era. The collapse of historical distance is a fundamental change in human experience. Digital networks, databases and hyperconnectivity 'don't just bridge historical distance: they crush it.'[109] 'The first thing' we need to appreciate, Philosopher Luciano Floridi explains, 'is a misunderstanding about ICT – digital technologies – we'll call them technologies of memory, but they actually wipe our memory. What they do is they are constantly presenting memory as an over-extended eternal present ... So the art of remembering, forgetting, recalling, closure, all those things that we skilfully developed over millennia have been completely disrupted.'[110] As a consequence, the way humans perceive the past and then position themselves in relation to it, their capacity to generate 'distance' as McKenna and Clark discuss, is also in a period of change.

---

106 Mark McKenna, 'The History Anxiety', in, *The Cambridge History of Australia*, eds. Alison Bashford and Stuart Macintyre (Cambridge : Cambridge University Press, 2013), 580.

107 Clark, 142.

108 Inga Clendinnen, 'The History Question: Who Owns the Past?', *Quarterly Essay* 23, (2006): 1-72.

109 Andrew Hoskins, *21st Century War: Media, Memory, History*, (Forthcoming). See also Andrew Hoskins and John Tulloch, Chapter 12, 'On Memory and Forgetting', in *Risk and Hyperconnectivity: Media and Memories of NeoLibealism*, (Oxford: Oxford Univeristy Press, 2016), 297-309.

110 Luciano Floridi interviewed by Zan Boag, 'Scuba Diving in the Infosphere,' *New Philosopher*. Retrieved from http://www.newphilosopher.com/articles/scuba-diving-in-the-infosphere/ (accessed March 24, 2016).

Historical understandings created in the twentieth century incorporated the ethical positions of earlier revolutions in human self-understanding. Now we are arguably on the verge of another revolution. After Turing, the present of emerging Artificial Intelligence considers a future where distinguishing from conscious and non-conscious entities is not precluded on a biological basis.[111] Connections with memory simulation – 'history' – are being uploaded in informational technologies. In the postdigital era, the distance between an online and offline world is blurred, and the past is constantly reconstituted in the present; we now exist in a new kind of environment. Postdigital Gallipoli recreations aim to encourage participants to feel like they are 'present' in the past in real time, while also being aware they are in the present here and now – creating 'uncanny' oscillations.

In her book *Cruel Optimism* Lauren Berlant defines the historical sense of the postdigital 'present' as a 'mediated affect,' 'a temporal genre whose conventions emerge from the personal and public filtering of the situations and events that are happening in an extended now whose very parameters… are also always there for debate.' The 'contours' of this 'shared historical present' are 'always profoundly political' because they outline which crises are considered 'urgent'.[112] Clearly, war is one of these crises. For historians, especially those engaged with understanding war's history, suggesting that empirical distance will suffice, historiographically, as an epistemic position in and of itself, may be increasingly difficult and possibly unproductive in a postdigital world. The 'critical understanding brought to the past by historians'[113] is now equally a responsibility to generate understandings of *how* the memory technologies of the present, and human interaction with them, are reframing the history of the future.

---

111 Michael Byron, 'Floridi's Fourth Revolution and the Demise of Ethics," *Knowledge, Technology, & Policy* 23, no. 1-2 (2010). Luciano Floridi, *The Fourth Revolution: How the Infosphere Is Reshaping Human Reality* (Oxford: Oxford univeristy Press, 2014). Luciano Floridi, 'Artificial Intelligence's New Frontier: Artificial Companions and the Fourth Revolution', *Metaphilosophy* 39, no. 4-5 (2008): 651-655.

112 Lauren Berlant, *Cruel Optimism* (Durham: Duke University Press, 2011), 4. Glen Fuller, 'Meta: Aesthetics of the Media Assemblage', *Platform: Journal of Media and Communication* 6, no. 1 (2015).

113 McKenna, 580.

Chapter 5

COMMENTARY

The New War Ecology

Andrew Hoskins

All forms of media have sat uneasily with the idea of the formation of authentic and deep memory and history. For example, Maurice Halbwachs who inaugurated the modern study of collective memory argues: 'Our memory truly rests not on learned history but on lived history'.[1] Under the governance of this formula it is not surprising that most of twentieth century (and earlier) media were seen as inevitably representational, always chasing living memory, the present never quite matching the past, no matter how much effort was invested in its recreation or re-enactment. A more nuanced perspective is to recognise media's functioning in what I have called 'new memory'.[2] That is to say that memory is constantly renewed by the media and technologies (and the metaphors) of the day, in this way it is always 'new' as well as through these same media reflexively shaping a reassessment of the very value of remembering and forgetting under these conditions.

Tom Sear's 'Uncanny valleys' chapter nicely illuminates the digital or 'postdigital's' intensification of new memory in two key ways. Firstly, he highlights the shift in media enabling a new kind of 'lived history' in the commemorative re-temporalising of the Gallipoli campaign in Australia, New Zealand and Turkey in 2015. And, secondly, Sear shows how the debate on the role of media in commemoration is no longer focused on the

---

1   Maurice Halbwachs, *The Collective Memory*, trans. Francis J. Ditter Jr and Vida Yazdi Ditter, Introduction by Mary Douglas, (London: Harper & Row, 1980), 57.
2   Andrew Hoskins, 'New Memory: Mediating History', *The Historical Journal of Film, Radio and Television* 21, No. 4 (2001): 191-211; Andrew Hoskins, *Televising War: From Vietnam to Iraq*, (London: Continuum, 2004).

cheapening effects of certain media seen as over-popularising the history of catastrophic twentieth century events, but rather with the compelling and uncanny character of the digital's collapsing of multiple modes of distance between then and now. And I now briefly expand on these two aspects.

To comprehend the impact of media on an array of events requires a shift in emphasis from 'representationality' (the objectivity and accuracy of an image) to that of 'mediality'.[3] Mediality refers to how media texts are interwoven into our lives through the familiarity of our media practices: how we routinely produce, post, filter, edit, share, reshape, remediate, message, archive, and delete digital media content. Essentially, this is part of a fundamental shift following the connective turn from a disconnected, anonymous and mostly passive mass media audience who consumed 'learned history' (in Halbwachs' terms above) to a new multitude of connected and visible users or participants who are entangled in the production of commemorative events, rather than merely observers of them.

But for Sear, the marking of the centenary of the Gallipoli campaign was something more than mediality, something beyond connected real-time participation, to a new way of living history. For example, News Corp Australia's Anzac Live project converted prominent Australian Gallipoli diarists into avatars, rescripting the event as though it was being witnessed for the first time through today's digital media ecology and facilitating interaction with 'followers' which seemed 'strange and impossible'. The uncanniness of this effect, however, is not only felt in the 'oscillations' in Sear's terms between an unfolding real-time present and a remediated unfolding real-time past. The media of the day imprints itself on events that shape how they are remembered in the future, as Geoffrey Bowker puts it: 'Each new medium imprints its own special flavor to the memories of that epoch'.[4] And Ingrid Volkmer's research into 'global generations media' demonstrates 'the relevance of the media environment for generation-specific perceptions of the world, despite national, cultural, and societal differences'.[5]

But whereas older media forms are often upgraded, where transferable, for consumption in the dominant media of the day, the Anzac Live project

---

3   Andrew Hoskins and Ben O'Loughlin, *War and Media: The Emergence of Diffused War*, (Cambridge: Polity Press, 2010); Richard Grusin, *Premediation: Affect and Mediality After 9/11*, (Basingstoke: Palgrave Macmillan, 2010).

4   Geoffrey C. Bowker, *Memory Practices in the Sciences*, (Cambridge, MA: MIT Press, 2005), 26.

5   Ingrid Volkmer (ed.), *News in Public Memory: An International Study of Media Memories across Generations*, (New York: Peter Lang, 2006), 7.

is an example of the *subversion* of earlier media ecologies, in Bowker's terms, by undermining the 'special flavor' imprinted by early twentieth century media on events, that help locate and distinguish them in time and as history. In other words, Anzac Live was not a commemorative event that merely extended, augmented, or protheticsied the memory of the Gallipoli campaign, but should be seen rather as a case of a new memory *entanglement* of human and technological remembrance. In this way, this commemoration is irreducibly *sociotechnical*, transcending the social and the technological, being part human, part algorithmic, in the continuous production of a new historical present.

In broader terms of the shifting relations between media, memory, war and history, Sear's concluding call for historians to 'generate understandings of how the memory technologies of the present, and human interaction with them, are reframing the history of the future', also speaks to the profound digital transformation of the start of the commemorative arc, as well as to its most recent re-configuration.

There is a pattern to the remembrances of some of the twentieth century's conflicts and catastrophes in their initial limited and awkward public markings and reflections. For example, the Holocaust, the Vietnam War, and the Falklands War, were all marked by following periods of limited and mostly private recollection, denial, unspoken trauma, and non-memory. But once their memorial dams had burst, these events were gripped by cycles of intensive commemoration and memorialisation of the late twentieth and early twenty-first century memory booms. For instance, Jay Winter identifies the time lag between mid- to late twentieth Century war and genocide and what he calls a second memory boom[6] from the 1970s as a shift in 'the balance of creation, adaptation, and circulation' of memory.[7] This shift was firmly embedded in the translation and remediation media of the day, with the new affordability of the personal video recorder in the 1970s and 1980s driving a new archival era of recorded witness testimony. But an explanation as to why this period also saw a revival of the commemoration of the First World War is provided by Eelco Runia in that: 'a generation after the First

---

6 The first memory boom for Winter is marked by the 1890s to the 1920s, when memory was central to the formation of national identities and the memorialising of the victims of the Great War (Winter, 18).

7 Jay Winter, *Remembering War: The Great War Between Memory and History in the Twentieth Century*, (New Haven: Yale University Press, 2006), 26.

World War we were too busy *making* history to be able to commemorate it'.[8] Thus, the emergence of commemoration (during the twentieth century) of the Great Wars was 'blocked' by the silencing of traumatic memory as well as by more war itself.

In this century, however, the digital reverses the memorial arc through a new structure of memorialisation that is near-synchronous with events themselves and war itself is emergent in a memory boom, almost pre-remembered. In this 'new war ecology'[9] there is a new urgency to memorial politics with memory actors who after earlier wars would have been scattered in time and space instead are connected through a kind of living archive.

The so-called 'collective memory' of war in this way is not something that is recalled but rather unfolds from war itself. The once hidden and official (military, government) record is pressured in a fluid war ecology in which individual soldiers, survivors, the bereaved, artists, journalists, museums etc. all contribute and compete in memorial acts of an immediacy and forms unimaginable in the aftermath of wars of the previous century. In this way, the deeply unpopular wars in Iraq and Afghanistan are both contested and legitimised through remembrances enacted at least a generation earlier than many wars commemorated through slower and more fragmented media ecologies.

Of course the major commemorations (particularly from the 1990s onwards) of the Great Wars mark the end of their memorial arcs in terms of the diminishment of the numbers of survivors (a shift from 'communicative' to 'cultural' memory in Jan Assmann's formulation).[10] Yet, Sear has shown that the postdigital offers new commemorative beginnings and imaginings which undermine the stability of generational horizons of memory and forgetting.

What remains to be seen, however, is the potential for the memory of war in the new war ecology. The new structure of memorialisation being too close to war itself may actually undermine the future of memory, with the postdigital disabling its capacity to change, transform and dissipate, in other words a kind of ironic blockage of commemoration, by commemoration.

---

8   Eelco Runia, *Moved by the Past: Discontinuity and Historical Mutation*, (New York: Columbia University Press, 2014), 11.

9   Andrew Hoskins, (forthcoming) *21st Century War: Media, Memory, History*.

10   Jan Assmann, 'Collective Memory and Cultural Identity', *New German Critique* 65 (1995): 125-133.

Part 3

Literary Representations

Chapter 6

TRAITOR/TRAITOR?

Peter Pierce

By the time his first novel, *Traitor*,[1] was published in 2010, Stephen Daisley was in his mid-fifties. As Ralph Waldo Emerson said of another unexpected literary eruption long ago, Walt Whitman's *Leaves of Grass*, 'it must have had a long foreground somewhere'. Born in 1955, Daisley grew up on the North Island of New Zealand. He served for five years in an infantry battalion in the New Zealand army. He also worked on sheep and cattle stations, oil and gas construction sites and drove trucks, both in his home country and in Australia, on whose west coast he now lives with his wife and five daughters. These experiences – of military life and rural work – and of the many implements and the skills required to use them, inform both *Traitor* and Daisley's recently released second novel, *Coming Rain* (2015)[2]. The two books show a deep assurance concerning the things that the author knows, whether of the material and visceral world – of loading rifles, shearing and delivering lambs, saddling horses – or of the emotional lives of characters who are articulate in their own terms, if in no fluently cosmopolitan way.

In 2011, *Traitor* won the Australian Prime Minister's Award for Fiction. Michael Heyward, the head of Text Publishing that had punted on the novel, has related how the esteemed New Zealand literary agent and short story writer, Michael Gifkins, who died in 2014, called the book – a touch wistfully perhaps – 'the great New Zealand novel',[3] as though this fabled creature had been sighted and certified at last, albeit on the wrong side of

---

1   Stephen Daisley, *Traitor* (Melbourne: Text Publishing, 2010).
2   Stephen Daisley, *Coming Rain* (Melbourne: Text Publishing, 2015).
3   Michael Heyward, e-mail to the author on Gifkins, 8 December 2014.

the Tasman Sea. These two judgments – by the award committee (of which I was the Chair) and by Gifkins – have the combined effect of making *Traitor* a decidedly ANZAC product, reinvigorating the acronym that was forged in the Great War from the time of the Gallipoli campaign of 1915. Now it could describe one of the most impressive of all the literary retrospects of the last century on the events of battle and of their much longer lasting domestic consequences. It is the case that both Australian and New Zealand literature of the Great War has more of substance to show from imaginative reconstructions of that conflict by those who were not there, than by those who had served.

Thus *The Oxford Companion to New Zealand Literature* (1998)[4] glumly declared that 'the First World War, for all its devastating casualties and patriotic fervour, produced little literature of lasting or distinctive quality'. Or, perhaps, one had to be patient. John A. Lee's *Civilian Into Soldier*, an autobiographically based account of his experiences on the Western Front, appeared in 1937. His later work, *Soldier*, about the loss of an arm in battle and a subsequent love affair in a military hospital in England, was not published until 1976. Other books that drew on their authors' experiences at war include Robin Hyde's novels, *Passport to Hell* (1936) and *Nor the Years Condemn* (1938), and Archibald Baxter's memoir, *We Will Not Cease* (1939).[5] The latter work, and the story that it tells of the author's field punishment (in part by a kind of crucifixion) in France on account of his conscientious objection to war, was a key point of reference for Daisley. The modest hero of *Traitor*, Sergeant David Monroe when we first encounter him, will hear at first-hand of Baxter's sufferings and judge him to be 'a brave and difficult man' before he endures similar travails of his own. Much later, and back in New Zealand, Monroe will learn of Hiruhurama, or Jerusalem, 'a place of cherry trees and nuns and a prophet poet whose father he had seen in the Etaples prison yard'. The poet was James Baxter.

If the Baxters' stories were primary New Zealand bearings for Daisley, he was also enrolling in a wider literary tradition. Monroe's crucial and instinctual decision both to befriend the Turkish doctor, follower of the Sufi tendency of Islam and prisoner of war, Mahmoud, with whom he has been wounded in a shell blast, and then to seek to escape with him from the Greek island of Lemnos, is a valiant and quixotic gesture. Monroe's

---

4   *The Oxford Companion to New Zealand Literature*, eds Roger Robinson and Nelson Wattie (Oxford: Oxford University Press, 1998).

5   *The Auckland University Press Anthology of New Zealand Literature*, eds Jane Stafford and Mark Williams (Auckland: Auckland University Press, 2012).

epiphany recalls what Ernest Hemingway's Lieutenant Frederic Henry, in the famous and poignantly titled war novel *A Farewell to Arms* (1929), described in audacious and soon enough blighted hope as the making of 'a separate peace'. In Australia, revisiting of the Great War in fiction, film and poetry began in the late 1960s. The main works are easy to name. They include such films as *Break of Day* (1976), directed by Ken Hannam, and Peter Weir's *Gallipoli* (1981); poems by Les Murray ('The Trainee, 1914', 'Visiting Anzac in the Year of Metrication'), Geoff Page ('Christ at Gallipoli', 'Trench Dreams') and Chris Wallace-Crabbe ('The Shapes of Gallipoli') and novels by Roger McDonald, *1915* (1979), David Malouf, *Fly Away Peter* (1982). A generation later came Bruce Scates's *On Dangerous Ground* (2012) and Steve Sailah's murder mystery, *A Fatal Tide* (2014). To what extent the earlier works were motivated by a last chance to speak in the name of survivors of the Great War, and how far they marked a recoil from the divisive conflict in Vietnam, remains debatable. (There is no place here to assess the seemingly unstaunchable flow of histories of Gallipoli and of the Great War more widely. Three only from last year suggest some of the range: Ross Coulthart's biography, *Charles Bean*, of the Official Australian War Correspondent and later the editor of the national history of the Great War; Raden Dunbar's *The Secrets of the Anzacs*, which deals with venereal disease and its treatments in Egypt, England and back in Australia; and another piece of febrile populism from Peter Fitzsimmons, *Gallipoli*).

In part in reaction to what he regarded as 'the easy nostalgia' of Weir's film and also to a desolating trip that he made to Gallipoli in 1977, New Zealand author Maurice Shadbolt abandoned plans for a novel about the conflict. Instead he wrote the play *On Chunuk Bair* (1982)[6] about the heroic and disastrous New Zealand action on 8 August 1915. Briefly, the Allied goal of the Dardanelles was sighted, but this was a literal high point that the rest of the campaign failed to repeat. Daisley has his David Monroe take part in that battle. Monroe would not have been out of place among the ageing contributors to the collection *Voices of Gallipoli* (1988)[7] that Shadbolt later edited. He described it as 'a collection of narratives which tell how humble and mostly simple New Zealanders lived and died on Turkey's Gallipoli peninsula for eight months in the year 1915'.

In his distinctive way, Daisley was also responding to Shadbolt's complaint that 'no significant poem, song, novel or painting – literally nothing in

---

6   Maurice Shadbolt, *Once on Chunuk Bair* (Auckland: Hodder & Stoughton, 1982).
7   Maurice Shadbolt (ed), *Voices of Gallipoli* (Auckland: Hodder & Stoughton, 1988).

our nation's cultural life – enshrined the New Zealand experiences of the Gallipoli campaign, and this though the Anzac Day, 25 April, remained conspicuous on our calendars'. Shadbolt quotes Ormond Burton, a soldier turned militant pacifist, from his book based on Great War service, *The Silent Division* (1935): 'How men were to die on Chunk Bair was determined largely by how men and women had lived on farms and in the towns of New Zealand'. Daisley's *Traitor* is deeply attuned to such a sentiment. The battles in which Monroe takes part at Gallipoli, and his wounding there with Mahmoud, are an essential preliminary portion of the novel. Where Monroe came from, and the world to which eventually he returns after being impressed into service in an ambulance corps on the Western Front, is the larger and in some ways its essential business.

The epigraph to this work titled, as it seems at first, bluntly and acridly *Traitor*, is from E.M. Forster and it will resonate through all that follows, not without ambiguity: 'I hate the very idea of causes, and if I had to choose between betraying my country and betraying my friend, I hope I should have the guts to betray my country'. That famous declaration informs, but does not altogether fit the choices that David Monroe makes. The novel opens on Lemnos in 1915, where Monroe, on the recommendation of an Australian doctor, is allowed to keep company with Mahmoud, who has been wounded with him on a spur of Ari Burnu by an errant British naval shell. (This was the same kind of misadventure that had killed Colonel William George Malone, commander of the Wellington battalion on Chunuk Bair, together with many of his men.) Almost at once, Daisley moves the action forward half a century to 1965 and to rural New Zealand. That country has just committed troops to Vietnam. However improbably, this means that the ageing shepherd who has worked on Papanui Station since 1920, has been called into the small police station at Ruatane on account of his distant, supposedly subversive and treacherous past.

This enables Daisley economically to outline what the military case had been against Monroe at his court martial. The officer in charge, Inspector Ogden, reads from Monroe's service record: 'in October 1915 you aided a POW to escape from detention in a camp on the island of Lemnos. That you also deserted with said prisoner'. He further asserts that 'You were a traitor to your country Mr Monroe is that right?' For his own part, Monroe explains how 'the Australian boys' refused to carry out his death sentence. Remembering Monroe's 'service at the Cove', they told the authorities 'to go fuck themselves they will not shoot one of their own'. After demotion and field punishment, Monroe was sent as a stretcher-bearer to France and

Belgium. In this second kind of war service, Monroe displays a quiet and inspiring Christian fortitude: 'God has not deserted any of us', he counsels a young soldier. After a further six months in Germany, he was granted a full pardon. 'And I came home then'. What is also revealed is Monroe's record at Gallipoli. Wounded on a Sari Bair ridge, he was 'mentioned in dispatches and recommended for field promotion by his battalion commander for actions on the Chunuk Bair heights'. Unfortunately, that recommendation was never given effect, because the commanding officer, Colonel Malone, had been killed. As Monroe remarks to the policeman, 'We all should have died but we didn't'.

There is one more crucial episode to be related of these events from long ago. Monroe's friend, Mahmoud, the Sufi, 'a man who wears wool and believes in God' has corresponded with him after the war. But the last letter that he receives from Turkey has been sent not by Mahmoud, but by his wife, Aisha, who relates that her husband has been hanged for his religious beliefs. That is, the former Turkish commander at Gallipoli, Kemal Ataturk, now first Prime Minister of the Turkish Republic, has cracked down on Sufis for their refusal to acknowledge a secular state. Mahmoud was 'the so-called enemy' not only for the ANZAC forces, but in his own country as well. Monroe dissents. As he recalls, 'I just felt an enormous affection even love for this man ... He kissed me on the mouth and called me God'. It was Mahmoud who led Monroe in an ecstatic whirling dance that he still performs in private on the sheep pastures near his home. Of course he has been seen, and thought mad, 'spinning around and around with his arms held out all alone on the Abernethy Flat. Falling and crying out to the sky'.

Monroe's connections to the district include Chung Moon, the Chinese owner of the general store where he used to buy birthday gifts for the child Catherine, who is now the widow Mrs Catherine McKenzie and owner of Rapanui Station. 'Old Dave', as he already seemed to be in his thirties, left those gifts at her door. Her mother, 'Sarah Mitchell the witch', had disappeared, leaving the baby girl in a basket on the front step of her Maori neighbours. Monroe knows the mother of his friend, Peter Whiting, whom he saw die in the rain on Mount St Quentin in the last months of the war. She tells him how – in one of Peter's letters home – he had said of Monroe that 'you were with him and that you were a blessed saint and not to take any notice of what anyone might say about you'. Among Monroe's threaded memories are those of his mother, born Mary O'Connell, who drowned when he was sixteen and she was only thirty – a casualty of some deep private pain unrelated to war. It was Eoin McKenzie, who still wore his captain's uniform with the right sleeve pinned up, who gave Monroe work on his property in 1920. Mrs McKenzie, whose father was killed at Gallipoli and whose brother went mad, spat at him. Too conveniently for her he was a criminal and a traitor, the worse because he had not perished.

The casualties of war do not end with the armistice. In making an accounting of them, of the sufferings of the damaged ones who return and of the grieving ones who have stayed behind, Daisley's novel has a deal in common with Chis Womersley's *Bereft* (2010), which relates the disruptive consequences of the homecoming of one presumed lost, the Great War veteran Quinn Walker, to the New South Wales country town of Flint. (Other disturbing revenants from that war are the protagonists of two earlier novels by Patrick White: Stan Parker in *The Tree of Man*, 1957, and Eddie Twyborn in *The Twyborn Affair*, 1979). Among Monroe's friends is the melancholy scholar and drinker Wit Abernethy, who has a soldier settler's block next to Papanui and who is tormented by how he had to shoot the horses that could not be taken away with the troops. Rehabilitated, he becomes a school teacher at New Plymouth, and now drinks only once a year on 'the anniversary of when the horses forgave him'.

With an unerring lightness of touch, Daisley weaves backwards and forwards between events during the war and their enduring legacy at home. For Monroe the essential episode was his decision – made suddenly but surely – to escape from their convalescence on Lemnos with Mahmoud, with no more considered plan that that 'I have a boat and a fisherman to take us'. The true traitor of the story is now revealed, the Limnion called Alexis who strands 'these two strange men who seemed to love one another' and then turns them over to the British. Three years later Monroe is in France, at Courcelles, with the Third Field Ambulance of the Australian Fifth Brigade: 'on the day it all ended he smelled burning gum leaves'. It is he who is chosen to kill the calf for the celebratory meal for those who have survived.

Back home he becomes the best shepherd in the district, tending to the 'lambing, the early ewes along the river flats'. He rides a horse called the John, 'named after a list of horses that had come before him. It was thus more than a name or an individual, it was an affirmation of memory, a respect for that which had been'. Monroe talks to Catherine McKenzie, who does not know that she is his daughter, and she tells him how 'I saw you once when I was a girl, turning in circles'. And he replies simply, with the quiet conviction that she will understand him, how 'a man called Mahmoud taught me this thing ... He was a Sufi. They are mad, crazed with the love of God'. All that should have been alien to him in the other man's belief and behaviour has not only been accepted as natural, but also as a guide and a benediction. This is the wonder at the heart of *Traitor*, a novel less concerned with the horrors of war than to the possibilities for redemption that they cannot foreclose.

Chapter 7

THE 'ENEMY' AT GALLIPOLI

Perceptions of the Adversary in Turkish, Australian and New Zealand Literatures

A. Candan Kirişci

One of the many ironies associated with the Gallipoli campaign is that it included parties that would otherwise have been least likely to have any contact with one another. Contrary to their initial expectations, the colonial troops from Australia and New Zealand found themselves not at the Western Front, but struggling instead to get a foothold on the steep hills of a little known peninsula. The defence force against them consisted mainly of Ottoman troops, a predominantly Turkish force. The infamous Hun, the adversary they had been taught to hate and trained to kill, did not have much visibility in the affair.[1] Likewise, the Ottomans also had to face an enemy thus far unknown to them. The term Anzac would in time acquire new meanings for the Turkish side, and mostly a positive connotation after the transition from the Ottoman state into modern Turkey.

This chapter will look at how this unexpected adversary was reflected in the literatures of Turkey, Australia and New Zealand. The body of literary

---

1   The defence troops at Gallipoli were recruited from various parts of the ethnically diverse Ottoman state, but the majority was Turkish. They were fighting under the joint leadership of Ottoman and German generals, and the technical assistance offered by Germany was a factor that strengthened the defence. But German presence did not extend to lower ranks. For the composition of the Ottoman army during the war, see Erik J. Zürcher, 'Between Death and Desertion. The Experience of the Ottoman Soldier in World War I', *Turcica* 28 (1996): 240-41. Information on the German assistance in Gallipoli can be found in Edward J. Erickson, *Ordered to Die: A History of the Ottoman Army in the First World War* (Connecticut: Greenwood Press, 2001), 76–82.

works published on the topic of Gallipoli constitutes today a sizeable volume, especially in the first two countries if not so much in New Zealand. The discussion below will mostly concern itself with the period that roughly covers the first fifty years of production, from 1915 to 1965. It will primarily dwell on some of the best known examples from these literatures without making any particular distinction with regard to the genres. Not all of these texts can be considered as having high literary qualities; some stand out by virtue of their place in popular memory rather than the canon. They are important, however, in that they still communicate certain patterns of thought and style with regard to the subject at hand, the perception of the enemy.

Gallipoli as a turning point in Turkish imagination

One of the best ways to understand the significance of Gallipoli in Turkish imagination would be to consider its timing. The battles were fought by the army of the Ottoman Empire which had entered the First World War on the side of the Central Powers. The country had long been struggling to reverse the military and economic decline that had weakened its former power. External threats were a major source of concern for its administrators, who also had to contain the rising trend of secessionism within the various ethnic communities under Ottoman rule. Shortly before the First World War, in 1912, the army had suffered a humiliating defeat in the Balkans where an important chunk of European territory was lost, triggering a series of social and economic problems that further destabilised the system. On the other hand, the experience marked a turning point for the strengthening of a Turkish national identity,[2] a trend also reinforced by the literature that followed from the war. But the success at Gallipoli would prove a more effective theme in that regard.

When the Ottomans joined the war it was a well known possibility that the Dardanelles would face an Allied attack. The initial round of bombardment in February 1915 was a sure warning for the military to step up the defence. Also, contingency plans were made to move the sultanate away from Istanbul in the eventuality of the Ottoman capital coming under occupation.[3] The

---

2   Zafer Toprak, 'Cihan Harbi'nin Provası Balkan Harbi' [The Balkan War as the Rehearsal of the First World War], *Toplumsal Tarih* 104, (August 2002): 44-51 (p.46).

3   The German commander Liman Von Sanders writes of the measures to support the defence systems near Istanbul in the event of the Allied navy passing through the Dardanelles, see Liman Von Sanders, *Türkiye'de Beş Yıl* [Five Years in Turkey] trans. Eşref Bengi Özbilen (Istanbul: Türkiye İş Bankası Kültür Yayınları, 2010), 73–74.

major offensive of the Allied navy on 18 March 1915 was, therefore, not unanticipated; if anything, it was much feared. To the great relief and delight of the Ottomans, the day of battle ended to their advantage, making it impossible for the British and French warships to force their way into the straits. The halt to the attempt was temporary, but it was enough to trigger a wave of patriotic literature which would continue until the end of the war, though with varying intensity. The dailies and periodicals of the time were the primary venue for this output, which mostly took poetic form. It should be underlined that these were publications that had to operate within the restrictions imposed by the war administration, and some enjoyed direct support by the War Ministry.[4] The link between propagandist pressures and the poetic medium was obvious, and the content and style of the literary output from the campaign would greatly be shaped by this phenomenon.[5]

This literature was mostly a celebration of the hero. He was invariably depicted as a man of courage, devotion and virtue and rewarded with the most lavish praises. His picture rarely emerged in isolation however, since a typical feature of these works was to place him in direct opposition to his adversary. The term 'enemy' contained a temporality that extended to a bygone era of glory. Reminiscing about old conquests quickly became a

---

Also the memoirs of the renowned poet Yahya Kemal reveal the anxiety felt by a circle of intellectuals in the days prior to the major naval expedition by the Allies and tell of their preparations in the case of a possible occupation, see Yahya Kemal [Beyatlı], *Siyasi ve Edebi Portreler* [Political and Literary Portraits] (Istanbul: Yahya Kemal Enstitüsü, 1976), 30–35. One of the original sources that mentions the plan to move the sultanate to the town of Eskişehir in Anatolia is Henry Morgenthau, *Ambassador Morgenthau's Story* (New York: Doubleday, Page & Company, 1918), 192. Morgenthau also elaborates on the sense of ominous anticipation of an Allied attack that reigned in the Ottoman government circles as well as the German and Austrian diplomatic missions in Istanbul, 184–201.

4   Some of the best known dailies that featured patriotic poetry were *Sabah* [Morning] *Tanin* [Echo], *İkdam* [Perseverant Effort] and *Tasvir-i Efkar* [Tablet of Thoughts]. *Türk Yurdu* [Turkish Homeland], a journal with a nationalist agenda and close ties to the Committee of Union and Progress which was in power during the First World War, was another venue for such literature. Two other important publications were *Donanma Mecmuası* [The Navy Review] and *Harp Mecmuası* [The War Review] which were known to be directly supported by the state administration. An important source on Ottoman press in the years leading to First World War is Ahmet Emin Yalman, *The Development of Modern Turkey as Measured by its Press* (New York: AMS Press, 1968).

5   For a comprehensive study on the role of literature in wartime propaganda, see Erol Köroğlu, *Türk Edebiyatı ve Birinci Dünya Savaşı (1914-1918): Propagandadan Milli Kimlik İnşasına* [Turkish Literature and the First World War (1914-1918): From Propaganda to the Making of National Identity] (Istanbul: Iletişim Yayınları, 2004). For a shorter version in English, see Erol Köroğlu, *Ottoman Propaganda and Turkish Identity: Literature in Turkey during World War I* (London: Tauris Academic Studies, 2007).

cliché, often foregrounding Europe in the image of a monolithic, eternal foe. The upper hand recently gained at the Dardanelles heralded a return to those days; as expressed repeatedly, this latest victory would 'erase the stain of the Balkan defeat'. After all, this was a defence put up by the sons of warriors that had 'roared' in Europe for five centuries.[6] The indignation was made most clear in imagery that projected a picture of the opponent as a horde of 'infidels', 'pirates', 'savages' and 'monsters'.[7] And the defender of the homeland was more of a hero because he fought against this most despicable enemy. In a way, he was exalted as much by way of this stark negation as the words of commendation lavishly heaped upon him.

The source for this initial outburst included a wide range from poetically inclined patriots to renowned poets. The emphasis on the enemy differed little, however. The same indignant, antagonistic tone ran through the whole output and similar imagery contributed to the effect. In the words of Mehmet Emin [Yurdakul][8], the prominent advocate of Turkish nationalism, the threat to the fatherland came from the 'white, black, red and yellow savages from five different worlds'. The poet did not specify these 'five worlds', instead elaborated on the enemy from a historical perspective. Russia, for instance, had extended its 'ferocious claws' into the Turkish land before; also the defeat at the Balkans had been the work of 'bloodsucking, rabies inflicted savages.'[9] As for the men at defence, Mehmet Emin, ever the nationalist-patriot, was quick to promote them as the best representatives of a race endowed with superior qualities. The famous lines of Mehmet Akif [Ersoy] who hailed from the other end of the ideological spectrum revealed different sensitivities. For this widely respected poet who favored Islamic unity at the expense of ethnic identity, Gallipoli was 'the last stronghold of Islam' and

---

6   Ali Rıza Seyfi, 'Kal'a-i Sultaniye' [Fortress of the Sultan], *Donanma*, no. 89-91 (15 April 1915), 652 quoted in Ömer Çakır, *Türk Şiirinde Çanakkale Muharebeleri* [Gallipoli in Turkish Poetry] (Ankara: Atatürk Kültür Merkezi Başkanlığı Yayınları, 2004), 36.

7   These were some of the terms generally used to refer to the enemy. They appeared abundantly in many poems of the time.

8   The poet will be referred to as Mehmet Emin hereafter as he was not yet known by his surname in this period. The practice of taking family names was introduced later during the 1930s, after the establishment of modern Turkey.

9   These quotations are from 'Ordu'nun Destanı' [The Epic of the Army] in *Mehmet Emin Yurdakul'un Eserleri – I* [The Works of Mehmet Emin Yurdakul], ed. Fevziye Abdullah Tansel (Ankara: Türk Tarih Kurumu Basımevi, 1989), 173-95. The poem was originally published in 1915 following a trip to the front. Mehmet Emin was part of a group commissioned by the Ottoman War Ministry to produce patriotic works based on observations at the front.

the heroes were 'the magnificent sons' of the Mohammedan army.[10] The enemy threatening it, however, came across with familiar emphasis: 'a pack of hyenas, running wild and away from their cage'.[11]

The composite nature of the Allied army escaped no poet's attention. This was sometimes expressed by spelling out the names of the big powers; fingers were pointed at the British and the French as the perpetrators of an unjust war. Their reliance on colonial troops was known to some of these poets but rarely figured in early examples.[12] The multinational character of the offence force was mostly mentioned in general terms, more like a rhetorical tool that emphasised the gravity of the odds facing the nation. In a rare instance, the Anzacs came into view in the lines of Mehmet Akif who described the conflict as a conspiracy of 'the old world' which put its dirty scheme in action with the help of 'the new world'. What followed was the cataloging of the Indians and Canadians along with the Australians. The poet somehow left out the New Zealanders, but this in no way overshadowed the main idea that Gallipoli was a defence against 'seven climes of the world'. However diverse they might be 'in their faces, languages and races', said the poet in a bitter voice, they all shared the same 'savagery'.[13]

Apart from indignation, the enemy also evoked a sense of disillusionment in these poets. This can be better understood when considered from a larger context. To that day, Europe had long represented to the Ottoman elite the

---

10   These quotations are from 'Berlin Hatıraları' [Memories of Berlin] where Mehmet Akif first mentioned Gallipoli. It was later included in his collection *Safahad* [Stages], ed. M. Ertuğrul Düzdağ (Istanbul: Nesil Yayınları, 2007), 283-306.

11   This line belongs to the poem 'Çanakkale Şehitleri'ne' [To the Martyrs of Gallipoli] which is widely accepted in Turkey as the best rendering of Gallipoli in literary form. It was originally published as part of a long narrative poem 'Asım' which first appeared in 1924, see Düzdağ, 363-405. It has also been reprinted separately numerous times.

12   As illustrated in the coverage of the battles in the daily *Ikdam*, little differentiation was made as to the ethnic identity of the enemy at this stage. The offence force was mostly referred to as the troops of the Allied army; the Australians were only mentioned in a few instances. The original coverage appeared in Ottoman Turkish, for a collection of the campaign reports in modern Turkish, see Murat Çulcu, *Ikdam Gazetesi'nde Çanakkale Cephesi: 3 Kasım 1914 – 3 Şubat 1916: haber-yorum-bildiri-röportaj-gözlem ve anılar* [The Gallipoli Front in the Daily Ikdam: 3 November 1914 – 3 February 1916: reports-comments-statements-interviews-accounts and memoirs], A. Candan Kirişci (Istanbul: Denizler Kitabevi, 2004).

13   These lines are also from 'Çanakkale Şehitleri'ne', in Düzdağ, 385. The awareness with regard to the identity of the colonial forces in the poem may be attributed to the fact that it was part of a publication believed to have been in the making from 1918 to 1924. This may have given Mehmet Akif more clarity as to the facts compared to those who wrote during the actual campaign.

ultimate level of human civilisation. Its achievements in arts and sciences were closely followed, at times copied and adopted at home. Perhaps more importantly, the ideas that emanated from its vibrant culture continued to inspire younger generations for many decades. And now, as these poets liked to express bitterly, the carnage that swept across humanity was also the work of the same civilisation. In addition to this, their fixation on a monstrous enemy figure pointed to yet another phenomenon. The Europe that they had long admired presented at the same time the most imminent and serious threat against Ottoman viability. Their take on the enemy was therefore prompted by more than a propaganda effort; it was also the manifestation of the unease created by these contradicting and powerful sentiments. The raging, contemptuous tone that marked their language whenever they turned their gaze to the opponent was perhaps their way of standing up against a power that had loomed so large in their imagination.

Gallipoli as a tune sung in harmony

As mentioned before, the timing played an important role in Gallipoli acquiring national significance. The Turkish nationalist movement , which had been gradually developing by then, was quick to seize the moment and promote it to advance the cause.[14] What followed thereafter was to further emphasise the place of Gallipoli in public consciousness. The battle was won, but the First World War ended with a catastrophic defeat for the Ottoman state which soon came under Allied occupation. A movement of resistance led by Mustafa Kemal who first achieved prominence at Gallipoli eventually paved the way for the establishment of modern Turkey in 1923. This was a new country, a republic, founded on the tenets of secularism and ethnic nationalism; as such it greatly diverged from the Islam-oriented, multi-ethnic structure that preceeded it.[15]

The republican era, especially in its early years, was marked by an obvious effort to distance itself from the Ottoman heritage. Gallipoli was

---

14 This was most evident in the publication of a special anniversary issue by *Yeni Mecmua* [The New Review] in 1918. For a later edition, see Muzaffer Albayrak and Ayhan Özyurt, eds., *Yeni Mecmua Çanakkale Özel Sayısı* [The New Review Special Issue on Gallipoli] (Istanbul: Yeditepe Yayınevi, 2006). For an assessment of the issue as well as its significance in the formation of national identity, see Erol Köroğlu, 'Yeni Mecmua Çanakkale Özel Sayısı' [The New Review Special Issue on Gallipoli], *Toplumsal Tarih* (March 2003): 94-99.

15 An important source giving a concise account of the transformation is Erik J. Zürcher, *Turkey: A Modern History* (London: I. B. Tauris, 2007).

cherished as a rare moment of pride nevertheless; it was often referred to as a self-defining experience for the young Turkish nation. At the same time, a growing emphasis was placed on Mustafa Kemal; in a well repeated metaphor, he represented 'the sun that rose at Gallipoli'. The famed battleground also acquired a new significance as the hallow site where the Turks first met their natural leader. It was the same person that led them through further struggle and hardship during the 'War of Independence', as the resistance against Allied occupation came to be known in Turkish history. This crucial link was often reiterated in the patriotic literature produced by a generation of poets and writers dedicated to the republican cause. Gallipoli mainly featured in this context, celebrated as the coming of age of a young nation, but generally overshadowed by the 'War of Independence', the last major trial on the path to independence. Some of the poems that had appeared during the First World War were republished after 1923, along with some new works that occasionally appeared on anniversaries.[16] But, in general, literary interest in Gallipoli fell short of reflecting the importance attributed to it in official mythology.

The era brought, on the other hand, a nuance with regard to the enemy. An initial instance was the famous conciliatory message to the Anzac side attributed largely to Mustafa Kemal.[17] The distinguishing of the Anzac soldier as a better enemy could also be seen in the limited number of literary works solely devoted to the theme.[18] One such title was *Gallipoli*, a verse volume published in 1939 by a professed patriot, Haluk Nihat Pepeyi, who sought to fill the void with an epic, the style which he deemed most appropriate for the subject matter at hand.[19] The effort brought the poet some acclaim at the time, but largely lacked the poetic qualities that could ensure a place in the canon. *Gallipoli* contains, on the other hand, some of the nuances mentioned above. The introduction signed by a renowned social

---

16 It is important to note that these later prints often appeared with revisions. For example, the words 'sultan', 'caliph' or 'crown' were either taken out completely or replaced by terms such as 'homeland', 'nation' and 'freedom', which reflected the preferences of the official discourse in the new republican era.

17 The history of this speech and the controversy surrounding its authorship is discussed in more detail in the chapter by Macleod and Tongo in this volume.

18 The emphasis on the Anzacs is mostly a phenomenon that has appeared in the novels of the past two decades which remain outside of the period covered in this paper. Two works that reveal a particular attention to the Anzacs are Buket Uzuner, *Uzun Beyaz Bulut: Gelibolu* [The Long White Cloud: Gallipoli] (Istanbul: Remzi Kitabevi, 2001) and Serpil Uras, *Şafakta Yanan Mumlar* [Candles at Dawn] (Ankara: Bilgi Yayınevi, 2003). Both titles have been translated into English.

19 Haluk Nihat Pepeyi, *Çanakkale* [Gallipoli] (Istanbul:Yeni Kitapçı, 1939).

scientist, Hilmi Ziya Ülken, presents the campaign as a scheme where the great powers pitted the weak against the weak. The Turks and the Anzacs, in his view, were driven to conflict not by their own choice but by others. The verse that follows revolves around the same theme, placing a particular blame for the war on the British and the French. Echoing the introduction, Pepeyi's own reference to the Anzacs conveys a similar tone of forgiveness. He calls them 'brave soldiers', but cannot keep from pitying 'these blind hordes' who would ask only too late: 'why and for whom did we die?'[20]

These lines were in fact the reflection of a mindset that prevailed throughout the Republican era. Independence was deemed sacred. The struggle put up against the threat of foreign rule after the First World War was a major theme in official discourse; great pride was taken in the fact that modern Turkey was a fully independent state. The same notion was further reiterated in school books as well as literary works. The term 'colony' generally evoked a simple form of domination, not much unlike the relationship between master and slave, and few distinctions were made in its use. As will be mentioned again, the particular circumstances of the Anzac nations, the levels of autonomy that they had achieved within the British Empire; more importantly, the ethnic, cultural and linguistic ties that they shared with the dominating power were largely overlooked. They were mentioned as members of the same unfortunate community as any nation that ever came under foreign rule. The best example that illustrated this point can be found in *The Epic of Gallipoli*, a collection of poems by the renowed poet Fazıl Hüsnü Dağlarca.[21] The volume was published in 1965 to mark the fiftieth anniversary. Among more than a hundred pieces that it contains, one is especially striking by virtue of its title: 'Song of the Brothers Exploited in the Army of the Exploiters'. It features a voice directed to the Senegalese and the Indians, asking them in the same compassionate tone, 'for whatever reason have you come?' to fight in this foreign land. When the attention turns to the 'brave' Australians, the question becomes 'what is it that your mountains want from mine?'.[22] Dağlarca's piece best captures a sentiment shared by many, that of astonishement at the turn of events that made enemies out of such distant and most unlikely nations.

As stated before, Turkish literary works treated Gallipoli with as much focus on the vilification of the enemy as on the celebration of the hero. A

---

20   Pepeyi, *Çanakkale*, 78.
21   Fazıl Hüsnü Dağlarca, *Çanakkale Destanı* [The Epic of Gallipoli] (Istanbul: Kitap Yayınları, 1965).
22   Dağlarca, *Çanakkale Destanı*, 77.

softer regard for the Anzacs, which emerged later, did not generally change this trend. The patriotic theme that was dominant in the period discussed here still resonates strongly. In fact patriotic fervor has always pervaded all forms of narration about Gallipoli, from its teaching in schools to commemoration ceremonies, and even to historical writing on the topic. The same stories, images and symbols have consistently appeared again and again in different forms of representation, offering little variation in terms of theme and style. In a way, Gallipoli has acquired an aspect similar to a tune sung in perfect harmony, with the rigid expectation that any mention of the affair should resound with the same intonation. Any slight deviation can be guaranteed to be frowned upon as a cracked voice. The pervasiveness of the official rhetoric across the cultural scene can partly account for this situation. Also, the very fact that public imagination as well as artistic inspiration has mostly been deprived of first-hand accounts about Gallipoli can be seen as a contributing factor. Compared to the Anzac side, the number of diaries, letters and memoirs on the Turkish side is fairly limited for the simple reason that the majority of the common soldiers in the Ottoman army were illiterate. Likewise, the voice of the combatants is conspicuously absent in literary representation. It goes without saying that such sources could have provided invaluable insights and perspectives in the study of the conflict, and shaped its perception differently. Compared to the Turkish experience, however, Australia offers a case where the same event was projected in literary form with more colour and variation.

Gallipoli as a turning point in Australian imagination

The significance of Gallipoli in Australian history and imagination has been the topic of a large volume of writings to this day. As often noted, the irony between the expectations before the war and the realities of the front experience is striking. Little did the Australian troops expect to fight at a site other than the Western Front and against an enemy other than the Hun. Little did anyone know that the date of the first landings at Gallipoli, 25 April 1915, would become so central in public imagination. Again, as for the Turkish side, the timing of the campaign was a particularly important factor in all this. The Australian troops had participated in colonial wars before but this was the first major involvement; neither would it be the last one. Subsequent battles on the Western Front would claim more lives and cause greater misery, but this initial impact was to be the strongest.

The Australians who found themselves forcing their way into Gallipoli were the members of a society long preoccupied with the issue of a distinct identity. Unlike their opponents, they hailed from a generally peaceful and prosperous land. The British influence was constantly felt in many aspects of life, from political and economic matters to arts and literature, but this was no obstacle to the development of an identity particular to the land and its people. This was a case where pride in one's ethnic origins did not generally conflict with the sentiment of being an 'independent Australian Briton.'[23] Nationalism gained particular strength in the 1890s, but mostly as a force that developed hand in hand with a strong sense of imperial allegiance. One notion that accompanied the trend was that Australia would eventually pay a blood sacrifice on its path to nationhood.[24] As compellingly put by the poet Henry Lawson, 'the Star of the South' could only 'rise in the lurid clouds of war'.[25] The idea resonated more forcefully in the rising militarism that swept the colonies in the decade before the First World War. Gallipoli would be the event that provided this long anticipated trial.

A glimpse at history displays little evidence to support the Turkish perception of the Australians as the helpless victims of a ruthless imperial power. It would show a more nuanced picture which reveals a certain distance from 'the older forms of domination, control and suasion exercised by the metropolitan power over the colonial society of settlement in the periphery'. What rather prevailed in the period leading up to the war were 'notions of cooperation and partnership, of alliance and mutual standing.'[26] Characteristically, independence in certain areas coexisted with strong loyalty to Britain as a new tide of immigrants rekindled interest in the imperial tradition.[27] When the war broke out, the ruling elite in Australia

---

23 Robert Cole, 'The Problem of 'Nationalism' and 'Imperialism' in British Settlement Colonies', *The Journal of British Studies* 10, no. 2 (May 1971): 160-82.

24 Patsy Adam-Smith, *The Anzacs* (London: Hamish Hamilton, 1978), 8.

25 The lines belong to the 1895 poem titled 'The Star of Australasia' in Colin Roderick, ed., *Henry Lawson Collected Verse*, 3 vols (Sydney: Angus and Robertson, 1967), vol. 1, 294-296.

26 John Eddy and Deryck Schreuder, eds., *The Rise of Colonial Nationalism* (Sydney: Allen & Unwin, 1988), 7-8. For a detailed account on the tensions between Australia and Britain, more specifically on the Australian assertions vis-à-vis the British colonial administration in matters of trade and security, see E. M. Andrews, *The Anzac Illusion: Anglo-Australian Relations during World War I* (UK: Cambridge University Press, 1993).

27 Andrews, *The Anzac Illusion*, 11-12. As also explained in the same source, the adaptation of the British school curriculum with strong focus on British literature, history and imperial unity was especially effective on young minds, 32-35.

was quick to commit troops and resources in support of the motherland. The initial enthusiasm demonstrated by the young men to enlist was striking, and the Australian Imperial Force would remain a volunteer army throughout the war.[28] As recounted in Bill Gammage's influential study *The Broken Years: Australian Soldiers in the Great War*, their motives were numerous and did not always reflect imperial ideals or notions of glory; the number of recruits driven by the expectation of good pay or a thirst for adventure was not negligible.[29] Clearly, this force of volunteers presented a different picture than the one painted in the Turkish examples above.

The word Gallipoli, largely unknown to the Australian public before the landings, quickly gained prominence as soon as dispatches from the front reached the local newspapers. An early poem by Henry Lawson, 'The Song of the Dardanelles', was published with the epigraph 'the wireless tells and the cable tells / How our boys behaved by the Dardanelles', which clearly recognised the praise that Australian soldiers had received in the media[30]. Lawson's work also features a much loaded refrain: '[we] knew they would'. The line was a response to those who doubted the courage and discipline of the colonial troops. As admitted by the poet, 'they got into scrapes', but also 'stormed the heights as Australians should.' These 'boys' stand out in his eyes as 'the youngest and the strongest of England's brood'. To make his point, Lawson did not need an adversary. Like many others, he was writing in a land which did not provide him with a past laden with war memories, nor a tradition that could readily evoke a stock enemy figure. The emphasis falls on the warrior who is pictured under a spotlight not reaching far enough to illuminate his opponent. What matters is how rather than against whom he fights.

---

28   A personal account that bears testimony to this phenomenon can be found in Susanna and Jake de Vries, eds., *To Hell and Back: The Banned Account of Gallipoli by Sydney Loch* (Sydney: Harper Collins Publishers, 2008).

29   Bill Gammage, *The Broken Years: Australian Soldiers in the Great War* (Canberra: Australian National University Press, 1974). For a more recent overview of the Australian support for war and a discussion of the motives behind enlistment, see Joan Beaumont, *Broken Nation: Australians in the Great War* (Sydney: Allen & Unwin, 2013), 15–26.

30   The poem first appeared in *The Bulletin* in June 1915. Sources on the early media coverage of the Australians at the front are many; some of the best accounts can be found in K. S. Inglis, 'The Australians at Gallipoli-I', *Historical Studies* 14, no.54 (April 1970): 219–230; Kevin Fewster, 'Ellis Ashmead Bartlett and the Making of the Anzac Legend', *Journal of Australian Studies*, no.10 (June 1982): 17-30; Jenny Macleod, *Reconsidering Gallipoli* (New York: Manchester University Press, 2004), 103-146.

Lawson was not alone in this respect. As elaborated by Peter Pierce in a comprehensive article, the ambiguity surrounding the antonyms of friend and foe in Australian war literature is a phenomenon in itself.[31] The way in which Lawson presented the Australian warrior also pointed to another characteristic of the cultural scene. The brave and rowdy colonial soldier described in his poem was no different than the bushman that he promoted earlier as typically Australian. The outback had long been part of the nationalist imagery along with the itinerant workers who struggled to lead an existence in that inhospitable environment. Lawson had greatly contributed to the acceptance of this figure in the popular mind. This was a practical and resilient man with a particular dislike for discipline and authority who could also demonstrate, at times of hardship, a great sense of camaraderie.[32] As such, he served as an ideal model after which the image of the Australian soldier would be developed.

Another type that emerged from the realities of Australian life was the larrikin, and it was also popularised in the context of Gallipoli. The term resonated until then with a negative connotation, mainly owing to its association with an urban life of crime and violence. But the man that C. J. Dennis presents in his 1916 verse narrative *The Moods of Ginger Mick*, is a kinder version of the stereotype; he is unruly perhaps, but also soft and sentimental.[33] And, at the front, he demonstrates the same courage as well as the nonchalant attitude as the 'boys' above. More importantly, this is the story of an Australian in the making; as Ginger Mick concedes in a characteristic vernacular, 'the reel, ribuck Australia's 'ere, among the fightin' men.'[34] The mateship that bonded them together at the front would also help forge a strong sense of identity. For the protagonist created by Dennis, this is a process which evolves with a particular emphasis on self perception rather than a persistent look across the trenches.

---

31 Peter Pierce, 'Perceptions of the Enemy in Australian War Literature', *Australian Literary Studies* 12, no.2 (October 1985): 166–181.

32 Russel Ward *The Australian Legend*, 2nd ed., (Melbourne, Oxford University Press, 1978), 16-17.

33 C. J. Dennis, *The Moods of Ginger Mick* (London: Angus & Robertson Publishers, 1976, first published in 1916). The work was also well known among the troops. See Amanda Laugesen, 'Australian Soldiers and the World of Print during the Great War' in *Publishing in the First World War*, eds. Mary Hammond and Shafquat Towheed (London: Palgrave, 2007), 93–109 (p.102).

34 Dennis, *The Moods of Ginger Mick*, 62.

The 'Enemy' as part of the myth

The works mentioned above were in line with the Anzac myth, a narrative based on the portrayal of the soldier as the embodiment of courage, resourcefulness, camaraderie along with an insubordinate streak and particular humour. The contribution of the journalist and historian C.E.W. Bean in the development of this myth is well known. One of his early efforts was to publish *The Anzac Book* (1916), a collection of writings and drawings by the actual combatants that bore his heavy stamp as an editor. A poem written by Bean himself is particularly revealing since it focuses on the enemy. Titled 'Abdul', after the nickname warmly attributed to the Turks, it reads as an appreciation for a man who knows 'the way to die'. As he is brought down by an Anzac bullet, the grief at his loss is felt on both sides of the trenches. In Bean's words, war is a 'beastly game' and both parties are equally helpless in it.[35] But as pointed out by David Kent, this seemingly genuine interest in the opponent can also be interpreted as Bean's way of promoting the Australian soldier as a gallant figure. This is not a faultless man perhaps but he certainly is magnanimous, and the respect and compassion that he displays for his opponent is the proof of it.[36] Bean's take stands, therefore, in clear contrast to the convention on the Turkish side to give a similar effect through a language of contempt and antagonism.

Brief instances of encounter with the enemy could also be seen in the prose of this period, a medium which further contributed to the development of the Anzac myth. The dominance of the nationalist theme, the exaggerated and self-congratulatory style in which this was related has already been noted in Robin Gerster's *Big-noting: The Heroic Theme in Australian War Writing*.[37] A volume titled *Trooper Bluegum at the Dardanelles* (1916) is one such example where the swaggering tone of the narrative conflicts sharply with its author's claim to objectivity. Written by a journalist in the form of dispatches from the Gallipoli front, the book illustrates a certain view of the opponent. 'It's the Germans we're up against' says one character, even though he now has to deal with the Turks who learned from them 'all sorts of nasty tricks'.[38] Even the

---

35   C.E.W. Bean, ed., *The Anzac Book* (London: Cassell and Company, Ltd., 1916), 58.

36   David Kent, 'Bean's 'Anzac' and the Making of the Anzac Legend' in *War: Australia's Creative Response*, eds. Anna Rutherford and James Wieland (Sydney: Allen and Unwin, 1997), 27–39 (p.34).

37   Robin Gerster, *Big Noting: The Heroic Theme in Australian War Writing* (Melbourne: Melbourne University Press, 1987).

38   Oliver Hogue, *Trooper Bluegum at the Dardanelles: Descriptive Narratives of the More Desperate Engagements on the Gallipoli Peninsula* (London: Andrew Melrose Ltd,

snipers do not seem to bother Trooper Bluegum who feels nothing but a sense of amusement at the sight of Turks charging with the cries of 'Allah Allah'. Perhaps most revealing in the collective attitude is a final note left for the enemy: 'Abdul', it says, 'you're a good clean fighter and we bear you no ill-will.'[39] A similar tone of respect for the adversary, though not as widely expressed, also resonates in William Baylebridge's collection of stories, *An Anzac Muster* (1921). The work, an illustration of 'big-noting' to the highest degree despite its author's earlier philosophical leanings, is not without a salute to the Turks. As the colonel says in 'The Deathless Dead', his soldiers 'harboured no malice' against him because he is deemed to be 'a foe worthy of them'.[40]

Gallipoli as a tune with many variations

One aspect that distinguishes the Australian representation of Gallipoli from the Turkish case is its inclusion of voices other than patriotic. This is especially apparent in recent literature which has taken a more critical tone. But even the period discussed in this paper, for all its emphasis on the Anzac myth, witnessed a certain regard for the human element. It is also telling that the best examples of this nature were the work of combatants. Leon Gellert's poetry collection *Songs of a Campaign* (1917) conveyed the perspective of a veteran who had survived the mayhem at Gallipoli, but felt no need to mythologise it.[41] His verse strikes a rare lyric tone that says more on the futility of war than heroism. The soldiers that he describes from the unique position of a fellow fighter are no more than victims of the circumstances. And it makes little difference whether or not they are portrayed in any opposition; the war itself is their biggest common enemy. Likewise, the work of Harvey Matthews, another Gallipoli veteran, remains largely aloof to the notions of national glory and loyalty. His poem 'Two Brothers' (1931) relates an encounter with a mostly invisible enemy, a figure again associated with the distinct cries of 'Allah! Allah!'.[42] Central in the narrative are the sensations that engulf the soldiers as they prepare for attack. The Turk features only briefly, as the source of anger and grief for the man

---

[1916]), 73–74.
39   Hogue, *Trooper Bluegum*, 278.
40   William Baylebridge, *An Anzac Muster*, ed. P. R. Stephensen (Sydney: Angus and Robertson, 1962, first published in 1921), 135.
41   Leon Gellert, *Songs of a Campaign* (Sydney: Angus & Robertson, 1917).
42   J. T. Laird, ed., *Other Banners: An Anthology of the Australian Literature of the First World War* (Canberra: The Australian War Memorial and Australian Government Publishing Service, 1971), 24-31.

who loses his brother and succumbs to a frenzy to 'Kill! Kill them all!'. It is clear that the urge manifests itself only momentarily and upon sudden horror, and not as the expression of long brewing hatred.

Some of the best known poetry from non-combatants is characterised by an elegiac tone. L. H. Allen's 'Gallipoli' expresses a 'tribute to those who brought their land to birth', where pride is quickly replaced by the repeated cry 'I weep the dead, they are no more, no more.' Mary Gilmore's little piece by the same title also features a mournful voice conveying, at the same time, a solemn statement against despair: 'Only above the grave of murdered faith / The grass grows never green.' J. Le Gay Brereton's 'Anzac' is a statement by a pacifist who follows 'only the flag of love, unfurled / For peace above a weeping world'. Yet it also reveals great respect for 'those whom other banners led' and mourns their loss.[43]

Clearly, the Australian response to Gallipoli emerged in a cultural environment that nurtured a thematic and stylistic variety despite the predominance of the heroic discourse. This was perhaps a natural outcome in a country where the war in general was subject to public debate. The very fact that dissenting voices, however limited these may be, could be heard in social and political platforms, and that the public had a say in matters such as conscription, painted a sharp contrast to the Turkish scene where the collective war experience was devoid of such dynamics.[44] It would not be wrong to say that in Australia the poets and writers enjoyed greater freedom to break out of the conformity imposed on them by the exigencies of wartime than their Ottoman/Turkish counterparts. But the Australian example also differed from that of New Zealand, the other partner of the Anzac phenomenon with whom it shared similar democratic practices. Despite their common involvement in the conflict, the representation of Gallipoli in New Zealand texts would feature different characteristics.

---

43   These three poems also appear in Laird, *Other Banners*, 47–51.
44   It has been shown that the anti-conscription movement was propelled more as a class issue than a popular disapproval for war. From a Turkish perspective, however, it is important in that it points to the presence of open space for debate regarding the war, its cost and effects on a larger population. An account of the conscription debate can be found in Beaumont, *Broken Nation*, 219-248. Also, however limited, the emergence of groups, such as the Womens's Peace Army, should also be noted as an indication of a society immersed in democratic practices, see Robert Bollard, *In the Shadow of Gallipoli: The Hidden History of Australia in World War I* (Sydney: NewSouth Publishing, 2013), 26-38. An important source that describes the economic, social and political conditions in the Ottoman state during war is Ahmet Emin Yalman, *Turkey in the World War* (New Haven: Yale University Press, 1930).

Gallipoli in New Zealand literature: A belated response

As in Australia, the psychological impact of this first major external war experience was also powerful on this young nation. Its reflection in literature, however, would appear later and with less intensity. This phenomenon contradicts the perception of the Anzacs on the Turkish side, which generally sees little difference between the two countries. During the First World War both Australia and New Zealand belonged to the British Commonwealth, but their colonisation had followed different paths. The first settlers in New Zealand were free men, mostly traders and missionaries, a fact which spared the future generations from the convict legacy that long preoccupied the Australian psyche. More importantly, this was a colony that developed in an environment largely shaped, especially in the early stages, by the nature of the relations with its native people. The Maori were more warlike and entrepreneurial than the Aborigines and their dealings with the 'white man' were initially based on mutual interest and interdependence. This would change as formal colonisation gained speed at the expense of the Maori, leading to violent clashes between the two communities. And this was another aspect of New Zealand that set it apart from the 'warless' Australia.[45] The diminishing numbers and weakening power of the Maori, however, did not keep them from looming large in the consciousness of the very community that had brought their end.

In the nineteenth century, the forerunners of literary nationalism in New Zealand looked to the Maori as a source that could add authentic colour to their writing. The image of the Maori as bygone, noble warriors was carefully incorporated in local literature which often celebrated them as the descendants of a race famed in courage and martial skills.[46] This was hardly a figure, however, that could serve as a template for the representation of the white colonial man fighting in a modern war. A continuity similar to the one

---

45 This passage draws on information from various sources: Michael King, *The Penguin History of New Zealand* (New Zealand: Penguin Books, 2003); Tom Brooking, *The History of New Zealand* (Connecticut: Greenwood Press, 2004) and Claudia Orange, 'The Maori People and the British Crown (1769-1840)' in Keith Sinclair, ed., *The Oxford Illustrated History of New Zealand* (New Zealand: Oxford University Press, 1997), 21-48.

46 The representations of the Maori in this early stage also included tropes such as 'the Maori in need of a father' or 'as a savage ready for enlightenement'. See Lydia Wevers, 'The Short Story' in Terry Sturm, ed., *The Oxford History of New Zealand Literature in English*. 2nd edition. (Auckland: Oxford University Press, 1998), 245-320.

established between the bushman and the soldier at Gallipoli was mostly absent in the New Zealand case. Neither did New Zealand poets have, at their disposal, a popular form as in Australia, such as balladry, that could have readily lent itself for the narration of war stories.[47] An additional factor was related to the limited size of the local readership. The situation had made the New Zealand writers heavily reliant on the tastes of the British audience, which in turn gave them little motivation to write about an imperial defeat with a particular focus on colonial nationalism.[48]

The silence of the literary community in New Zealand was not a manifestation of indifference on the part of the larger public. The First World War had hardly left a family untouched, the belief that Gallipoli had been a baptism of fire was widespread. The Anzac Days were solemn affairs that were underlied by the conviction that the heroes at Gallipoli had not only served the empire, but also established a nationhood.[49] The Anzac legend had taken hold here as well, but, in the absence of a mythmaking force such as C.E.W. Bean, this would develop as a more subdued version. It was aided, nevertheless, by a number of histories that aimed at telling the public of the glorious deeds of their men at war.[50]

War would be treated in New Zealand literature after a lapse of time. It was in the 1930s that a literary interest became evident in the subject, a time which also gave rise to a new orientation in New Zealand literature. As put by the renowned poet Allen Curnow, the country now began 'to look to its own creative resources, not this time to provide it with something national to brag about, but to satisfy a real hunger of the spirit.'[51] It was obvious that war as a nation-maker would not be a dominant theme in this literature. Even a book dedicated to the story of the New Zealanders at war would end with a pacifist note. *The Silent Division* (1935) by Ormond Burton, himself a Gallipoli veteran, was one of the few works that gave considerable attention

---

47   J. O. C. Phillips, 'Musings in Maoriland –or was there a Bulletin School in New Zealand?', *Historical Studies* 20, no.81 (October 1983): 520-35 (p.524).

48   This point was kindly brought to my attention by Jock Phillips in an interview on 2 August 2007 in Wellington, New Zealand.

49   R. Maureen Sharp, 'Anzac Day in New Zealand: 1916-1939', *The New Zealand Journal of History* 15, no.2 (October 1981): 97-114.

50   Ormond Burton's *Our Little Bit: A Brief History of the New Zealand Division* (1918) as well as his history of the Auckland Regiment (1922) can be counted among such works. Another well-known title was *New Zealanders at Gallipoli* by Fred Waite (1919). Both Burton and Waite were Gallipoli veterans.

51   Allen Curnow, ed., *The Penguin Book of New Zealand* (Middlesex, Great Britain: Penguin Books Ltd., 1960), 38.

to the campaign.⁵² In a narrative that bordered on fact and fiction, it aimed to relate 'the adventures and sufferings, the good fun and fellowship, the self-sacrifice and valour of our men as a mass.'⁵³ Published in a period overcast by the clouds of another approaching war in Europe, it also expressed a warning against future involvement in armed conflict.

An important feature of *The Silent Division* lies in the nuanced view of the opponent. The Turk is treated by Burton in the same matter-of-fact tone that he employs to narrate the heroic deeds of his fellow soldiers. What the author sees across the trenches is a fellow human being who accidentally found himself in the opposing camp; an enemy only because the role has somehow been thrust upon him. Admittedly, 'there was anger, and hatred and a bitter longing for revenge' among the New Zealanders who survived the first day of landing. But these sentiments are quickly dismissed by Burton as the outburst of a reaction to the horrors of war rather than the manifestation of a particular animosity.⁵⁴ The man across the trenches is sometimes warmly referred to as Johnny the Turk, even pictured fraternising with the Anzacs. The sniper is also given some degree of attention, but mostly to highlight the ease with which he will be thwarted by his New Zealander counterpart.

The few glimpses afforded to the Turks in Robin Hyde's *Passport to Hell* (1936) are coloured by the wit and humour which characterise the rest of the novel.⁵⁵ It tells the story of Starkie, a man constantly at odds with authority who also demonstrates exceptional skills in fighting. As such, he shares some of the traits associated with the bushman-turned-into-Australian-soldier figure, but his adventures are narrated by a writer who did not display the same *engagé* attitude for nation-making as Lawson. Hyde had heavily invested in the effort to give New Zealand literature a distinct character and she sought to do it by telling stories particular to her land in a voice that could only be her own.⁵⁶ Starkie's portrayal reflects this predisposition; he is the product of the New Zealand society, but his story is conveyed as a personal rather than a communal affair. At Gallipoli, he is mainly pictured as part of a rowdy party that seems to care more about retrieving moneybelts from the

---

52   O. E. Burton, *The Silent Division: New Zealanders at the Front, 1914-1919* (Sydney: Angus and Robertson Limited, 1935).

53   Burton, *The Silent Division*, vii.

54   Burton, *The Silent Division*, 46.

55   Robin Hyde, *Passport to Hell*, ed. D.I.B. Smith (Auckland: Auckland University Press, 1986), first published in 1936). The editor's introduction in this later edition is especially informative on the origins of the story as well as the writing process.

56   Robin Hyde, 'The Singers of Loneliness', *T'ien Hsia Monthly*, 7 (August 1938): 9-23.

bodies of dead soldiers than shooting at the enemy. On the other hand, against the Turkish sniper, 'the aristocrat of No Man's Land', he holds a particular grudge. This 'cold killer', who does not allow the regular soldiers 'their decent modicum of rest', is the spoiler of a war game to which Starkie easily adapts himself.[57] His encounter with the Turks also reveals moments of sympathy for the men across the trenches, especially when he hears them uttering their 'long-drawn-out floating cries of 'Allah Allah".[58] These words are not only chanted during charge, Starkie quickly realises, but they also come out from the mouths of dying men, signifying thus to him human vulnerability rather than belligerence.

A more loaded image of the Turkish opponent can be found in a later work, a play staged in 1982. Maurice Shadbolt's *Once on Chunuk Bair* falls outside of the period taken up in this paper; it calls attention, nevertheless, as a work solely devoted to the theme discussed here.[59] As professed by the playwright, the creation process was prompted by the realisation that 'no significant poem, song, novel, painting – literally nothing in our nation's cultural life enshrined the New Zealand experience of the Gallipoli campaign'.[60] Shadbolt's work is based on a brief episode during the August offensive, the capture of the strategic crest of Chunuk Bair by a predominantly New Zealander force and its loss thereafter. Fittingly named after the famous heights that host today a monument in honour of the fallen, the play foregrounds the notion of Gallipoli as a self-defining experience for a young nation. On the other hand, this does not keep Shadbolt from questioning the New Zealand involvement in the campaign. The Turkish enemy features in this context as a man who dies gloriously for the defence of his own land, and not fighting somebody else's war.

The critical tone becomes more pronounced as the focus turns to British leadership. In Shadbolt's take, the Chunuk offensive fails only because of the inability of the incompetent generals to provide desperately needed help at a crucial time.[61] The central character Colonel Connolly, modeled after the

---

57   Hyde, *Passport to Hell*, 81-82.
58   Hyde, *Passport to Hell*, 83.
59   Maurice Shadbolt, *Once on Chunuk Bair* (Auckland: Hodder and Stoughton, 1982).
60   Maurice Shadbolt, *Voices of Gallipoli* (Auckland: Hodder and Stoughton, 1988), 9. The playwright also explains his motives in Phillip Mann, 'The First Production of *Once on Chunuk Bair*: Extracts from an Interview with Maurice Shadbolt on ANZAC Day, April 25, 1987', *Illusions* no. 11 (July 1989): 14-18.
61   A source that presents the failure at Chunuk Bair as the outcome of poor leadership on the part of the British command is Christopher Pugsley, *Gallipoli: The New Zealand Story* (New Zealand: Sceptre, 1990). A later study, Robin Prior, *Gallipoli: The End of the*

well revered Colonel Malone, remarks tellingly: 'I'd give an arm to have Mustafa Kemal as my commander'. The sense of betrayal by the biggest ally is thus conveyed with much emphasis, and with a respectful salute to the enemy. The *coup de grâce* also comes from the friend rather than the foe as the whole party dies in an accidental salvo by a British ship. Its significance resonates in the words of a dying man: 'the Turks couldn't do us. Only *they* could.'[62]

Conclusion

The questioning approach in Shadbolt's play points to a larger reality on the Anzac side. The significance of the Gallipoli campaign in the histories of Australia and New Zealand is indisputable, nor is the dominance of the Anzac myth that surrounds the perception of the war. Nevertheless, the same myth has also come to signify a whole host of meanings, complexities and contradictions that exist simultaneously.[63] Literary representations of Gallipoli have been one of the threads in this discourse, revealing national pride on the one hand, while acting as a medium for critical attitudes on the other. Works of literature nourished the myth at times, especially in the period discussed in this paper. But Alan Seymour's *The One Day of the Year*, a product of the anti-war era of the 1960s, strikes with its strong criticism of the notion of war as a nation builder. Roger McDonald's poem '1915' expresses pity rather than pride for the boys who 'totter to their knees'. In the New Zealand poet Kevin Ireland's 'Anzac Day, Davenport', on the other hand, Gallipoli is remembered as a vague distant memory, a far cry from the founding myth.[64]

As briefly reiterated in these later examples and noted before with regard to earlier works, literary representation of Gallipoli in Australia mainly, but also in New Zealand, reveals a thematic richness that cannot be observed on

---

Myth (New Haven: Yale University Press, 2009), gives a more nuanced account.

62 Shadbolt, *Once on Chunuk Bair*, 85; 100.

63 Two important sources that relate both the evolution of the myth as well as the complexities involved in it are: Bill Gammage, 'Anzac' in *Intruders in the Bush: The Australian Quest for Identity*, ed. John Carroll (Melbourne: Oxford University Press, 1982), 54-66; Graham Seal, 'ANZAC: The Sacred in the Secular', *Journal of Australian Studies* 31 no. 91 (2007): 135-144.

64 Alan Seymour, *The One Day of the Year* (London: Angus & Robertson Publishers, 1976); Roger McDonald, '1915' in Chris Wallace-Crabbe and Peter Pierce, *Clubbing of the Gunfire: 101 Australian War Poems* (Melbourne: Melbourne University Press, 1984), 89; Kevin Ireland 'Anzac Day, Davenport' in *Anzac Day: Selected Poems* (Christchurch: Hazard Press, 1997), 68-69.

the Turkish side. The thematic and stylistic trend set in the initial Turkish output, which emerged at the height of war propaganda, defined the literary production that would follow thereafter. This can partly be attributed to the Turkish perception that this was an unjust assault on their homeland which was successfully repulsed, the victorious closure thus making pointless any attempt to probe further into the affair. The whole phenomenon stands in sharp contrast to the Anzac experience where a defeat has lent itself to a myriad of interpretations with the apparent effect on literary representation. Artistic creation in Turkey has also developed in the virtual absence of first hand accounts, the kind of narratives that could have provided a unique insight into individual perceptions, or informed the later generations on personal loss and grief. Turkish response has evolved in a rather restricted environment therefore, and its character was largely defined by a national myth that posited not only the hero in the centre but also the foe. This highlights a major difference with the Anzac side where the enemy has almost been invisible. The Turkish emphasis on the opponent is still dominant, as made evident in the wave of popular novels that emerged in the last two decades. One significant phenomenon, on the other hand, is that the indignant and contemptuous tone that usually marks any mention of the enemy subsides when the attention turns to Anzacs. The occasional displays of sympathy for them, however, are rarely conveyed without a pitying look at what is perceived to be the misfortune of fighting somebody else's war. It is our hope that the centenary marks the beginning of an attempt to narrate and represent Gallipoli in Turkey with a closer look at the human dimension, and as a collective experience not only for one community but for many others as well.

Plate A

The Seeds of Friendship Memorial

Raised in Melbourne by the Australian Turkish Community in 2015, the Memorial takes the form of an arching crescent lifting into the sky. Constructed of woven steel, it has a kind of weightlessness about it, a grace and verticality altogether absent in in the Shrine of Remembrance (Victoria's State Memorial), situated immediately opposite. At its centre stand two symbolic seedpods – a cone from one of the pines that grows to this day on the heights of Sari Bair – and the seed of a plant indigenous, indeed unique to Australia, the casuarina. And woven into its base are the words of Anzac and Ottoman alike; extracts from diaries, letters and journals; epitaphs chosen by grieving mothers; Hugo Throssell's eloquent condemnation of war, and the much-cited words attributed to two architects of Gallipoli's abiding mythology, Mustafa Kemal Ataturk and CEW Bean. The closing paper at the conference explored the two memorials as an instance of 'dialogical memorialisation'. It also alerted historians to the strength as well as the dangers of reconciliation narratives: the beauty and elegance of the memorial at odds with the cruel reality of war.

Photograph courtesy of Bruce Scates.

Plate 4.1

From *Anzac Cove and Gallipoli: then and now – interactive*.
Courtesy of Mike Bowers for *The Guardian*.
Australian War Memorial P10140.004.

Plate 4.2

Exhibition Giant, *Gallipoli: The Scale of Our War*, Private Colin Airlie Warden (1890–1915),
Auckland Infantry Battalion.
Photograph by Michael Hall.
Courtesy of the Museum of New Zealand Te Papa Tongarewa.

Plate 8.1

George Lambert, *Anzac, the landing 1915*, painted 1920-22 oil on canvas, 199.8 x 370.2 cm. Australian War Memorial ART02873.

Plate 8.2

Hubert Wilkins, *Looking from the crest of Plugge's Plateau which was first reached on the morning of the landing across the Razorback to the Sphinx*, c.17 February 1919 glass whole plate negative.
Australian War Memorial G01872.

Wilkins took this photograph as Hedley Howe led the group over the Gallipoli site. George Lambert later used it as reference material as he painted his large canvas of the landing.

Plate 9.1

Ellis Silas, *Roll Call*, oil on canvas. 1920 101.8 cm x 153.1 cm; framed: 131.8 cm x 183.5 cm x 13 cm.
Australian War Memorial ART02436.

Plate 9.2

Sidney Nolan, *Gallipoli Landscape* c.1961 textile dye, wax on coated paper 25.4 x 30.4 cm.
Australian War Memorial ART91235.

Plate 9.3

Sidney Nolan, *Gallipoli Landscape*, c.1960 textile dye, wax on coated paper 30.4 x 25.4 cm.
Australian War Memorial ART91291.

Plate 9.4

Sidney Nolan, *Drowned soldier at Anzac as Icarus* 18 November 1958 textile dye, sgraffito, coloured crayon on coated paper 25.4 x 30.4 cm.
Australian War Memorial ART91309.

Plate 10.1

Volunteers take a break during their four month task installing 888,246 ceramic poppies in the Tower of London's moat. Courtesy of Kevin Fewster.

Plate 10.2

Crowds throng to see the near completed installation. Courtesy of Kevin Fewster.

Plate 10.3

Students from the Royal Hospital School carry the school's 1914-18 Honour Boards into the Queens House, Greenwich, 11 November 2014.
Photography courtesy of Greenwich Hospital.

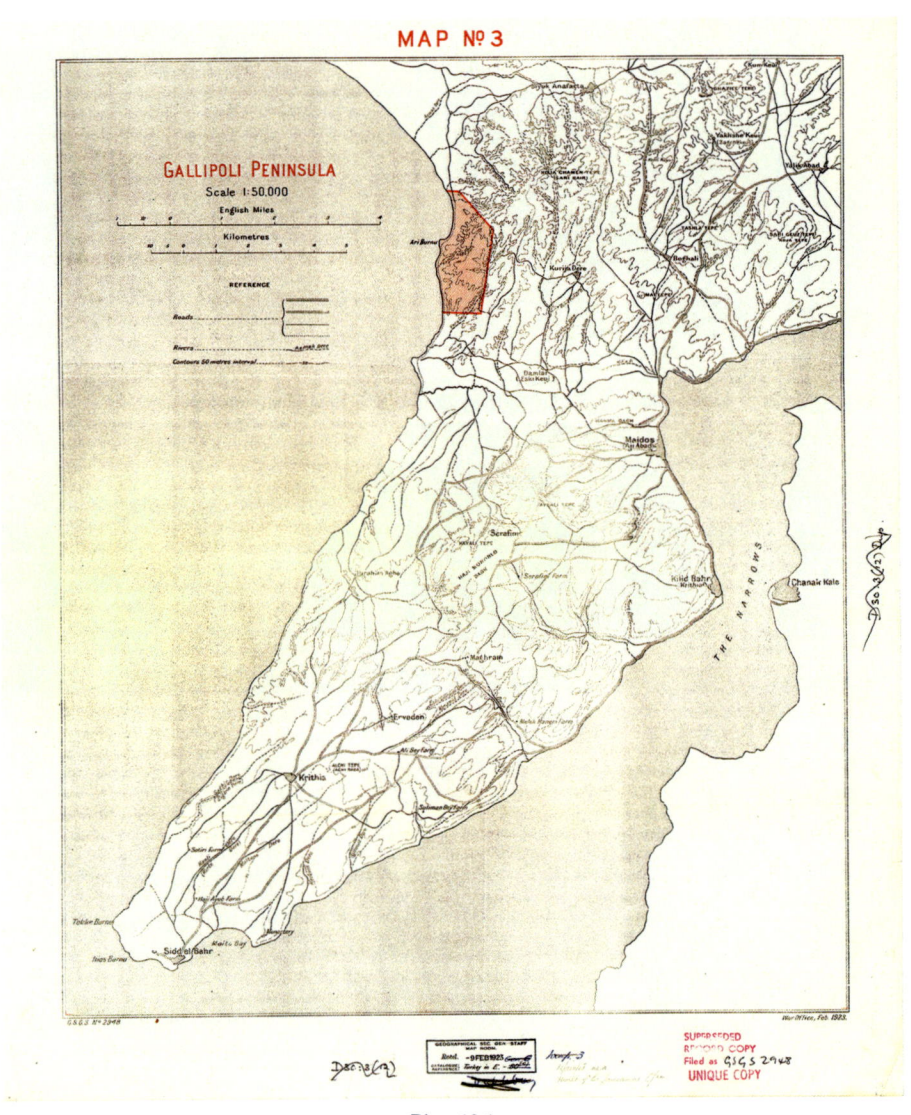

Plate 13.1

Map 3 from the Treaty of Lausanne, showing the 'Anzac Area' to be reserved.
Courtesy of the National Archives, London, WO 301/653/001.

Plate 13.2

Turkish map of Arıburnu/Anzac Area, 1:5000 scale, annotated with an English translation of Ottoman placenames. Courtesy of the Australian War Memorial Collections, ID number RC03163.

Plate 13.3

The boundaries and key placenames within the JHAS survey area. Courtesy of Jessie Birkett-Rees.

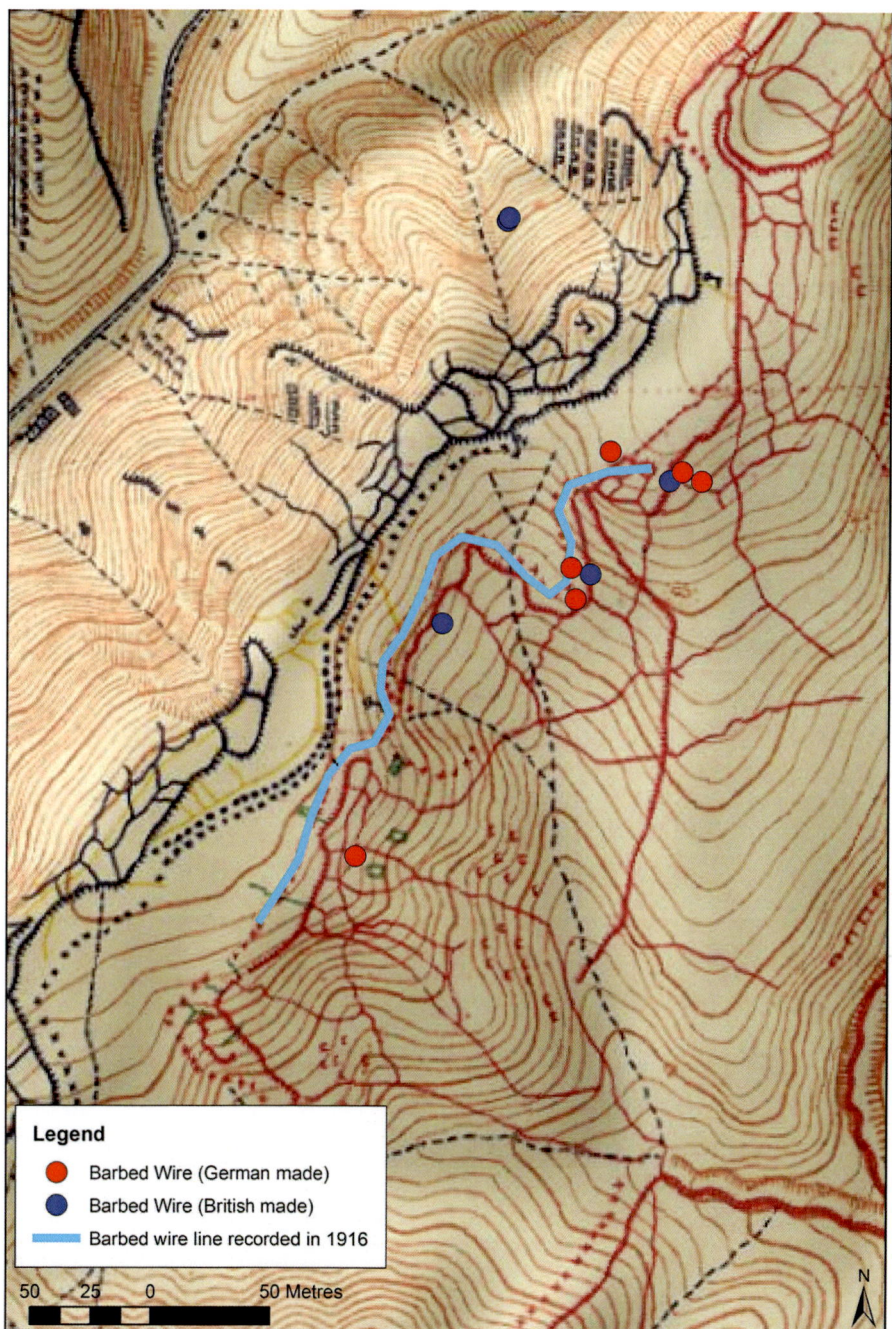

Plate 13.4

Map depicting the positions of barbed wire recorded by the JHAS in 2010-14 overlayed on a georeferenced copy of the Turkish 1:5000 scale map produced under the direction of Brigadier General Mehmet Şevki Pasha in 1916. Courtesy of Jessie Birkett-Rees.

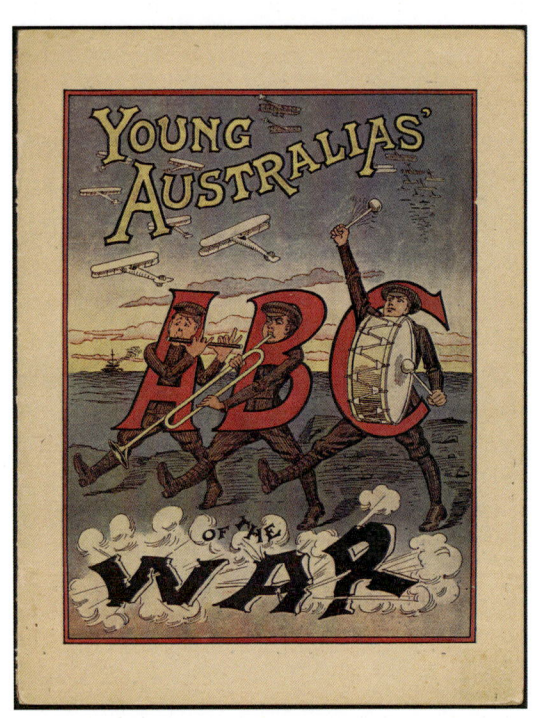

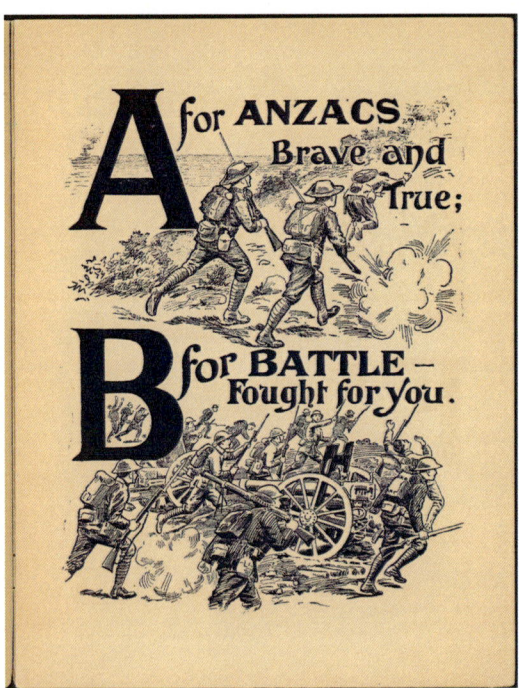

Plate 15.1

Images from *Young Australias'* [sic] *ABC of War* ([Australia], Gordon and Gotch, n.d. [c. 1918]). Courtesy of National Library of Australia.

Part 4

Art, Museums and Artefacts

Chapter 8

'A FINE IDEAL AND AN IMPERISHABLE MEMORY'

George Lambert's Painting *ANZAC, the Landing 1915*

Janda Gooding

In the years immediately after the First World War, Australian families cherished in private ways 'memory objects' that reminded them of relatives that died in the war. Photographs, diaries, letters and keepsakes sent from the front lines, commemorative scrapbooks and personal possessions packaged up and sent to the next of kin after a death, became physical reminders of loss.[1] Objects and images provided real and tangible connections that helped people commemorate a loved one and potentially situate the personal cost of war within the broader context of national endeavour. In the public sphere, memorials, commemorative boards and cemeteries brought together symbolic meaning with the powerful and simplified messages of nationhood and sacrifice. These public forms of expression served to honour the individual dead, as well as justify the war and the nation's loss.

Many scholars have written of the First World War and the memorialisation of people, places and events in public monuments, battlefield sites and cemeteries.[2] Jay Winter, in describing community memorials, has noted that 'communal commemorative art provided, first and foremost a framework

---

1 See Bruce Scates, *Return to Gallipoli: Walking the Battlefields of the Great War* (Cambridge: Cambridge University Press, 2004), 15-26.
2 See Jay Winter, *Sites of Memory, Sites of Mourning: The Great War in European Cultural History* (Cambridge: Cambridge University Press, 1995); Ken Inglis, *Sacred Places: War Memorials in the Australian Landscape* (Melbourne: Melbourne University Press, 1998); Tanja Luckins, *The Gates of Memory: Australian People's Experience and Memories of Loss and the Great War* (Fremantle: Curtin University Books, 2004).

for and legitimation of individual and family grief'.³ But while stone and concrete memorials served a specific purpose of reconciling an individual death in the greater context, the capacity of most memorials to deliver visual information was limited.

Mourners in Australia sought out photographs of battle sites and grave markers as a way to locate their personal loss within a specific landscape. However, photography at the time of the First World War was primarily documentary and most people still expected a photograph to be a reliable and trustworthy image of a particular place at a particular time. Photographs gave many viewers an insight into the grim reality of war, but for some this was just too overwhelming – there was nothing left to the imagination. Attempts by Frank Hurley and other photographers to combine multiple negatives to construct a more representative image were considered artistic interpretations and criticised by some as 'faked' or 'misleading' depictions of war.⁴

On the other hand, early twentieth century audiences were very familiar with traditional narrative paintings that were both emotive and instructional representations of an event. Painters combined a unique set of storytelling and technical skills. When representing historical events, artists could select and then blend individual elements from the remembered past into single and coherent narratives. And, they could draw together multiple memories and overlapping events from the real world to represent drama, action and emotion in a convenient two-dimensional format.

By situating war stories in a specific setting, artists helped viewers to visualise and imagine the actual physical landscape in which an event or a death may have occurred. People who were grieving could see a context for their loss while returning veterans found that paintings were sometimes a less-confronting vehicle to stimulate memories or a starting point from which to retell their testimony to others. As Australian service men and women who died overseas were buried in cemeteries mostly across the northern hemisphere, few Australians were capable of making the costly pilgrimage to the cemeteries and battlefield sites.⁵ An artistic interpretation could therefore provide an imaginative and emotional substitute for many Australians.

---

3   Jay Winter, *Sites of Memory*, 93.
4   An account of the dispute between Frank Hurley and Charles Bean over composite photographs can be found in Shaune Lakin, *Contact: Photographs from the Australian War Memorial Collection* (Canberra: Australian War Memorial, 2006).
5   Bruce Scates, *Return to Gallipoli*, 27.

Some commemorative paintings so ably captured the essential core of a story that they moved beyond just representing a specific battle scene. They became a repository of a community's shared memory. The subject of this chapter is one such painting that came to exemplify the national narratives round Anzac that strengthened in the post war years in Australia.

This painting, *Anzac, the Landing 1915*, by George Lambert, has remained fixed in people's minds across successive generations as an iconic representation of the Australian landing at Gallipoli. It was a central feature in the first galleries created by the fledgling Australian war museum in 1922 and is still a fixture in the newest displays opened by its successor, the Australian War Memorial in late 2014 to mark the centenary of Anzac. My interest is in how a painting's meaning and relevance might transfer through multiple generations of visitors. And, potentially remain relevant despite the fluctuations of public and political interest in the Gallipoli story, a story that has been constantly challenged and reshaped by politicians, historians, media and the public over the last one hundred years.

I have written elsewhere of the detailed circumstances around the creation of this painting and the context of the Australian Historical Mission to Gallipoli in 1919.[6] As stated by Charles Bean, the main aim of the party was to solve the many riddles of Anzac including the exact details of the Australian landing, how far Australian troops had reached that first day, and what the Turks could see from their positions.[7] To do this, the party would walk the ground, make detailed inspections of positions and collect battlefield objects that would reveal where Australians had fought as well as help future museum visitors understand the personal cost of war.

In selecting men for the Historical Mission, Bean chose those who had served at Gallipoli and could explain events that he had not witnessed or others he had worked with during the war. The official photographer for the group was Hubert Wilkins, who had worked alongside Bean on the Western Front and the official Australian artist, George Lambert, had previously fulfilled a commission for Bean when he travelled in early 1918 to Palestine to record activities of the Australian Light Horse units.

---

6   Janda Gooding, *Gallipoli Revisited: In the Footsteps of Charles Bean and the Australian Historical Mission* (Melbourne and Canberra: Hardie Grant and the Australian War Memorial, 2009). Charles Bean also published in 1948 a very detailed and highly readable account of his return to Gallipoli in C.E.W. Bean, *Gallipoli Mission* (Canberra: Australian War Memorial, 1948).

7   C.E.W. Bean, *Gallipoli Mission*, 5-9.

Wilkins's and Lambert's roles as visual artists were pivotal in Bean's conception of the future historical displays of the war museum.[8] Art and photography were integral components of a much larger collection that would reveal Australian service men and women 'each with his or her own character, feelings, problems and interests'.[9] As Bean stated, it was important to represent Australians who served in the war as individuals, not just 'ciphers in the huge total'.[10] This was one of the reasons that he advocated combining personal testimony with art, photography, documents, and objects to make an emotional and unique experience for visitors to the Australian War Memorial.

Lambert was well known before the war, for his portrait paintings of society men and women but he considered that his best contribution to the war was to record the efforts and achievements of the Australian soldiers. His eagerness was not completely altruistic as he haggled relentlessly for a larger commission fee. However, there is enough evidence to indicate that he genuinely admired the Australian fighting men and wished to contribute his skills and time. In late 1918, Charles Bean on behalf of the Australian government offered George Lambert a commission to visit Gallipoli to prepare for two large paintings – one on the 3rd Light Horse Brigade charge at the Nek on 7 August 1915 and the other painting to show the Australian landing of 25 April.

Lambert knew that the Gallipoli paintings were destined to be centrepieces of the national war museum and it appealed to his vanity as well as his pocket that he was asked to paint them. The subject of the Australians landing at Gallipoli presented him with a great personal opportunity to expand his interest in nationhood and narrative. It was also what many people at the time would agree was the most important commission for the future war museum.

The experience of walking the ground with Charles Bean and Gallipoli veterans gave Lambert insights into individual experiences and the emotional drama of the event that would eventually be incorporated into his painting. For the main narrative framework of the painting though, he was reliant

---

8   The history of the Australian War Memorial and its collections can be found in Nola Anderson, *Australian War Memorial: Treasures From a Century of Collecting* (Sydney: Murdoch Books, 2012).

9   C.E.W. Bean, 'The Beginnings of the Australian War Memorial' [n.d. but later in his life], C.E.W. Bean Papers, AWM38: 3DRL 6673/619, 18, Australian War Memorial, Canberra.

10 C.E.W. Bean, 'The Beginnings of the Australian War Memorial', 18.

on the account of his companion, Hedley Howe of the 11th Battalion (3rd Brigade).

On the Historical Mission's first day of fieldwork, Howe led them over the course that he had taken nearly 4 years before when he had been in one of the first Australian boats to reach the shore. He talked to the group about his anxiety as they were towed and then how the shingle grated as they pulled into the shore. His platoon ran across the beach, threw off their packs at a bank where vegetation started just as the sky was growing light. Howe could see Ari Burnu leading up to a bigger and steeper hill: 'Obviously the active enemy in this sector was on top of the higher plateau, though no Turk could be seen; and the men from the boat therefore began immediately to climb one of the scrubby ridges or ribs which led steeply, like a buttress, direct to the higher summit'.[11] Significantly Howe described the moment when they had come across two Turkish soldiers, 'one dead, the other with his brain exposed, but apparently conscious, reaching for his water-bottle. An Australian put it in his hand'.[12] Pausing for a moment in Rest Gully his group noticed 'the first enemy shell most of them had seen burst in a fleecy white puff and scatter its shrapnel upon the gravel of the Razor Edge'.[13]

Lambert utilised much of Howe's personal account but also added other elements that gave poignancy and potency to the image. For example, the young lad in the centre – beautiful but dead – is suggestive of John Masefield's description of ANZAC troops as the 'finest body of young men brought together in modern times'; marked by their 'physical beauty and nobility of bearing'.[14]

George Lambert's painting of the landing was first revealed to the public on ANZAC Day 1922, when the new displays of the Australian War Museum in Melbourne opened to the public. If you had known a man or woman in the war, or had yourself served, this was the first chance to see the items collected from the battlefield, read the letters and messages from the frontline, and see in photographs and artworks, the events of the war. In fact, for many it would be the opportunity to see all constituent elements brought together to represent in its totality, Australia's part in the war.

Not surprisingly, *Anzac, the Landing 1915* dominated the Gallipoli Court. From a distance, viewers would have registered how big it is and the strong

---

11 Hedley Howe's account can be found in C.E.W. Bean, *Gallipoli Mission*, 75-80.
12 C.E.W. Bean, *Gallipoli Mission*, 78.
13 C.E.W. Bean, *Gallipoli Mission*, 79.
14 John Masefield, *Gallipoli* (Toronto: S.B. Gundy, 1916), 19.

diagonal composition that rises out of the left corner to the upper right. Overall, the lower half of the painting seems to be an undifferentiated mass of muddy reds, browns and sagey greens while the upper portion appears to be a washed out dawn sky with a couple of small dirty cloud puffs. As visitors come closer, the confused foreground starts to resolve into men and earth, bushes and rocks. Stand in front of it and the individual details emerge, each conveying part of a larger narrative that was undoubtedly already familiar from press reports and personal accounts: the boats on the beach; a man scrambling up the steep slope trying to get a handhold and using his rifle butt for more purchase; the young lad lying dead as others rush past him; here a Turkish soldier grasping his water bottle while two Australians glance back before going on.

Onwards and upwards you scan the picture as you follow the path of the men: on the skyline there is a scurry of small figures running across open ground. Your eye follows the jagged outline of the cliff face across to the other side of the gorge and that small cloud now appears likely to be an artillery explosion. The upper half of the painting is almost devoid of human figures, dominated only by the ragged and precipitous edges of cliffs. As you follow the line of these downwards, you are taken back to the beach where men are landing on the narrow shore. Clearly much of this painting's narrative is based on Hedley Howe's personal account. But the artist has also managed to create the impression of an endlessly repeating film loop, as more men land, climb the slopes and run into the distance at the top right.

The 1922 guidebook to the Museum displays highlighted that the painting was surrounded in the Gallipoli Court by 'some of the sacred mementoes of this first, most tragic, and in some ways, most glorious, of the Australian campaigns'.[15] A brief statement – probably written by Charles Bean – gave further context:

> The picture of the Landing, which dominates the court, was painted by G.W. Lambert, the noted Australian artist, who went minutely over the ground four years later with some of those who were present when the heights were stormed. It shows the 3rd Brigade making the first rush up the steep slope to Plugge's Plateau in the dim light of dawn, in the teeth of heavy fire from an almost invisible enemy. Unlike many traditional battle pictures, this painting is an almost exact representation of the

---

15   *Australian War Museum: The Relics and Records of Australia's Effort in the Defence of the Empire, 1914-1918* (Melbourne: Australian War Museum, 1922), 11.

actual scene on that fateful April morning, when the Glory of Anzac was revealed.[16]

The guidebook refers to *Anzac, the Landing 1915* as a traditional battle painting, or a history painting as it might be termed. Before we move on, I want to outline some of the essential characteristics of history paintings. Importantly, in this category – size does matter. Most are very large – this one is nearly four metres wide. After all, a painting of this monumental size proclaims itself as an 'important' picture and therefore the event it depicts must be important.

History paintings are determined by their subject matter, not the style of painting. They are didactic in nature and usually show heroic events from the past, weaving 'together the heroism of individuals with universal moral messages embodied by those individuals at particular moments'.[17] Ultimately, they demonstrate the value and continuity of traditions that connect the past to the present.

When Lambert was developing the painting from 1920 to 1922, he portrayed the morning's events but imbued the scene with the heroic themes that had become embedded in the Anzac legend from the first reports of the landing published in Australia by the war correspondents in May 1915. Ashmead Bartlett had described the landing as 'There has been no finer feat in this war than this sudden landing in the dark and the storming of the heights'.[18] Bean placed a similar emphasis on the Australian achievement in landing in such a place: 'the feat which will go down in history is that Sunday's fighting when three Australian Brigades stormed, in face of a heavy fire, tier after tier of cliffs and mountains …'.[19]

Lambert made this a focus in his painting; in particular, the struggle of the Australian men as they battle through the landscape towards their objective. The enemy are virtually invisible – the wounded Turkish soldier with the water bottle in the lower right corner is the only representation of the Turkish troops. Otherwise, the picture reinforces the already established theme of the Australian soldier battling against the steep and inhospitable terrain, a theme that conveniently linked the recent narrative of Anzac to

---

16   *Australian War Museum: The Relics and Records*, 14.
17   Steven Conn, 'Narrative Trauma and Civil War History Painting, Or Why are these Pictures so Terrible?' *History and Theory* Theme Issue 41, December 2002, 23.
18   Ellis Ashmead Bartlett, 'Mr. Ashmead Bartlett's Story', *Sydney Morning Herald* 8 May 1915, 13.
19   Charles Bean, *Commonwealth of Australia Gazette* 39, 17 May 1915, 932.

the past Australian bushman and pioneer narratives. As Robin Prior has pointed out, however, it is not just the difficulties presented by the landscape but the fact that 'the setting allows the warrior-like qualities of the soldier to be exhibited. Hence we can have the resourceful soldier making sense of a landing that went awry, the fit, bronzed soldier scaling cliffs with ease and beating back the enemy'.[20] Indeed, as the British commander, General Sir Ian Hamilton later described the events at Gallipoli; it is the conquest 'by our soldiers and sailors over every man's enemy – "The Impossible!"'[21]

Apart from highlighting heroic effort, the central story of Lambert's history painting had to be well known and easily recognised by viewers. Lambert's job was to convert a tale understood mainly through written accounts into something that could be seen and experienced. He used the full array of artists' skills to make it the most affective image he could.

At first glance, the landscape background of this painting seems a familiar rendering of the Anzac Cove area. It is in fact a totally fabricated landscape. Lambert pushed and pulled the physical terrain to show both the beach and the upper heights together. The broad canvas covers an arc of about 240 degrees. This is much more than the human eye can see in one glance, but this distortion was necessary to convey the entire story as it unfolded over space and time. The apparent specificity of the landscape, the cycle of men landing, climbing and disappearing across the crest, collapse all this into one scene that gives the impression of representing only a moment. No camera on the day of the landing could ever have captured the entire sweep of the landscape and the sequence of events.

An often-underestimated contradiction in history paintings is the balance an artist needs to achieve between accuracy and interpretation. We have already seen that Lambert deliberately constructed a false landscape and brought together elements of an event stretched across a few hours. This license helped him create the imaginative field on which all the elements could be enacted. But, he was aware that errors of detail could undermine the viewers' confidence and he needed to demonstrate that he was reliable and had done the necessary research. To help, Lambert made a few detailed 'on the spot' sketches of individual components of the landscape such as the arbutus shrub and the distinctive landscape feature of the Sphinx. Interestingly, he

---

20 Robin Prior, 'The Heroic Image of the Warrior in the First World War', *War & Society* 23, special number, September 2005, 49.

21 General Sir Ian Hamilton, 'One More Drop of Blood!', *John Bull* 30 Jan 1932 quoted in Jenny Macleod, *Reconsidering Gallipoli* (Manchester and New York: Manchester University Press, 2004), 13.

did not during his field trip to Gallipoli complete a comprehensive visual record of the 'field of action' that would later appear in the large painting.

On some things, he chose to discard strict accuracy. He was subsequently criticised for elements that viewers thought were incorrect, notably whether Australians in the first landing group wore caps or slouch hats. Lambert sought advice from Bean who said both caps and hats had been worn. Lambert then proceeded to paint nearly all the men with slouch hats as he said it gave the painting a uniquely 'Australian' character. But it is clear that desire for historical accuracy only went so far. More importantly, Lambert wanted to give viewers an 'authentic' and moving experience. To capture people's imagination, all good stories must be told with drama and enthusiasm so the balance for Lambert was to make sure he got most of the details right but also conveyed atmosphere and excitement to his audience.

Most of Lambert's artistic licence went unnoticed and it is clear that the painting hit the mark in 1922. It represented Australian men as many viewers wanted them to be remembered – determined, heroic and conquering apparently overwhelming odds. It was seen by over 14,000 visitors in Melbourne during the first week of the museum and 770,000 by the time the displays closed in early 1924. A report in May 1922 noted that the displays were mostly viewed by 'returned soldiers accompanied by friends and relatives'.[22] Attendants and staff of the Museum were also returned soldiers and undoubtedly took a further role in interpreting and embellishing museum displays for the visitors.

Lambert's painting of the landing was described as instructive and illustrative – even an object lesson of a 'fine ideal and an imperishable memory' that would encourage young people to 'maintain those same traditions in peace, and carry them on, if need be, in war'.[23] People were also reminded in advertising that it was 'a truthful portrayal of this brilliant achievement'[24] while one art critic described it as a 'declaration of sacrifice and achievement in a way that no other war picture has done.'[25] *Anzac, the Landing 1915*, had helped some people make sense of their lives, to place their own experience in the much larger whole or as Samuel Hynes has described

---

22   *The Herald* (Melbourne), 8 May 1922.
23   *Sun News Pictorial* (Melbourne), 25 April 1924, 1.
24   Advertisement for reproductions of the painting in *Descriptive Catalogue: Official War Photographs* (Melbourne: The Australian War Museum, c.1922), 30.
25   A. Colquhoun, 'Battles in Oils. Artists Depict the Spirit of Anzac. Fine Show at War Museum', *Herald* (Melbourne), 4 May 1922.

it, make 'sense of the muddle of images that most men bring back from their wars.'[26]

As historians such as Joan Beaumont and many others have demonstrated, by the end of the war, the Gallipoli campaign – despite its failure – was well on its way to becoming 'the signifier of national identity and discourse within which all later experiences of war would be positioned.'[27] It was cemented into Australian history as a 'passage of arms'.[28] And, as Prime Minister Billy Hughes asserted in 1918 it was 'the day the Australian nation was born. Before that we were New South Welshmen, Queenslanders, Victorians, – but on that day we became Australians'.[29] In simplifying, dramatising and sanitising the events of the Australian landing in an uncritical way, Lambert's painting represented the essential heroic and romantic story of Anzac that was firmly established in the immediate post war years.

It would be natural to expect that this painting would reduce in prominence as Australian audiences became more absorbed in other world events and distanced from the details of 1915. However, this was not the case. As Caroline Winter has observed 'once a memory has been selected and articulated it will be slowly forgotten unless the information is regularly rehearsed or recalled'.[30] And *Anzac, the Landing 1915*, as a central object in the growing institution of the Australian War Memorial, was in the perfect place for continued renewal. Enshrined in Anzac day ceremonies, visited by hundreds of thousands of visitors each year and repeatedly published and cited as an 'authentic' visual record of the landing, the painting remained a central visual reference to the Gallipoli story as it morphed to suit changing times.

This brings me to my final point, the possible relationship between this painting and the formation of cultural memory, also variously termed collective or social memory. Cultural memory can be simply described as an iterative process by which a society selects what to remember based on its framework of values, beliefs and behaviours. It is important to note, that

---

26   Samuel Hynes, 'Personal Narratives and Commemoration', in *War and Remembrance in the Twentieth Century,* eds. Jay Winter and Emmanuel Sivan (Cambridge: Cambridge University Press, 1999), 207.

27   Joan Beaumont, *Unbroken Nation: Australians in the Great War* (New South Wales: Allen & Unwin, 2013), 52.

28   John Masefield, *Gallipoli*, 55.

29   Billy Hughes to troops in France, 2 July 1918, noted in Charles Bean diary no 116, C.E.W. Bean Papers, AWM 38/606/116/2, Australian War Memorial, Canberra.

30   Caroline Winter, 'Tourism, Social Memory and the Great War', *Annals of Tourism Research*, 36, no. 4, 2009, 615.

in the process of remembering, other things must either be forgotten or pushed into the background. This process of selection enables the chosen memory to become dominant while others, that perhaps provide counter narratives, gradually fade.[31] Remembering is only one part of the formation of a cultural memory, it then has to be maintained and transferred through generations, and that process is dependent on the particular group's attitudes to history, the past and remembering.[32] Not surprisingly, each society will use slightly different vehicles to carry and transmit a dominant memory. In general though, cultural memory is often stored away in places and in things that are tangible reminders – monuments, museums, libraries and archives are prime examples. Symbolic forms like written texts or in this case, a painting, are relatively stable 'carriers' of memory and their messages are easily transmitted from one generation to the next.

By 1922 when George Lambert completed his massive painting of the Australians landing at Gallipoli, he was visualising the core elements of the Anzac story that Australians had already chosen to remember – the heroic and romantic story of Australians fighting an unseen enemy, overcoming the impossible to make an amphibious landing on hostile shores. Despite the failure of the campaign, the artist visualised a 'victory' over the impossible that served to blur the boundary between 'myth and history'.[33]

By using the lenses of history painting and cultural memory, I have tried to demonstrate that an important cultural object such as George Lambert's painting *Anzac, the Landing 1915*, is not necessarily passive. It may illustrate an historical event or reflect the artist's individual interpretation of it, but it also is formed within a cultural context. It is shaped by the interaction of the artist with their immediate environment, by influential associates such as Charles Bean who we know had a strong hand in the creation of the Anzac myth, and the general themes being discussed in the society in which the artist works. Lambert's strong admiration for the Australian soldier is also very evident in this picture.

But by synthesising multiple memories and events, and articulating the essential core of the Anzac story, this history painting has also become an

---

31   Jan Assmann, *Religion and Cultural Memory*, trans Rodney Livingstone (California: Stanford University Press, 2006, first published in German, 2000), 3.

32   Jan Assmann and John Czaplicka, 'Collective Memory and Cultural Identity', *New German Critique*, 65, Spring-Summer 1995, 133.

33   Jan Assmann, 'Communicative and Cultural Memory', in *Cultural Memory Studies: An International and Interdisciplinary Handbook* eds. Astrid Erll and Ansgar Nünning (Berlin and New York, 2008), 113.

active agent in promulgating one of Australia's most dominant and enduring memories – that of the Gallipoli campaign. Its centrality to the Anzac story is demonstrated by its continued display in multiple iterations of the 'Gallipoli Court' of the Australian War Memorial stretching from the first in 1922 to the most recent in 2015. Through its longevity in the public arena George Lambert's *Anzac, the Landing 1915* also contributes to and reinforces a popularly held belief that the Australian nation and national identity were forged in a battle on the shores of a foreign sovereign country. This painting can tell us much about the formation of the Anzac myth and its perpetuation in cultural objects and in so doing, perhaps offer insights into the broader question about the centrality and longevity of that myth in Australia.

Chapter 9

'FILLING THE VOID'

Artistic Interpretations of the Empty Battlefield

Paul Gough

This chapter has three parts: the first offers a critique of the idea of 'emptiness' and its application to the apparently deserted battlescapes of the First World War. The second part explores how this concept of emptiness was understood and applied by artists who witnessed the action, or the aftermath, of campaigns in Gallipoli, France and Belgium. To do so it focuses on the war diaries, sketches and post-battle paintings by Australian artist and Australian Imperial Force (AIF) signaller Ellis Silas, and also recounts the challenges faced by official war photographer Frank Hurley during the Third Battle of Ypres in 1917. Part Three reflects on more recent work by the Australian painter Sidney Nolan who for two decades later in the twentieth century was deeply engaged with the powerful memoryscapes of Turkey.

Part one: Filling the void

None but those who have endeavoured can realise the insurmountable difficulties of portraying a modern battle by camera. To include the event on a single negative, I have tried and tried, but the results are hopeless. Everything is on such a vast scale. Figures are scattered — the atmosphere is dense with haze and smoke — shells will not burst where required — yet the whole elements are there could they but be brought together and condensed. The battle is in full swing, the men are just going over the top — and I snap! A fleet of bombing planes is flying low, and a barrage burst all around. On developing my plate there is disappointment! All I find is a record of a few figures advancing from the trenches — and a background of haze.[1]

These are the words of the incorrigible Australian photographer Frank Hurley describing the challenges of both equipment and opportunity as one of two official war photographers with the Australian Imperial Force's Australian War Records Section, established in June 1917. Hurley became deeply frustrated by the practical difficulties of taking meaningful photographs on the battlefield and by the diffuse character of the war on the Western Front. The massive scale of the fighting around the trench lines, the noise, dust, cacophony of action, and the barren emptiness of so much of the battlefield did not lend themselves to the busy, action-filled iconography that he felt befitted the incredible efforts and heroism of his countrymen.[2]

Later we explore some of the creative ploys he used to meet his vision of this war. First, however, we examine the spatial, aural and sensorial nature of the conditions faced by many front-line combatants in Turkey, France and Belgium at that time in an attempt to understand the many challenges facing the artists and photographers whose objective was to record, and interpret, the face of total modern warfare.

Hurley, like many who tried to make a record of the First World War battlefield, realised his photographs fell short of capturing the immense emptiness of the modern battlescape. Even when risking the dangerous vantage of a trench parapet, photographs could not visualise emptiness; they could only allude to absences. Words also failed to convey the null and void, the intensity of emptiness:

> It seemed quite unthinkable that there was another trench over there a few yards away just like our own ... Not even the shells made that brooding watchfulness more easy to grasp; they only made it more grotesque. For everything was so paralysed in calm, so unnaturally innocent and bland and balmy. You simply could not take it in.[3]

1　See Robert Dixon, *Photography, early cinema and colonial modernity: Frank Hurley's synchronized lecture entertainments* (London: Anthem Press, 2011).

2　Alasdair McGregor, *Frank Hurley: a photographer's life*. (Camberwell, Victoria: Viking Books, 2004).

3　Reginald Farrer, *The void of war: letters from three fronts*. (London: Constable, 1918), 113.

In Europe the Great War (the First World War) continued a process of emptying the battlefield that had begun with the introduction of smokeless powder and the invention of the machine rifle which allowed infantry to fire from well-concealed and distant positions.[4] Improved detection and registration devices, refinements in the use of camouflage, and the weight of firepower that could be bought to bear on a fixed front, meant that for long stretches of time the battlefield of the First World War was deserted during daylight hours. Nonetheless, however empty, it was always being scrutinised. A complete photographic record of the entire Western Front was shot twice each day by the Royal Air Force (RAF) as a mechanical eye systematically gridded once, and then re-gridded, what many considered to be unmappable spaces. Becca Weir has called this 'the paradox of measurable nothingness'[5] in which the blasted topography had to be located, fixed, calibrated and then named:

> I learnt the names of every wood and all the villages (wrote one soldier) I knew the contour of the hills and the shapes of the lakes in the valley. To see so much and to see nothing. We might have been the only men alive, my two signallers and I. And yet I knew there were thousands of hidden men in front of me ... but no one moved, everyone was waiting for the safety of darkness.[6]

In Turkey, the compressed scale of the Gallipoli battlefield meant that even the most insignificant topographical feature would be named, recorded and scrutinised incessantly. On the inhospitable slopes above the beaches of the Dardanelles, small gullies, mounds, and isolated trees were soon given appellations that were widely adopted; places associated with particular individuals were named and promptly became part of the localised cartography. Naming, gridding, and cartographic logic tried to get a fix on the seemingly empty spaces that characterised the battleground.

While the battlescape may have appeared deserted, the dead lay just beneath its ruptured surface and the living led an ordered and disciplined (although often very perilous) existence in underground shelters and deep

---

4   James J Schneider, 'The theory of the empty battlefield'. RUSI Journal, 132:3 (1987), 37-44.

5   Becca Weir, "Degrees in nothingness': battlefield topography in the First World War'. *Critical Quarterly*, 49:4, (2007), 40-55.

6   Richard Talbot Kelly, *A subaltern's odyssey: a memoir of the Great War*, 1915-1917 (London: William Kimber, 1980), 5.

chambers.[7] It was one of the greatest contradictions of modern warfare, a landscape that gave the appearance by daylight of being empty but was emphatically not: it teemed with invisible life. Few paintings or photographs have captured the immensity of that void; even the most inventive narrative fails to convey the intensity of its emptiness. Faced with the phantasmagoric lunar face of No Man's Land, the imagination froze. Writer and painter Wyndham Lewis recalls the dreadful panorama of nothingness:

> I turned to look back at this obnoxious death-trap, as one turns to look back at a mountain whose top one had just visited, once one is down below. The sunset had turned on its romantic dream-light and what had been romantic enough before was now absolutely operatic. A darkening ridge, above a drift of Saharan steppe, gouged and tossed into a monotonous disorder, in a word the war-wilderness; not a flicker of life, not even a ration-party – not even a skeleton; and upon the ridge the congeries of 'bursts', to mark the spot where we had been. It was like the twitching of chicken after its head had been chopped off. We turned away from this brainless bustle, going on all by itself, about an empty concrete Easter-egg. In a stupid desert.[8]

Reflecting on his uncanny sight of a deserted but deeply dangerous battlefield, the writer Reginald Farrer insightfully notes that it was actually misleading to regard the 'huge, haunted solitude' of the modern battlefield as empty. 'It is more', he argues, 'full of emptiness ... an emptiness that is not really empty at all'.[9] The young English artist (and front-line officer) Paul Nash visualises this idea – borrowing Farrer's phrase the 'Void of War' – populating its emptinesses with latent violence.[10] Artists from Australia, Canada, and New Zealand (as well as Britain) faced similar challenges in trying to pictorialise the vacuum of the deserted battlefield.

The phenomenon of 'emptiness' was accentuated by factors peculiar to the charged spatiality of the Dardanelles battlescape. Factors included the comprehensive inversion of night and day – the night was inevitably busy

---

7   William Redmond, *Trench Pictures from France*, 1917, 39, cited in Paul Gough, 'The Empty Battlefield: Painters and the First World War', *Imperial War Museum Review*, 8 (London: Imperial War Museum, and Leo Cooper, 1993), 38-47.

8   Percy Wyndham Lewis, *Blasting and Bombardiering.* (Berkeley: University of California Press, 1967), 159.

9   Reginald Farrer, 25.

10 For an exploration of Paul Nash and the void see Paul Gough, *'Brothers in arms', John and Paul Nash, and the aftermath of the Great War* (Bristol: Sansom and Company, 2014), 49-63.

and industrious; daylight hours were outwardly calm, with opposing soldiers remaining out of sight of each other, hearing became more important than sight. Scrutiny of the 'other' had to be gleaned using proxy measures such as trench periscopes or primitive listening devices. During the Gallipoli campaign every human sense was attuned to the tract of land that lay between the front-lines. In places No Man's Land was little more than a few metres wide and became a 'debatable', fluid, and near-mythical zone that soldiers learned to fear, but it also exercised a dread fascination for many. Although the soldier-poet David Jones may not have been typical of many in the Anzac force, some may have shared his poetic understanding of the liminal qualities of No Man's Land, the threshold between two different existential spaces:

> The day by day in the wasteland, the sudden violences and long stillnesses, the sharp contours and unformed voids of that mysterious existence profoundly affected the imaginations of those who suffered it. It was a place of enchantment.[11]

At the intersection of these two worlds – the hazardous emptiness of the daylight battlescape and the crowded busy-ness of the benighted No Man's Land – came one of the critical moments of any soldier's experience of war: the moment he left the relative safety of the front-line and stepped up into the danger zone:

> The scene that followed was the most remarkable that I have ever witnessed. At one moment there was an intense and nerve shattering struggle with death screaming through the air. Then, as if with the wave of a magic wand, all was changed; all over 'No Man's Land' troops came out of the trenches, or rose from the ground where they had been lying.[12]

Moving from the horizontal to the vertical, from subterranean security to maximal vulnerability, was an ultimate transformation for every combatant. It compounded the central tenet of militarised service; the transformation from civilian to soldier, from innocence to experience, and, in many cases, from youth to adult. The peculiarly strict proximity of the Allied and Turkish trenches on the Dardanelles battlefield, and the imperative for

---

11   David Jones, *In Parenthesis* (London: Faber, 1937), x.
12   A. Stuart Dolden, *Cannon Fodder: an infantryman's life on the Western Front, 1914-1918* (Blandford: Blandford Press, 1980), 39.

the Allies to maintain the offensive or be pushed back into the sea, has made the sight of Anzac soldiers charging over the tense tract of No Man's Land the leitmotif of this particular conflict. This recurrent theme informs many of the most memorable post-war canvases in the major collections of Australian and New Zealand war art, and has entered the 'high diction' of battle iconography, also recounted in movies, documentaries and still photography.[13]

Significantly the landscape of the Dardanelles peninsula plays a very different pictorial role to that of the flat [and further flattened] terrain of much of northern France and Belgium where the Anzac forces would fight later in the war. In glaring contrast to the grim and deadly terrain immediately around the trenches and dug-outs, the picturesque hills, the vast Aegean sea, and the distinctive features of the headland were a striking backdrop to war: a beautiful place with 'cliffs carpeted with flowers'. The headland around the small town of Krithia was described by the British official historian as looking onto 'a smiling valley studded with cypress and patches of young corn'.[14] This rich visual topography became a powerful visual context for painters when they came to compose vivid re-enactments of momentous skirmishes and infamous attacks on the Turkish lines.

From a military point of view, what the battlescapes of Flanders and the Dardanelles had in common was the urgent need by the opposing armies to dominate the physical terrain and control scopic space. As the fixed trench warfare became more drawn out and intractable, there grew an urgent need to control the enemy line and the hazardous zone beyond. However, the enemy space could not always be seen: it might be heard, or smelt, or experienced in some other non-visual way. In describing their term 'smooth space' Deleuze and Guattari say 'It is a space of affects more than one of properties. It is haptic rather than optical perception'.[15] In the 'smooth space' of No Man's Land things are felt, intuited, located by sound and smell, or grasped in the dark while crawling across the tortured ground during night patrol. In stark contrast, exacting observation by trained soldiers sees the enemy lines ceaselessly scrutinised, recorded, registered and calibrated whenever possible.

---

13 See for example Peter Weir's seminal feature film, *Gallipoli* (1981).
14 Garrie Hutchinson, *Pilgrimage: A traveller's guide to Australia's battlefields* (Melbourne: Black Inc., 2006), 29.
15 Gilles Deleuze and Felix Guattari, *A thousand plateaus: capitalism and schizophrenia*. Trans. Brian Massumi (Minneapolis: University of Minnesota Press, 1987), 479.

Military sketching for reconnaissance purposes (or to aid artillery fire through target indication carried out by Forward Observation Officers) played an important part in how a significant number of artist-combatants turned their skills to military purposes.[16] In the Gallipoli campaign a number of drawings and watercolours – made on land but also significantly from the decks of naval vessels offshore –aimed to schematise the act of looking, using basic and well-tested methods of measuring and calibration by eye and hand. In the hands of a trained observer, even the most complicated terrain could be simplified, its salient features clarified through a process of careful analysis, and rendered as a drawn panorama which could inform and augment other surveillance work. Through this approach, graphic information often proved to be superior to coastal or land-based photography because it eliminated unnecessary or distracting detail, using a pictorial language to identify essential elements, relying on shared graphic codes to inform tactical actions.

Finally, there is a further understanding of the battlescape to note, one as true of Gallipoli as it was of Flanders or Salonika. Combatants came to be wary of being attracted to, or gathering around, distinctive landscape features. In France the well-known cartoonist Bruce Bairnsfather recalls, 'A farm was a place where you expected a shell through the wall any minute; a tree was the sort of thing the gunners took range on; a sunset indicated a quality of light in which it was not safe to walk abroad'.[17]

Battle immediately brings about a new order in any landscape. The nondescript, the contingent, the marginal, and the apparently featureless space quickly became prioritised and valued. Danger spots soon became well known, widely shared and greatly feared. In the Anzac trenches at Gallipoli there were many notorious points which were open to enemy sniping, where little could be done to screen soldiers as they undertook the potentially deadly act of passing them.

As a consequence, terrain was rarely neutral; it was divided unequally between the safe and the unsafe; between refuge and prospect. An officer recalls one terrifying foray into No Man's Land where everything seemed suddenly (and almost irreversibly) inverted:

> Straight lines did not exist. If one went forward patrolling, it was almost inevitable that one would soon creep around some hole or suspect heap

---

16   Paul Gough, 'Calculating the future – panoramic sketching, reconnaissance drawing and the material trace of war', in *Contested Objects: Material Memories of the Great War*, eds Nicholas Saunders and Paul Cornish (London: Routledge, 2009), 237-251.

17   Bruce Bairnsfather, *Bullets and billets* (Pen and Sword, London, 1916/1993).

or stretch of wired stumps, and then, suddenly one no longer knew which was the [enemy] line, which our own ... Willow-trees seemed [like] moving men. Compasses responded to old iron and failed us.

At last by luck or stroke of recognition one found oneself.[18]

Although straight lines rarely existed on any battlefield, there was a strong awareness of a spatial 'other', especially the tract of unknown land that existed only in the future tense: this has many spatial manifestations:

> This side of the wire everything is familiar and very man a friend; over there beyond their wire, is the unknown, the uncanny, there are the people about whom you accumulate scraps of irrelevant information but whose real life you can never penetrate ...[19]

If in front lay the unknowable, beyond that lay the unreachable. Soldiers in the few privileged elevated positions on the Western Front could glimpse a green, distant strip of land – always out of reach, forever locked in an unattainable future:

> I could ... see unspoiled land beyond the Hindenburg Line, undulating hills ... woods, villages fit to live in, trees that had leaves, a hillside without shell-holes. It was a Promised Land.[20]

This idea of a 'promised land' that could only be mentioned in the future tense became a standard trope amongst many memoir-writers; a recognition that they were somehow irreversibly situated in an irreversible 'here and now'. On the Dardanelles Peninsula the distant hills of the Sari Bair Range played the same role, tantalisingly offering the ultimate prize and prospect, but cruelly denied.

Part two: Artistic interpretations

Here we look at these spatial, aural and haptic phenomena through the eyes of two artist-practitioners, Frank Hurley in Belgium in late 1917 and Ellis Silas on the slopes above Anzac Beach in May 1915.

Photographer and cinematographer Frank Hurley had arrived in London in early 1917 as a national Australian hero, having sensationally survived the

---

18 Gough, 'Calculating the Future', 242.
19 Edmund Blunden, *Undertones of war* (London: Penguin, Penguin Classics 2000, 1928).
20 Charles Carrington, *Soldier from the wars returning* (London: Hutchinson, 1965), 87.

catastrophe that beset Shackleton's Imperial Trans-Antarctic Expedition of 1914-16. Commissioned by the Australian War Records Section when it was formed in mid-1917 and attached to the AIF as an honorary Captain, he was quite overwhelmed by the horrors of the Western Front, stunned by its scale, complexity and omnipresent dangers. Although his imagination was ignited by the spectacle of war he struggled with its speed and intensity. Hurley and his assistant Hubert Wilkins did what they could scenographically to embrace the battlescape's visual sweep, on one occasion they hazarded out of their fragile shelter to capture the random instantaneity of an aerial bombardment, but it was a futile business, 'In spite of heavy shelling by the Boche, we made an endeavour to secure a number of shell burst pictures. ... I took two pictures by hiding in a dugout and then rushing out and snapping'.[21]

Fig. 9.1 Frank Hurley, A composite photograph, originally known as "a hop over", constructed by official war photographer, Australian War Memorial E05988B

---

21 Frank Hurley, *The diaries of Frank Hurley, 1912-1941*. Robert Dixon and Christopher Lee (eds.), London: Anthem, 2011, (6 October 1917). The establishment of the Australian War Records Section is given in the Australian War Memorial record as May 1917. However, elsewhere (usually sources in the UK) give the date as June. See https://www.awm.gov.au/blog/2007/06/12/the-australian-war-records-section/

Despite his determined pursuit of a good image, for Hurley the results were disappointing. He realised that the face of modern war was too elusive for a single snapshot, 'Everything is on such a vast scale. Figures are scattered — the atmosphere is dense with haze and smoke — shells will not burst where required — yet the whole elements are there could they but be brought together and condensed'.[22]

Hurley acknowledged that the difficulties were 'insurmountable' and proposed that he create composite photographs. He later told an audience 'Now if negatives are taken of all the separate incidents in the action and combined, some idea may be gained of what a modern battle looks like'.[23] Composite printing was a well-established, indeed staple, technique of photographers at the time, used extensively for mural-sized exhibition prints for display. Hurley was aware that the Canadian Expeditionary Force (CEF) had recruited photographers who willingly embraced the technique and he was determined, in his words, to 'beat them'. However, as is now widely known, the official war historian for Australia Charles Bean firmly prohibited the practice. Officially responsible for an eyewitness record of the Australian effort, Bean wanted nothing to do with 'scoops, competitions, magnification and exaggeration' which he regarded as falsifying the authentic evidence of war and out of harmony with 'what is best for the country'. Photographs were regarded as sacred records – standing for future generations to see forever the simple plain truth'.[24]

Hurley refused to regard his photographs as either a sacred relic or an indexical account of the front, nor did he think Bean's reductive ruling could reflect the extraordinary bravery of the Anzac soldiers he witnessed in action on the front-line. Their row was a bitter one:

> Had a great argument with Bean about combination pictures. Am thoroughly convinced that it is impossible to secure effects, without resorting to combination pictures ... Had a lengthy discussion with Bean re pictures for exhibition and publicity purposes. Our authorities here will not permit me to pose any pictures or indulge in any original means to secure them ... As this absolutely takes all possibilities of producing

---

22 Martyn Jolly, 'Composite propaganda photographs during the First World War'. History of Photography, 27:2, Summer, 2003, 154-165. Discusses Hurley, Press cuttings, *Sydney Morning Herald* (20 March 1919), n.p.

23 Frank Hurley, Press cuttings, National Library of Australia, MS883, series 2, items 29-36, n.d.

24 Charles E.W. Bean Diary, Australian War Memorial, AWM38, cited in Michael McKernan, *Here is Their Spirit* (Brisbane: University of Queensland Press, 1991), 42.

pictures from me, I have decided to tender my resignation at once. I conscientiously consider it but right to illustrate to the public the things our fellows do and how the war is conducted. They can only be got by printing a result from a number of negatives or re-enactment. This is out of reason and they prefer to let all these interesting episodes pass. This is unfair to our boys and I conscientiously could not undertake to continue to work.[25]

Hurley eventually reached a compromise with Bean and AIF Headquarters and retracted his resignation. Hurley was allowed to make six composites for a London exhibition devoted to Australia's fighting in France, provided they were captioned as composites. In later exhibitions and publications these captions somehow disappeared and the public began to assume that all of Hurley's pictures were real. For his London show in May 1918 he showed these composites enlarged to mural size, and a further 130 further images describing military activity and actions on the Western Front and Palestine where the AIF was stationed and where Hurley was posted in November 1917.

Hurley revelled in the public and press attention, delighted by the success of his 'action pictures'. He regarded them as truly authentic visions of a war that had proved absurdly elusive:

> The exhibition was well patronised today. The colour lantern is working excellently. The colour slides depict scenes on the Western Front, Flanders and also Palestine. They are gems and elicit applause at every showing. A military band plays throughout the day. ...
>
> ... Another sensational picture is 'DEATH THE REAPER'. This remarkable effect is made up of two negatives. One, the foreground, shows the mud splashed corpse of a Boche floating in a shell crater. The second is an extraordinary shell burst: the form of which resembles death. The Palestine series are magnificent .... It is some recompense to see one's work shown to the masses and to receive favourable criticism after the risks and hardships I have taken and endured to secure the negatives.[26]

---

25 Frank Hurley, 26 September 1917.
26 Frank Hurley, 4 June 1918.

Fig. 9.2 Frank Hurley, *An advanced aid post*, Australian War Memorial 1917E01202A

Hurley would always assure his audiences that the elements of each composite picture were taken at great risk during battles, and were not 'fancy pictures faked from a safe position behind the lines'. No one questioned his front-line credentials. Even Bean recognised that Hurley had 'been nearly killed a dozen times'.[27]

---

27 Charles E.W. Bean, *Wilkins and Hurley recommendations*, Australian War Memorial, AWM38, DRL6673, item 57, 24 October 1917.

But do these vast collages actually capture the face of total war? Do they compete with the works of front-line painters who set out to interpret what they had seen as Official War Artists? Do they, in fact, tell us much about the unique conditions of the front-line? The answer to each of these questions is probably no, not as much as Hurley believed as they add little to the iconography of modern warfare. Hurley's composite works are, to echo one historian's critique, little more than 'quaint historical footnotes'.[28]

Hurley's large composite works fell into the same trap as the epic cavalry-laden tableau of the high Victorian and Edwardian battle art they mimicked, being over-anxious to promote heroic gesture and martial zeal. In wishing to be counted as equal to the vast canvases that lined the walls of the Royal Academies, Hurley's mural size prints may seem little more than overblown compendiums in absurdly ornate frames. In retrospect none of the effort seems necessary. Hurley was an impressive documentary photographer – deeply committed, fearless and authentic. His technical innovations, particularly in flash photography, establish him as a pioneer. His single-shot photographs of the battle front help visualise some of the intangible, virtually indescribable, aspects of modern war. When seen alongside his powerful war diary Hurley's documentary photographs recount an extraordinary tale of commitment, zeal and pictorial innovation.

Born in 1885, the same year as Hurley, painter Ellis Silas sailed to Australia from England in 1907. He painted in Sydney, Melbourne, and Adelaide before settling in Perth. In 1914 he joined the AIF as a signaller, was trained in Egypt and landed in Gallipoli with the 16th Battalion in the early evening of 25th April 1915. His unit went straight into action at Pope's Hill at the head of Monash Valley where they spent the night hurriedly digging in while under intense enemy rifle-fire. Ellis later recorded these first traumatic hours in his memorable painting *The End of the Great Day*.[29] His unit held its precarious position, without relief, for the next five days and nights. Later, Ellis found time to record his reactions in a diary and to make drawn records of the events enveloping him 'The repetition of shrapnel in each sketch is not a fad of mine, but just the natural order of things'.[30]

---

28 Martyn Jolly, 'Australian First World War photography'. *History of Photography*, 23, number 2, Summer, 1999.

29 Ellis Silas, 'The End of the Great Day: The 16th Battalion, AIF digging the original trenches on Pope's Hill on the evening of the landing at Anzac, 25 April 1915' – By an eyewitness (Signaller Ellis Silas, 16th Battalion AIF).

30 Ellis Silas, *Crusading at Anzac AD 1915* (London, 1916).

Fig. 9.3 Frank HURLEY *No title (Supporting troops of the 1st Australian Division walking on a duckboard track)* (1917) (recto) gelatin silver photograph 14.0 x 19.0 cm (image and sheet) National Gallery of Victoria, Melbourne 2003.371

He recalls that, only hours after coming ashore, there was a curious phenomenon in the midst of 'this frightful hell of screaming shrapnel and heavy ordinance', birds were chirping and buzzing from leaf to leaf'.[31] Such bucolic dissonance was a common feature of the Great War battlefields, characterised as 'ridiculous mad incongruity!' by Nash, another painter on a very different battleground some two years later.[32] As a signaller Ellis had constantly to expose himself in full view so as to relay his messages to others on distant parts of the battlefield. It is a highly fraught occupation. In contrast to his fellow combatant, a signaller's reading of space and distance has to be finely and uniquely attuned.

As Ellis took in his surroundings, his artist's eye was drawn to the few distinctive motifs of the sandy landscape – the single fir tree, for example, on the ridge opposite where a New Zealand unit was advancing. But he became quickly aware that danger lurks most in those places identified by enemy

---

31   Ellis Silas, Diary entry, 26 April 1915.
32   Paul Nash, *Outline: an autobiography and other writings*, with a preface by Herbert Read (London: Faber and Faber, 1948), 186.

snipers as patently empty, most obviously the gaps in the breastworks and temporary defensive lines. And he later made a drawing of one such danger spot known as 'Dead Man's Patch', a notorious open space so well covered by Turkish sharpshooters that 'few men have been able to get across it – a stream of dead marks its length'.[33]

> All along the route, scrambling along the side of the exposed incline, my comrades offered me a dug-out for me to take cover as the snipers are getting our chaps every minute, but as the messages are important I must take my chance. All along the route I keep coming across bodies of the poor chaps who have been less fortunate than I.[34]

To Ellis and his fellow combatants the Gallipolean landscape is a truly malign place, offering little succour or respite, where every element seems to conspire against them. On one occasion Ellis was about to make a dash from the cover of bushes to cross a bare patch when he found himself momentarily ensnared by a sharp branch 'The seat of my pants caught in the bushes, and I hung by them! I was in a terrible funk, for then the snipers got busy'. Illustrated in his book *Crusading at Anzac* Ellis's drawing creates an extremely dissonant impression, for sprawled among the picturesque scene of flowering foliage and billowing clouds are the prone bodies of his comrades, impaled and forlorn in grotesque Goyaesque postures.[35]

Despite the intense dangers and the deliriums that befell him after a week of non-stop sniper fire Ellis managed to maintain a record of what was happening around him, though he apologises to himself that he was keeping little but notes and 'making no effort to keep a concise diary.' He did however find time to sketch, amusing himself one evening in Rest Camp[36] by designing stained glass windows, and on another making a reconnaissance sketch of a position for his superior officers possibly, he thinks, for General Birdwood. He complains frequently in his diary that as day light recedes 'his sight is going', a terrible dilemma for Ellis the signaller, let alone Ellis the fine artist.

He describes an occasion when he mistakes the shifting spatiality of the narrow battlefield when returning from delivering a message and takes the 'wrong side' of a road, one that is open to enemy observation. 'Keep to the

---

33   Ellis Silas, Diary entry 26 April 1915.
34   Ellis Silas, Diary entry 26 April 1915.
35   Reproduced as Dead Man's Patch' in Ellis Silas, *Crusading at Anzac AD 1915*.
36   Ellis Silas, Diary entry, 11 May 1915.

right!', his Captain shouts out, 'Don't you know which is the right side? Run for it...'[37] As battle continues Ellis observes one of the characteristic fusions of the new order of things: 'The shrapnel is now ever in the sky, it is as much a part of the landscape as the clouds.' and in less than a fortnight, on 7th May, he records that the distinction between day and night is becoming blurred, 'All last night the Turks have been bombarding heavily with shrapnel; a quite unusual occurrence, as they never used to commence before dawn'.[38]

Ellis lasted at the front little more than three weeks. His nerves were shredded and he was evacuated. By his own reckoning he felt he had played a part, had done 'his bit' with his fellows and shown 'a sneering world that artists are not quite failures on the battlefield', though he freely admitted that 'we are not quite cut out for this sort of work'.[39] Ellis saw out the war first in Egypt, as a medical orderly with those evacuated from the Dardanelles, and then as a convalescent himself in England. In 1916 he gathered together his battlefield notes and sketches which were published as *Crusading at Anzac AD 1915*, a searing but also compassionate account of the landing, its aftermath and his recovery. The ink drawings trace a traumatic account of his brief time on the headland and conclude with an image of a wounded soldier comforted by a nurse at Palace Hospital, Heliopolis entitled 'Heaven!'[40]

Ellis Silas holds the distinction of being the only participant in the Battle of the Landing to produce paintings from his personal experiences. The Australian War Museum purchased three of his large paintings, where Silas focuses on the combatants and their heroic plight. By focusing almost entirely on the figures the emptied battlescapes offer little more than background colour and context.[41]

---

37 Ellis Silas, Diary entry, 2 May 1915.
38 Ellis Silas, Diary entry, 7 May 1915.
39 Ellis Silas, Diary entry, 28 April 1915.
40 Ellis Silas, *Crusading at Anzac AD 1915*. With an introduction by General Sir William Birdwood, and foreword by General Sir Ian Hamilton. Hamilton wrote a rather back-handed compliment in the Foreword, that although Silas' drawings might seem a little 'slight, they seem solid and serious enough to such of us as were there'.
41 For a brief but thorough account see: http://www.anzacsite.gov.au/1landing/s_biography.html). 'Roll Call', Ellis Silas, 1920, oil on canvas, 101.8 x 153.1 cm [AWM ART02436]. Silas executed this painting in London in about 1920 on commission for the Australian War Records Section, and along with two other works, 'The Attack of the 4th Brigade, AIF' and 'Digging in at Quinn's Post or the End of a Great Day', it went to the Australian War Memorial, where it currently hangs in the Gallipoli gallery. 'Roll Call' was based upon an earlier sketch of his that appeared in 'Crusading at Anzac', titled 'The Roll Call – Quinn's Pôst'. According to Silas, the roll call after a battle was 'always a most heart-breaking incident. Name after name would be called; the reply a deep silence.'

Fig. 9.4 Silas Ellis *Dawn, 3 May 1915* 28 x 15 cm (irreg.) Australian War Memorial ART90803

Part three: Memoryscapes as an exploration of the void

Today few painters can approach the topic of Gallipoli without reference to the extraordinary suite of images created by the Australian artist Sidney Nolan during a period between the mid-1950s and the late 1970s. These images are very different from anything thus far considered and offer a wholly new perspective, unlike the eye-witness accounts by Ellis Silas, the post-war topographical views by Horace Moore-Jones, or indeed the epic canvases depicting infamous battle charges recreated by George Lambert after the war. 'The power and the energy of Nolan's Gallipoli works', claims Lola Wilkins 'are palpable. It is as if Nolan found a way to breathe life into what had become a long-repeated story, giving a uniquely personal perspective on a subject that has been largely treated as history'.[42]

In 1978 Nolan donated 252 pieces from his Gallipoli series to the Australian War Memorial in Canberra. Much has been written about Nolan's mythical treatment of the campaign, how he had long wanted to explore heroic themes, had delved into Homer's *Iliad*, and visited the archaeological museum in Athens where he became fascinated by classical Greek black vases exquisitely painted with representations of warriors in combat.

In 1956 he took an opportunity to visit the preserved site of Troy and spent a single memorable day on the peninsula of Gallipoli, a visit that left its indelible mark on his keyed-up imagination:

> I stood on the place where the first ANZACs had stood, looked across the straits to the site of ancient Troy, and felt that here history had stood still ... Here and there I picked up a soldier's water bottle or some other piece of discarded equipment ... I found the place on top of the hill where the ANZAC and Turkish trenches had been only yards apart and the whole expedition balanced between success or failure.
>
> I visualised the young, fresh faces of the boys from the bush, knowing nothing or war of faraway places, all individuals, and suddenly all the same – united and uniform in the dignity of the common destiny. And that is how I came to paint the series.[43]

---

42 Lola Wilkins, 'Sidney Nolan: The Gallipoli Series', essay in *Sidney Nolan: The Gallipoli Series*, exhibition catalogue (Australian War Memorial, Canberra, 2009), 1-14, 2-3.
43 Sidney Nolan, 'The ANZAC Story', *The Australian Women's Weekly*, 17 March 1965, 3.

A substantial number of the Series are empty. Charles Green describes them as 'fields of colour from which soldiers are almost wholly absent'.[44] Sombre and tonal they depict the barren topography of the headland, its impenetrable scrub, remnants of trenches, sharply-cut gullies, and low distant hills, and the ocean that engirdled the peninsula.

Through his sustained preoccupation with the Gallipoli campaign Nolan took his fascination with the landscape myths of his homeland and merged them with the idea that Australia's national identity was born with the Anzac legend of Gallipoli. This became a potent combination.

Nolan fused the bare hills of Asia Minor with the harsh landscape of the Australian bush, blurring 'one iconic landscape with another'.[45] He recognised in the ancient Turkish landscape similar qualities to the Australian outback; he was familiar with its colours, tone and texture, and recognised it as innately inhospitable as had contemporary commentators such as British journalist and war correspondent Ellis Ashmead-Bartlett in his written dispatches, at first full of life and colour:

> It is indeed a formidable and forbidding land. To the sea it presents a steep front, broken into innumerable ridges, bluffs, valleys, and sand spits, which rise to a height of several hundred feet. The surface is either a kind of bare yellow sandstone which crumbles when you tread on it, or else is covered with very thick shrubbery about six feet in height.[46]

Nolan absorbed these narratives and other eye-witness accounts, he talked lengthily to eminent historians, and spent time in London at the Imperial War Museum viewing contemporary photographs of the campaign. Embedding, indeed saturating, himself in the milieu of a theme was a standard approach for the artist before embarking on any series. 'Experience, knowledge, and imagination', writes Laura Webster, 'would interact in his mind before he got down to the business of creating the work. In this way the works became ruminations, but produced with great rapidity and arising

---

44 Charles Green, 'The Gallipoli Series: An Artist's Perspective', essay in *Sidney Nolan: The Gallipoli Series*, exhibition catalogue (Australian War Memorial, Canberra, 2009), 24-29, 25.
45 Charles Green, 'The Gallipoli Series: An Artist's Perspective', 25.
46 Ellis Ashmead-Bartlett, *Despatches from the Dardanelles* (George Newnes, London, 1916), 72.

out of an almost unconscious, emotional response'.[47] Having steeped himself in the geographical and mythological history of Gallipoli, Nolan painted a succession of memoryscapes that exude the core ideas of a crowded emptiness.

He was both in awe of the place and assured in his creative process. Using his trademark materials – textile dye, polymer medium, coloured crayon, coated paper – he created bare, almost minimal, images suffused with colour, executed hastily, without any wasted effort. They eschew perspective or depth, they have no detail or anecdotal touch points, the planes are distorted and bent. As with so many of his landscapes they are 'geographically tentative and uncertain'.[48]

What is it that makes this Series so convincing? Is it because they are so elusive and stripped down, little more than a wash of saturated red and pink on striated cliffs, or because they seemed to have been achieved so effortlessly, with their pleats of colour folded over and over to miraculously recreate the friable geology of the beachhead and the burrow-holed ravines and gullies where the soldiers endured a fragile troglodyte existence? Or is it that Nolan recognised that every landscape – the bush, outback, or beachhead – had its own story to tell, each with its own innate power of embedded, multiple, narratives?

Absorbed by the mythological intensity of Gallipoli, Nolan knew that less was more in presenting the emptiness of the battle and the landscape that still remained on his visit decades later. Interviewed at the Australian War Memorial in 1982 he voices a sense that threat, menace, unease lay close to the surface, just as the personal detritus of the retreating armies had once littered it. 'The landscape', he reflects of that distant boneyard, 'becomes darker and more fissured'.[49] Nolan's bleak minimal vistas impart to the viewer a knowledge that something awful had happened on this fractured ground. They evoke rich layers of memory and emotion that render the landscape silent witness to both historic and contemporary events.

In the past two decades as the mystique surrounding the Gallipoli Campaign broadens, deepens, intensifies, other Australian and New Zealand artists have been stimulated to create equally pared down representations of the scarred cliffs and once-fatal ridges of the peninsula. Idris Murphy's representation of a *Gallipoli Evening* (2013), for example, borrows much of

---

47 Laura Webster, 'Nolan's Gallipoli Landscapes', essay in Sidney Nolan: *The Gallipoli Series*, exhibition catalogue (Australian War Memorial, Canberra, 2009), 44-51, 49.

48 Daniel Thomas, *Outlines of Australian art: the Joseph Brown Collection* (New York: Harry N. Abrams, 1989), 37.

49 Interview with Gavin Fry, 26 February 1982, Australian War Memorial recording 359.

its stripped back and simplified design from Nolan's example.[50] However his is a hard act to follow, and most comparable painting pales through poor imitation.

Nolan's dozens of landscapes speak eloquently of the crowded emptiness of fated ground, indeed they may represent the most distilled essence of a brutalised and blighted battlescape since Paul Nash told a 'bitter truth' without resorting to legions of soldiers and hackneyed narratives. Nolan would have known such paintings, and he would have been keenly aware of Australian precedents by First World War artists at Gallipoli, such as George Benson, Frank Crozier, and George Lambert, but at the end of the day they meant little to him:

> I'm very interested, in fact, compelled and dedicated to transmitting emotions and I care for very little else. I care for that process so much that I'm prepared to belt the paint across the canvas much faster than it should be belted. I don't care as long as I can get that emotional communication. I will sacrifice everything to it – and that I've done.[51]

In exploring the idea of emptiness and its application to the battlescapes of Turkey and Europe in the First World War, each of these three artists, Hurley, Ellis and Nolan respond to both the scenes before them and to the 'smooth space' of the sensorial landscape, where the senses – haptic, visual and aural – entwine in the complex layers of an horrific battleground. While Hurley and Nolan knew already the stark, empty and threatening landscapes of the Australian outback and polar wastelands, nothing prepared them for the wasted boneyards of Gallipoli, the Somme or Ypres. They responded imaginatively and with unique creative vision. After months in recuperation from the traumas of his service in the Dardanelles, artist and signaller Ellis Silas was finally able to use his unique experiences to ask the pertinent question of the 'legacy of emptiness', a dense legacy that would gradually suffuse the desolate landscape of that doomed peninsula:

> Fighting still continuing with unabated vigour – will this frightful noise never cease? I wonder what this valley will be like when there is no longer noise of fighting, no longer the hurried tread of combating forces – when the raw earth of the trenches is o'erspread with verdant

---

50 See http://www.smh.com.au/national/gallipoli-letters-add-poignancy-to-idris-murphys-20000-art-prize-win-20140423-374hc.html Accessed 1 February 2016.

51 John Buckley, *Sidney Nolan: works on paper* (Sydney: Australian Gallery Directors' Council, 1980), 3.

grass. Perhaps here and there equipment of War will be lying with fresh spring sprouts of grass threading through interstices – underneath the sad little mounds resting sons of a great nation – in the clear sky overhead, instead of the bursting shrapnel, little fleecy clouds – the scream of shrapnel, the Hell noise of the firing, giving place to an unbroken stillness save for the chirping of a bird or the soft buzzing of the bee! I wonder would it be thus![52]

---

52   Ellis Silas, 'The Diary of an Anzac', typescript, ML MSS.1840, Mitchell Library, State Library of New South Wales, 5.

Chapter 10

LEST WE FORGET

Presentation, Commemoration and Memorialisation of the Great War[1]

Kevin Fewster

The centenary of the outbreak of the Great War in 2014 was marked across Britain by a veritable bombardment of events and programmes. As one commentator writing in the *London Evening Standard* newspaper reflected just before Remembrance Day:

> This year's centenary of the Great War seems to have lost all proportion. It has become a ritualised overlay to any and every public activity. The BBC cannot get away from it. Not an evening is allowed to pass without footage somewhere of trenches, barbed wire, explosions and bodies.... We have Great War dramas, proms, poetry readings, fashion shows, gardening programmes, even Great War bake-ins... and, last weekend, Great War Antiques Roadshows.[2]

Not surprisingly, museums were very much to the fore. Both the Imperial War Museum and the Royal Navy Museum, Portsmouth, underwent major overhauls in preparation for the centenary (although, surprisingly, the

---

1   I wish to thank Henrietta Probert for alerting me to Adam Gopnik's review article about the 9/11 Museum and Memorial. I am also especially grateful to Dr Michael McKernan for his comments at the Çanakkale conference regarding the *WW1: Love & Sorrow* exhibition at Museum of Melbourne and to Dr Richard Gillespie and Deborah Tout-Smith from Melbourne Museum for subsequently sharing materials with me regarding this exhibition.
2   S. Jenkins, 'The poppies are glorious but let's learn their lesson', *London Evening Standard*, 4 November 2014.

National Army Museum is closed for rebuilding until 2016). Museums up-and-down the country were (and still are) staging exhibitions, large and small, reflecting their own particular link to the war and its commemoration. My own institution, Royal Museums Greenwich (which includes Britain's National Maritime Museum) is mounting a five-year programme of exhibitions, programmes and online projects to shine light on the war at sea.

Britain played a central role in the 1915 Gallipoli campaign, but commemoration of the battles has been muted: the last surviving Royal Navy gunboat that served off Gallipoli is being restored in dry-dock at Portsmouth and was augmented by a Gallipoli exhibition at adjacent Royal Navy Museum, the BBC commissioned a television documentary examining Australian journalist Keith Murdoch's role in the campaign, and public commemoration focussed, as always, around the annual wreath laying event at the Cenotaph, Whitehall, followed by the magnificent annual Service of Commemoration and Thanksgiving at Westminster Abbey. Yet, for most Britons, Gallipoli is but one more name in a long list of British battles down the ages.

Amidst the barrage of Great War centenary programming, one project captured the public's attention like no other – the art installation, *Blood-Swept Lands and Seas of Red* at Britain's most famous military establishment, the Tower of London. Jointly conceived by sculptor Paul Cummins and theatre designer Tom Piper, the work filled the moat surrounding the Tower with 888,246 individually-made ceramic poppies – a poppy for every life lost by British and Dominion forces in the war. The red poppies seemed to pour, like blood, out of a window in one of the Tower's famous turrets. It took four months for a team of volunteers to install all the poppies which, upon their removal after Remembrance Day, were individually sold off for armed services charities, raising over £10m.

Many people returned time after time to watch the 'red sea' spread as the weeks progressed. 'The art work', one newspaper reported in early November, 'has been a London sensation… The watching crowd seemed solemn and genuinely moved, not the usual London rubber-neckers.'[3] The Queen added her own floral tribute and later reflected in her annual Christmas Message: 'The only possible reaction to walking among them was silence'.[4] As Remembrance Day drew near, the numbers of people became so great that the nearby Tower Hill Underground station was

---

3   Jenkins.
4   http://www.royal.gov.uk/imagesandbroadcasts/thequeenschristmasbroadcasts/christmasbroadcasts/christmasbroadcast2014.aspx, accessed 15 April 2015.

regularly closed in an effort to control the throng and organisers, fearing possible crushes, asked people to stay away during the busy school holiday week. Yet still they came, with national papers carrying adverts for special two day coach trips: 'Don't Delay – Book Now – Ends Tuesday 11 November 2014'[5] – wording akin to a West End musical! In all, it is estimated that between four and five million people saw the poppies in situ.

But amidst all this acclaim, the *Guardian* journalist, Jonathan Jones, spoke out against the work, condemning it as:

> a deeply aestheticized, prettified and toothless war memorial. It is all dignity and grace. There is a fake nobility to it…. What a lie. The first world war was not noble. War is not noble. A meaningful mass memorial to this horror would not be dignified or pretty. It would be gory, vile and terrible to see. The moat of the Tower should be filled with barbed wire and bones.[6]

Other papers were quick to condemn the 'sneering *Guardian*', leading Jones to retaliate with a second article declaring:

> What we owe the youth of that generation is to attend to the details of the history that caught them in its hungry jaws. We need to smell the rotting earth and gunpowder, feel the boots falling apart in muddy water, the pounding of the chest as the guns started up. The installation at the Tower is abstract, and tells us nothing about history. It is instead a representation of grief as such – a second hand evocation of feelings about the dead.
>
> It doesn't matter now how sad we are about those the first world war killed. Our soulfulness won't bring back a single slaughtered soldier. What can make a difference is our historical understanding of the Great War, its causes and consequence. History is worth far more than the illusion of memory, when none of us today actually have a memory of being soldiers in 1914-18…. A true work of art about the first world war would need to be as obscene as cancer.[7]

---

5   Omega Holidays, *Daily Mail*, http://hulldailymail.reader.travel/tour.php?c=65&s=473&t=2780, accessed 15 April 2015.

6   J. Jones, 'The Tower of London poppies are fake, trite and inward-looking – a Ukip-style memorial', *Guardian*, 28 October 2014.

7   J. Jones, 'Mail and PM are wrong. The poppies muffle truth', *Guardian*, 1 November 2014

His comments drew one of the installation's creators – theatre designer Tom Piper – out on to the field of battle. Piper responded to Jones:

> This is not an installation about war or an illustration of its violence and barbarity; it is about loss and commemoration that has given individuals a unique way to tap into their own family history and appreciate some of the human cost…
>
> Just because a play is about World War 1 you don't fill the stage with bones – that would be a crass clichéd thing to do. You find the metaphor and you allow people in.[8]

This war of words, and the art work itself, made me reflect on my own profession: how museums represent war, memory and commemoration. In today's world, museums (along with the print and electronic media) are the means through which most people outside formal learning receive and engage with history, whether that be war or any other subset of history. Museums generally do this through displaying and interpreting objects they have collected or borrowed. Adam Gopnik put it succinctly in his review article, 'Stones and Bones – visiting the 9/11 memorial and museum' in *The New Yorker* magazine: '[Museums] display an unusual object and explain its original meaning'.[9] Good museums try (as Jones would wish) to tell the stories of history, indeed some with big budgets will seek to realise Jones' ambition 'to smell the rotting earth and gunpowder'. But, no matter how large the budget or how convincing the special effects, how often do museums actually succeed in 'cutting through' and really engaging or challenging visitors as Jones' demands? It's one thing to present an historical story and or display objects that illustrate this; it's quite something else to make our visitors truly stop and reflect on what they are seeing and reading.

Royal Museums Greenwich (RMG) is the world's largest and most visited maritime museum. In 2013/14 we welcomed 2.8 million visitors across our four sites, all located within the Maritime Greenwich World Heritage Site in suburban London. Perhaps the most iconic set of objects in the National Maritime Museum at RMG is the uniform Admiral Lord Nelson was wearing when he has mortally wounded by a French marksman at the Battle of Trafalgar. Ever since the Museum opened in 1937 generations of visitors have stood in awe in front of his coat (the musket ball entry hole

---

8   *Daily Mail*, 7 January 2015
9   A. Gopnik, 'Stones and Bones', *The New Yorker*, 7 July 2014. www.newyorker.com

Fig. 10.1. The coat Admiral Lord Nelson wore at the Battle of Trafalgar, 21 October 1805. The fatal musket ball entry point is clearly visible just below the left epaulette. Photo: Royal Museums Greenwich.

clearing evident just below the left epaulette), his trousers raggedly cut open by the surgeon, and his heavily blood-stained stockings. Jonathan Jones has praised this exhibition for 'paint[ing] a harrowing picture of what war was like at sea in the early 19th-century and retell[ing] the sorrowful story of the admiral who died at his moment of victory in a suitably touching way'.[10] To many, Nelson's uniform is something akin to the Turin shroud, a national holy relic. In truth, most visitors, I suspect, are more fascinated by the uniform's remarkable survival and preservation than repulsed or overwhelmed by any associations with his actual death.

Just as the Museum's Nelsonic collections are truly remarkable, we also hold fine materials pertaining to the Great War. Drawing on these, the Museum's World War One centenary programme is rich and diverse:

---

10   J. Jones, 'Has sentimental remembrance met its Waterloo?', *Guardian*, 4 March 2015

> *Forgotten Fighters – the war at sea*, a semi-permanent exhibition built around objects from our collections that will run across the full five years of the centenary
>
> *War and Memory*, a contemporary art installation by Rozanne Hawksley that showed through the second half of 2014
>
> *War Artists at Sea*, drawing on the Museum's superb holdings of paintings and sculptures by Britain's official war artists from both WW1 and WW2, running for 16 months from March 2014
>
> A temporary exhibition in 2016 to mark the Battle of Jutland centenary
>
> A massive digitisation project that indexes and uploads online for the first time the crew lists of all 39,000 British mercantile voyages undertaken in 1915, including personal data for 775,000 individual crew members, plus
>
> A stream of lectures, performances, special days and other activities.

Forgotten Fighters is an excellent exhibition, showcasing over 150 objects, including models, medals and images, drawn from the national maritime collection, supported by iPad technology which gives the visitor far greater depth of interpretation than is provided in a traditional museum exhibition. Our *War Artists at Sea* exhibition is equally good, displaying powerful art works of battle and everyday depictions of life at sea and on the home front in both world wars. But, as Quintin Colville, the curator of *Forgotten Fighters* observed in a paper given to an RMG staff seminar: 'Objects freeze-frame the war ... [The intention] is for the viewer to do the talking and imagining.'[11] Much the same could be said of the art works in our *War Artists* exhibition. The artists have captured a moment in the war, but this is not necessarily the same as capturing the essence of the experience. Colville's paper made a similar point about the many gallantry medals he had included in *Forgotten Fighters*:

> Within the Museum the challenge for naval history is to expose the onion-skin meanings of these objects and perhaps to ensure that the experiences they obscure also receive our attention.[12]

---

11 Q. Colville, 'Panning for gold: representing the First World War at sea through word and object', unpublished paper, 9.

12 Colville, 16.

Fig. 10.2. Rozanne Hawksley's 1987 work, *Pale Armistice: in Death only are we United*, displayed at the Queen's House, Royal Museums Greenwich, 2014. Photo: Royal Museums Greenwich.

How, he asked, could any object convey the reality of, for example, the diary entry of an unnamed sailor returning from the Mediterranean in 1918:

> Last week an American oil tanker caught fire here. One man tried to escape thro' a port, and was jammed half way. A rope was put round him but all efforts to shift him proved unsuccessful. He begged them to shoot him, the fire burning his legs inside and the heat intense. A fitter from the dockyard offered to cut him out with a blow lamp, but was not allowed as an explosion was expected. A doctor then gave him…[a lethal] injection and he died.[13]

The most powerful, most confronting of our exhibitions, I would contend, was Rozanne Hawksley's art installation, *War + Memory*. Hawksley was a World War Two child evacuee from the naval city of Portsmouth, where her grandmother was an outworker sewing sailors' collars for the Royal Navy from the end of the First World War until she was killed during an air raid in 1944. Hawksley constructs her art works with fabrics and stitching, often

---

13   Colville, 8.

recycling materials from the period. Much of her work explores the nature and meaning of the commemoration and memorialisation of war and her pieces have been collected by institutions such as the Imperial War Museum as well as conventional art galleries.

The main theme panel for the exhibition stated:

> THE EMOTIONAL SCARS LEFT by the experience of war are the enduring theme in Rozanne Hawksley's work. Some of her most disturbing images convey the impact of these experiences: they aim to look beneath the calm exterior that is maintained to the emotional damage created by war. Taking inspiration from diaries, poetry and the work of war artists and photographers, the pieces in this room illustrate the way in which sailors have been represented ... Their stoicism is contrasted with the work of Rozanne Hawksley, who attempts to represent the unspeakable.

The exhibition included older works as well as a full-room installation she created especially for the RMG exhibition. Her 1987 piece, *Pale Armistice: in Death only are we United*, commemorates the Great War by creating a memorial wreath composed of white gloves with bones and wax lilies to add further poignancy. A more recent work, created in 2006, consists of two pieces:

> *He always wanted to be a soldier I*
>
> *He always wanted to be a soldier II*

each based on 'sweetheart pieces' that sailors and soldiers made for their loved ones. The object label stated: 'The first illustrates the romanticised view of heroism and sacrifice held by the untried soldier – indicated by unspent cartridges, gold fringe and purple taffeta. The bleak reality of war is portrayed in the second piece, with its spent cartridges and burnt corps suspended from medal ribbons.'

I found her works challenging and disturbing.

War + Memory would not meet Jonathan Jones' demand for a Great War exhibition to display only 'barbed wire and bones' or to be as obscene as cancer. Yet, to my mind, it was confronting and thought provoking in ways that I rarely experience with conventional museum exhibitions. The rooms felt cold and desolate, the works conveying both poignancy and power.

As with *Blood-Swept Lands and Seas of Red*, the *War + Memory* exhibition season peaked on Remembrance Day, 11 November, when students from a naval school that had been based on the Museum's grounds until the 1930s, ceremonially carried back into the building the school's World War One

Fig. 10.3. Rozanne Hawksley's work, *Full Fathom Five*, commissioned by Royal Museums Greenwich and displayed in the Queen's House, 2014. Photo: Royal Museums Greenwich.

Honour Boards. A fourteen year-old bugler, the same age as one of the boys lost all those years ago, accompanied the procession as the young students walked the boards back into the hall where they had hung for many years. The panels have not been displayed for many decades; the columns of gold leaf names now so faded as to be almost illegible. It was a poignant metaphor of lives now almost totally faded from memory.

In my experience, museum visitors rarely like being confronted by uncomfortable realities. Exhibitions about climate change, for example, do not attract large attendances. Museum exhibitions can explain and illustrate what happened, although the severe restrictions of exhibition text length greatly restrict the amount of detail that can be conveyed (put bluntly, today's museum visitors don't want to read books on walls). But museum curators and designers generally like aesthetically pleasing designs thus, in my experience, the sort of display that Jonathan Jones' demands is rarely attempted because, in truth, people generally won't engage with it.

So, I ask, are conventional object-based museum exhibitions the best way of conveying the awful reality of war? Similarly, are thematic, narrative museum exhibitions best able to reflect the loss and memories that flow from war? Indeed, is it ever appropriate for museums to seek to convey emotions as well as so-called 'facts', or is art a better medium for expressing these emotions and responses? It seems to me that the art installations, *Blood-Swept Lands and Seas of Red* and *War + Memory* engaged audiences viscerally in ways that rarely happen with more conventional museum exhibition techniques. Right or wrong, museums generally shy away from displaying emotion.

A notable exception to this is the subtheme 'Honouring the Dead – The Wall' in the Smithsonian Institution's National Museum of American History's permanent exhibition *The Price of Freedom: Americans at War* which displays objects and messages left at Washington's Vietnam Veterans Memorial over the years since it opened in 1982. I have chosen just three of over 90,000 pieces left before 2006. A note, left with a ring attached, simply asks:

> Uncle Sherman
>
> Please take care of Grandpa up there.
> I'm sorry I never knew you.
> Please keep an eye out for me.
>
> Love,
>
> Candy

A handwritten card left at the Wall in 1995 proudly declares:

> Manzelle A. ("Howdy") Ford 3/25/95
>
> Dear Howdy – YOU'RE A GRANDPA!
>
> IT'S A BOY!
>
> Your son, Eddie has a beautiful son of his own. Justin is his name. You would be proud of the fine father your son has become. You are missed.
>
> Love, John & Shari

One vet. left a six-pack of empty beer cans with the note:

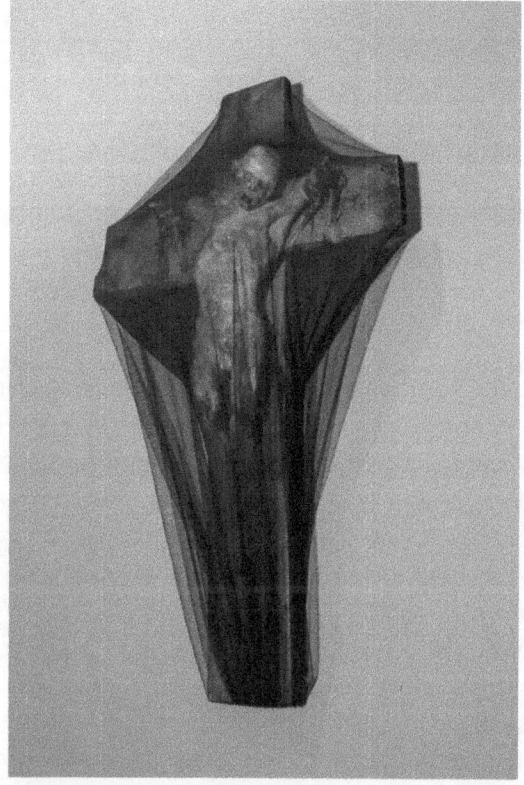

Fig. 10.4. Rozanne Hawksley's 1987 work, *Sir Galahad*, displayed at the Queen's House, Royal Museums Greenwich, 2014. Created in response to the sinking of HMS *Galahad* in the Falklands War, 1982. Photo: Royal Museums Greenwich.

Dear Michael

Here's some beer to go with the food and smokes (sorry, no Ba Muoi Ba is available in Raleigh).

Bernie Birenbaum's (3E52) got the smokes and Eddie Blumer's (29E38) got real food.

Love Jeff 8/5/94[14]

The objects and messages are intensely personal, the very antithesis of the ceramic poppies at The Tower, yet both manage to convey with equal power an overwhelming sense of loss and lives cut short. The Tower's ceramic

---

14 M. Sofarelli, *Letters on the Wall. Offerings and Remembrances from the Vietnam Veterans Memorial* (New York: Collins 2006), 8,66,111.

poppies, totally different to the Washington polished granite in so many ways, were nevertheless similar in that they managed to personalise the scale of loss, even though individuals were not identified. In his *New Yorker* article about the 9/11 Museum and Memorial, Adam Gopnik reflected on the success of Maya Lin's design for the Washington memorial:

> Understatement permitted individual statement; the roadside memorial met the war grave. An arena that sad gave permission to a thousand small cries. It was as if the pockets of the boys at Gettysburg had been turned inside out and their contents shown to the world.[15]

Aside from *War + Memory* the nearest that an exhibition has come to capturing this emotional power in any of the four museums I have had the privilege to lead was the touring exhibition, *Anne Frank: a history for today* staged in 2001 by the Powerhouse Museum, Sydney, in collaboration with Anne Frank House, Amsterdam. This photo-based exhibition had toured widely around the world, but we enlarged and augmented it by adding stories and objects drawn from Sydney's sizeable Holocaust survivor community (after World War Two Australia became home to the largest number of Holocaust survivors outside Israel). But what gave the Sydney show a unique immediacy was our decision to mark what would have been Anne's 72nd birthday by staging an uninterrupted, continuous public reading of the entire diary. We invited children, clergy, Holocaust survivors, diplomats, politicians and others to each read two pages from this remarkable testament. Much to our surprise, the Director of Anne Frank House told us that this was, to his knowledge, the first ever public reading of the complete diary. The 14-hour event was, I sensed, deeply moving for all 120 readers and the many others who sat through any part of the proceedings. The reading touched people personally, regardless of any Jewish links they may or may not have. Regretfully, the Australian War Memorial declined to be part of the exhibition's Australian tour as, their Director told me, it did not relate to Australia.

Jonathan Jones and his detractors agreed on one point: *Blood-Swept Lands and Seas of Red* was a work of artistic abstraction, not a literal history lesson. But I, like many others, would disagree with Jones' contention that this weakens the work's relevance or value. When all is said and done, what is the point of marking the centenary of the Great War? Undoubtedly, as Jones would contend, it is to improve people's understanding and awareness of a

---

15   Gopnik.

war that now – a hundred years later – directly means little if anything to the overwhelming majority of people or their immediate loved ones. Through exhibitions and public programmes, museums can play a leading role in educating people about such things.

I am less sure that conventional museum exhibitions can fulfil the other, equally important aspect of the Great War centenary; namely, honouring the past and the sacrifices of those who died. Museums are good at telling stories, but generally struggle to convey deeper emotions that lie beneath. Contemporary artists seem better able to connect with audiences at an emotional level, perhaps because they are more sensitive to the rhythms of their generation and their society. Through art installations such as *Blood-Swept Lands and Seas of Red* and *War + Memory*, audiences have been able to find points of personal connection and public reflection which, combined with more literal retellings (at least in Britain) are making the centenary of the Great War a powerful and uplifting community experience.

As human beings we rely in equal measure on both the head and the heart to gain a rounded understanding of things. As such, the museum exhibition and the artist's interpretation both have a place to play in giving people a rich understanding of complex stories and the emotions that go with them. Lest we forget.

Postscript

The above text created lively discussion when presented to a conference initiated by Monash University in collaboration with Çanakkale Onsekiz Mart (March 18) University in Turkey in May 2015. Dr Michael McKernan, an historian of the Great War and former Deputy Director of the Australian War Memorial, while agreeing with my central premise that museums are generally reluctant or unable to present stories in ways that elicit strong emotion, pointed me towards the exhibition *WW1: Love & sorrow*, currently showing at the Melbourne Museum in Australia. Part of the museum's Anzac Centenary 2014–2018 programme, this temporary exhibition has been extended through until 2018, so strong has been the public response. In reviewing the exhibition for the National Museum of Australia's magazine, *reCollections*, McKernan wrote:

> *Love & Sorrow* is in a class of its own. Working at the Australian War Memorial many years ago I became aware that the Memorial, from its inception, had deliberately, and perhaps properly, avoided much engagement with the emotions of the museum visitor. Many

war museums and interpretation centres, even in recent times, have gone down exactly the same path. *Love & Sorrow* entirely rejects this approach. This is an exhibition that openly and deliberately works on the emotions of its visitors to proclaim its strong and powerful message: war is an unmitigated and abhorrent disaster and we need always to be conscious of its enduring impacts across subsequent generations…

Put simply, [*Love & Sorrow*] is the most exquisite, moving, and intense exhibition on aspects of the First World War that I have seen anywhere in the world.[16]

Since returning from Çanakkale I have been in email communication with the exhibition's curator, Deborah Tout-Smith, who informs me that

In developing the exhibition we started with the view that after 100 years a more honest and complete story about the impacts of World War 1 could be told. That meant that we wanted to embrace some of the most difficult (and largely hidden) impacts of the war: facial wounds, psychiatric impacts, suicide, sexually-transmitted disease and the 'white plague' (TB). We also wanted to create a deeply personal, emotional story of the war, connecting more intimately with feelings and expressions of personal impact.

…the exhibition explores the real cost of World War 1 through eight real-life stories, illustrated with powerful, poignant objects, images and audio-visuals: a nurse, butcher, a coach-builder, an orchardist, a teenage telegraph messenger, Aboriginal brothers and German Jewish brothers. It includes graphic, confronting content about what the violence of war does to bodies and minds, and the long term effects that have stretched across 100 years. The exhibition ends with moving testimonies of descendants.[17]

The response to the exhibition, both from the public and in the media, has, in Tout-Smith's words been 'absolutely extraordinary… Our visitor comments section (hand-written cards in an area adjacent to the exhibition's exit) is overwhelmingly positive and sometimes breathtakingly personal and moving'.

Melbourne Museum has generously allowed me to see the exhibition's Summative Evaluation Report. Two thirds of visitors interviewed after

---

16   Michael McKernan, 'WWI: Love & Sorrow', *reCollections* 10, no. 1 (April 2015).
17   Personal email, D Tout-Smith to author, 3 June 2015.

going through *Love & Sorrow* had been unaware of the exhibition before they arrived at the museum, yet few seem to have been put off by its graphic content. When asked about what part they found most memorable, 21% thought it the objects on display, 21% the life stories told, 16% the facial reconstructions section and 13% the effects of war content. Thus, nearly 30% of interviewees were most struck by the graphic imagery and disturbing stories that museums have traditionally shied away from. One visitor responded to this question: 'Facial reconstruction exhibit and following the life of one of those soldiers. These were real people, not just photographs on a wall.'[18] McKernan's reaction to the exhibition experience had been not dissimilar:

> One of the intriguing things about *Love & Sorrow* is that the emotion arises, largely, from the interactives and video presentations, more than from the traditional museum objects and original letters.[19]

When shown a list of words to describe the exhibition experience, 75% of visitors highlighted 'moving', 75% 'thought provoking', and 56% 'distressing (but we need to hear these stories)'. Only 1% agreed with the statement 'distressing (because these stories should not be told)'.[20]

I will certainly try to see *WW1: Love & Sorrow* when next I return to Australia. Melbourne Museum is a large, multi-themed general museum attracting broad audiences, especially school groups and families. Given its audience profile, one admires all the more the museum's courage in developing this moving, confronting exhibition. It seems their courage has been richly rewarded. The strong attendances and reaffirming visitor responses the exhibition has received suggest enough time has passed that people are now interested and able enough to confront the realities and terrible legacies of this catastrophic event through imaginative museum exhibition approaches.

In the concluding paragraphs of my paper in Çanakkale I questioned if conventional museum exhibitions can truly engage visitors emotionally with subjects like war. It seems that *Love & Sorrow*, like *Honouring the Dead – The Wall* at the Smithsonian Institution, demonstrates that this challenge can be met in ways that engage both the head and the heart. I look forward to others having the imagination, courage and confidence to follow their example.

---

18 WW1: Love & Sorrow Summative Evaluation Report, Museum of Victoria, February 2015
19 McKernan.
20 WWI: Love & Sorrow Report.

Chapter 11

BROTHERS IN ARMS

Gordon and Robin Harper and the Anatomy of Bravery

Jock Phillips

Fig. 11.1 Gordon and Robin Harper in the Sinai desert 1916. Harper collection.[1]

---

1 All photos and objects illustrated are from the private collection of the Harper family.

This is the story of two brothers, Gordon and Robin Harper, who joined up with the Canterbury Mounted Rifles in August 1914. They fought side-by-side at Gallipoli and in the Sinai Desert where the older brother, Gordon, was fatally injured in August 1916. The two were not nation-wide heroes. But they were unusually brave soldiers. This paper seeks to explain that bravery.

Normally historians start with an intellectual problem and then look round for evidence to test it. This story did not begin that way, but through the accident of my marriage. I first became interested in the Great War in the 1980s while exploring the nature of the New Zealand male stereotype. To illustrate the power and costs of the stereotype, I read soldiers' letters and diaries. I gravitated to those who had had been victims of the war mythology – soldiers who had become disillusioned, those who were malingerers, or conscientious objectors. I was interested in war heroes only in terms of their mythology. Yet the Harper Brothers were in many respects Boys Own heroes. Their story was not well-known, but they believed in the military traditions of the British Empire and achieved actions on the battlefield that their peers applauded. So when I read their letters in the 1980s I gave them less attention than perhaps they deserved.

Then I married into the family and discovered that my brother-in-law had been conscientiously collecting material about the brothers in the Great War. He asked me to produce a family publication. Initially, prejudices intact, I resisted. But not for long. I took another look at the letters, mostly written by Gordon to his mother. I was struck by the quality of the writing – rich descriptions, powerful sentiments. Gordon took the epistolary task seriously. His major complaint was shortage of paper and on one occasion at Gallipoli he wrote to his mother immediately because he had found some paper in a raid on a Turkish trench. He composed two different accounts on Gallipoli – one written immediately which passed through the military censor; and a second long diary/letter which he wrote up periodically and sent once he was away from the front to avoid censorship. Then there were the photographs – four albums and a number of loose ones which had been kept in a bottom drawer. Some were taken by the younger brother Robin – we have a photograph of Robin with his Kodak camera on the beach at Gallipoli. The photos were put together in albums, at least one by their mother because they are captioned in her writing, and a second by Robin. In my experience it is unusual to find photographs which showed the people and incidents described in accompanying letters. What clinched my interest was when I crawled into the family attic to look at the objects there. They included two guns – a Maxim machine gun originally used by a territorial unit, the Canterbury Yeomanry Cavalry (CYC), taken to Egypt and used by Gordon throughout his war; and a German-made machine gun captured from the Turks. There was a photo of it back in the New Zealanders' trench an hour later. Loaned to the Canterbury Museum, the gun was returned to the family as of no interest in the 1950s. There were other remarkable objects – Robin's prayerbook with the path of a bullet which had been in his breast pocket presumably saving his life; an artillery marking flag from Gallipoli; the last orders issued to Robin as one of the final 'C' party at the evacuation from Gallipoli; Gordon's bivvy bag from his time in the desert. For a historian these sources were simply too rich to resist. I agreed to put together a book combining the letters, photographs and objects and tell the story of Gordon and Robin at Gallipoli and the Sinai Desert.

Fig. 11.2: Robin Harper with camera at Anzac Cove, Gallipoli.

As I began to know the brothers well, especially Gordon, I became intrigued, and a bit horrified, by their bravery. What had made them unusually courageous? This paper provides my answer. I describe their background and war, and then explore various explanations.

Gordon and Robin Harper were the two youngest of seven boys, who with one girl were the children of George and Agnes Harper. George was a lawyer in Christchurch and his father was the first Anglican Bishop of Christchurch. Agnes, however, was a devout Roman Catholic and the boys were brought up as Catholics. George's law firm failed spectacularly in the early 1890s, and as a result the two younger boys were sent, not to the elite Anglican school of Christ's College, but to the state secondary school, Christchurch Boys High. The red-haired Gordon was obviously a character. One of his teachers, O.T.J. Alpers, later a prominent judge, wrote in the school magazine in 1917:

> The 'gay Gordon', with his close-cropped ginger hair, his firm set jaw, the twinkle of humour in the eye that never left him, – his was the individuality that impressed me most strongly of all the boys I ever taught. I suppose it was partly because he was a rebel. On the morning after he left school he walked up and down Worcester Street in front of the windows of the Masters' room for a full hour – puffing at a huge pipe to show his independence; that was characteristic of him.[2]

Gordon, despite his rebellious streak, was a monitor (prefect), captain of cadets, and editor of the school magazine. His younger brother Robin spent his last four school years at Christ's College.

On leaving school Gordon drifted. Failing to qualify as a dentist, he became a cowboy in Canada and finally joined Robin to go farming in north Canterbury.[3] When New Zealand found itself at war on 5 August 1914, the two boys took little time to offer their services. In less than three weeks they had sold the farm and come into Christchurch to enlist. Already members of the volunteer unit, the CYC, and with experience riding horses, they joined the Canterbury Mounted Rifles as machine gunners. In October they sailed with the Main Body of the New Zealand Expeditionary Force and set up camp at Zeitoun near Cairo. They did what most Anzac soldiers did – trained in the desert, visited the pyramids, enjoyed time off in Cairo.

---

2   Reprinted in O.T.J. Alpers, *Cheerful Yesterdays* (Auckland: Whitcombe and Tombs, 1930), 80-82.

3   ed. Jock Phillips with Philip Harper and Susan Harper, *Brothers in Arms – Gordon and Robin Harper in the Great War* (Wellington: NZHistoryJock, 2015), 14-23.

When the infantry left for the Gallipoli Peninsula in April, the Mounteds were left behind – the peninsula's steep slopes were no place for men with horses. But as casualties increased, they were summoned and landed on the peninsula on 12 May, 1915.

Three incidents highlight the brothers' considerable bravery. The first was the offensive of early August 1915. The Canterbury Mounteds' task was to clear the foothills. At 9.30 pm on 5 August they stepped out of their trenches to be met by rifles and machine guns, but, writes Gordon, 'the line never wavered'. They climbed up the open hillside leapt the parapets and, in his words, 'the silent swish of the bayonet did its work.'[4] The Mounteds had won the foothills, 'a magnificent feat of arms, the brilliance of which was never surpassed, if indeed equalled during the campaign' was Charles Bean's judgement.[5] In the accounts of the action the Harper Brothers are not singled out. They carry out the task which their fellow members of the Mounteds had also been asked to do.

But in two other actions, their particular achievement is noted in the accounts. One came two weeks later. The August offensive had failed – the heights of Chunuk Bair were held for 36 hours but then abandoned. Yet Sir Ian Hamilton had not given up. He wanted to strengthen his position for possible future attacks by capturing Hill 60, a small knoll north of the foothills. Hamilton believed it might improve the boundary between Anzac Cove and Suvla Bay where British troops had landed. Most subsequent observers have considered it a pointless exercise. It was territory which had been captured in the earlier offensive and then abandoned; and was unlikely to provide much gain.

Despite their exhaustion and injuries, Andrew Russell's mounted regiments were asked to capture Hill 60 on a hot Saturday, 21 August. The artillery fire, significantly curtailed, did little damage but warned the Turks of an impending attack. The Canterbury and Otago Mounted Rifles had to cross 700 metres and two minor ridges to reach the Turkish trenches in broad daylight without covering fire. The men were weakened by dysentery and fatigue, but they kept going forward – in Fred Waite's words 'a triumph of resolute minds over wasted bodies.'[6] The survivors raced downhill and then

---

4   Gordon Harper, diary letter to Mother, May-August 1915 reprinted in ed. Phillips, *Brothers*, 82-83.
5   Quoted in ed. C.G. Powles, *The History of the Canterbury Mounted Rifles 1914-1919* (Auckland: Whitcombe and Tombs, 1928), 49.
6   Fred Waite, *The New Zealanders at Gallipoli* (Christchurch: Whitcombe and Tombs, 1919) 252. For Hill 60 see also Terry Kinloch, *Echoes of Gallipoli in the words of New*

climbed up the slopes of Hill 60 to reach the forward trenches. They leapt into them, bayonetting the defenders and throwing grenades. Gordon and Robin captured a machine gun and immediately used it on the Turks. Eventually the Canterbury and Otago rifles were able to hold about 100 metres of Turkish trench, but it was well below the summit. The next morning there were under 20 Canterbury men in the trenches. One veteran, D. Templar, remembered: 'Luckily we had Robin Harper there with a machine gun'. An 'elderly Otago Major' gave orders that when the Turks counter-attacked, fire was to be held until he gave orders. 'However', the veteran continued, 'at last Robin Harper let fly with his machine gun. Then we all let fly and those we didn't hit vanished in the dark. The first one that Robin bowled over was so close that the blast of the machine gun set his clothes on fire.'[7] With the help of Australian reinforcements the Mounteds held on until the evening of the 23rd August.

The two South Island regiments had gone into the battle with 400 men; they left with only 191 unwounded. Among those wounded was Gordon Harper, hit in the neck. Robin carried him out of the trenches, and down to the beach. He boarded the *RMS Franconia* and sailed for England to recover.

As for Hill 60, General Birdwood was determined to claim it; so on 27 August 150 men of the Canterbury and Auckland Mounteds, Robin among them, were ordered to jump out of their trenches and advance uphill in broad daylight towards the Turkish trenches above. Three times they captured a line of trenches, wrestled with the Turks there and then advanced once more to the next line. Casualties were high, and the survivors totally exhausted. By the time the operation was called off on August 29 with the highpoint still uncaptured, the Canterbury Mounted Rifles had only 18 fit men left, from the 119 who had set off on the 27th. Robin was one of the injured.

Hill 60 was the tragic climax of Gallipoli for the Mounteds and the Harper brothers. It showed extraordinary bravery on their part, despite the exhaustion and pointless nature of the exercise. Their efforts were clearly recognised as worthy of note. Both were awarded a DCM (Distinguished Conduct Medal) for their efforts and mentioned in despatches, and on 21 October 1915 both became commissioned officers as Second Lieutenants.

Zealand's Mounted Riflemen (Auckland: Exisle Publishing, 2005), 237-251; ed. Powles, *Canterbury Mounted*, 55-66; Christopher Pugsley, *Gallipoli: the New Zealand Story* (Auckland: Hodder and Stoughton, 1984), 301-320.

7   Quoted in Pugsley, 319.

Fig. 11.3: Robin Harper injured and awaiting evacuation from Gallipoli, late August 1915.

The third incident, this time in the Sinai Desert, came a year later. After being injured at Gallipoli Gordon spent almost four months recovering in England and Wales; Robin recovered from his injuries in Malta and returned to Gallipoli where he was chosen to be one of the 'C' party, the last group to depart Gallipoli on the early morning 20 December 1915. The brothers were then reunited in Cairo with each other and their horses in January 1916. Gordon was serving under Robin who was now commanding the machine gunners in the Canterbury Mounted Rifles. Their job was to defend the canal from the Ottomans. In May the Mounteds went eastwards to Romani in the Sinai desert.[8] The heat was extreme – regularly over 40°C –, the water brackenish, and eating was, as Guy Powles said, 'one long fight between hungry men and hungry flies'.[9] Gordon wrote 'I have not the same 'internals' that I started with'.[10] On 4 August the Ottomans attempted to capture Romani, and although they took two high points, the Mounteds responded. The next day the Mounteds attempted to capture Katia and two days later unsuccessfully attacked Oghratina. The Turks withdrew to Bir el Abd. So on 9 August, for the fourth time in six days, the Canterbury Mounteds were in action, this time attempting to defeat the Turks at Bir

---

8   See ed. Phillips, *Brothers*, 94-126 and Terry Kinloch, *Devils on Horses in the words of the Anzacs in the Middle East 1916-1919* (Auckland: Exisle Publishing, 2007).

9   C. Guy Powles, *The New Zealanders in Sinai and Palestine* (Auckland: Whitcombe and Tombs, 1922), 15.

10 Gordon Harper to mother, 19 June 1916, in ed. Phillips, *Brothers*, 155.

el Abd. They set off at 5.30am and advanced before the Turks counter-attacked. The temperature was reportedly 38°C. Eventually, at 5.30pm, the order was given to withdraw. It was a perilous operation. The men held on until night began to fall, and then withdrew section by section, with the Canterbury Rifles in the rear-guard. They had lost the help of supporting troops on both flanks, so the machine gunners kept up a fierce protective fire to allow the squadron to withdraw. Robin wrote later, 'The accepted practice in a withdrawal is for the squadron to cover the machine guns as they came out of action, but Gordon who was never orthodox, kept his guns firing at point blank range – thereby saving the lives of many of the squadron.'[11] According to J.H. Luxford's history of the machine gunners, 'The bold decision of 2nd Lieut. Harper to hold his dangerous position in order to cover the Canterbury Regiment's withdrawal, with the slight chance of successfully fighting his guns back to safety, was an outstanding example of self-sacrifice.'[12] Then the machine gunners withdrew a pair at a time. As they did so, they became obvious targets. At some point Gordon was hit, either by a bullet or by the intense Turkish artillery shellfire. Robin, who was commanding the machine guns, rode a mile under fire to rescue him. Gordon made it back to a hospital in Cairo, but died three days later, on 12 August 1916.[13]

Fig. 11.4: Spent bullets from Gordon's last position in the Sinai Desert 9 August 1916

---

11   Robin Harper, undated notes in family's possession.
12   Major J.H. Luxford, *With the Machine Gunners in France and Palestine* (Auckland: Whitcombe and Tombs, 1923), 185.
13   ed. Phillips, *Brothers*, 160-162; Robin Harper to mother and father, August 1916, in Phillips, *Brothers*, 163-167.

Robin stayed on with the Mounteds in the advance across the Sinai and into Palestine before he too was wounded in November 1917 – this time a sergeant rescued him and carried him across a river to safety. He returned to New Zealand in 1918.

So there is no question about the extraordinary bravery of both brothers. Three times, in the August 1915 offensive at Gallipoli, in the attacks on Hill 60 and at Bir el Abd a year later, the two brothers showed a denial of fear, which to someone brought up in a relatively benign world appears incomprehensible. How do we explain their actions? We recognise of course that many soldiers at that time displayed considerable bravery. But the two brothers were seen as exceptionally courageous. What made them different?

There has been much investigation of the reasons for men's abilities in war, especially the First World War – a considerable body of writings about how men endured the horrific conditions of the Western Front; and some writings about how to explain courage on the battlefield. Explaining endurance and explaining unusual courage are slightly different problems, but they both throw up interesting theories. Let's test some of these ideas to try and isolate the factors behind the Harper brothers' bravery.

There is general agreement that belief in a larger cause strengthens men's commitment on the battlefield.[14] In the Harpers' case, at least initially, they were strong believers in the values and traditions of the British Empire. In 1900 New Zealand was overwhelmingly settled by people of English or Scottish background, and the proportion of Irish Catholic origin was comparatively low (about 14%[15]). Christchurch was deservedly known as the most English and Anglican part of the country. In school, pupils in the years before the war had a steady diet of British history and were well-schooled in the heroic military traditions of the British Empire.[16] What strengthened this broad cultural environment were the Harpers' strong family links with the old country. On their father's side their grandfather had been the first Anglican Bishop of Christchurch; and three of his sons, the boys' uncles, were living in England at the time of the war. Gordon visited them while recovering there in late 1915. On the mother's side her father had been a

---

14   e.g. S.D. Wesbrook, 'The potential for 'military disintegration'' in *Combat effectiveness: Cohesion, Stress and the Volunteer Military*, ed. S. Sarkesian (Beverly Hills: Sage Publications, 1980), 244-278.

15   Rory Sweetman. 'Catholic Church – The Catholic Church in the 2000s', Te Ara – the Encyclopedia of New Zealand, updated 16-Dec-14 URL: http://www.TeAra.govt.nz/en/interactive/29307/number-of-catholics-in-new-zealand.

16   E.P. Malone, 'The New Zealand School Journal and the Imperial Ideology,' *New Zealand Journal of History*, vol. 7 (April, 1973): 12-27.

judge with the East India Company and after spending time in Canterbury the judge had returned to London. In 1915 Gordon visited his widow who was living in Kensington in her 90s, and stayed with two of her daughters, Gordon's aunts. Gordon had been named after General Gordon, the hero of the seige of Khartoum who was killed the very year (1885) that Gordon was born. The boys' uncle on their mother's side, Robert Loughnan, had written an enthusiastic account of the visit of the Duke and Duchess of Cornwall to New Zealand in 1901. Gordon had been a member of the school cadets when the Duke, son of the Queen, had inspected them.[17] There can be no doubt of the boys' commitment to the British Empire. Evidence for this became apparent once news of the war's outbreak arrived. Gordon with his old teacher O.T.J. Alpers immediately organised a patriotic meeting in the aptly-named Victoria Square, Christchurch. The meeting featured waving Union Jacks and speeches by both Gordon and Alpers. Gordon was by this time a parliamentary candidate for the conservative party, Reform – a position he quickly resigned in order to enlist.

So initially the two boys, and Gordon especially, were staunch upholders of imperial values. As with so many New Zealand soldiers the war experience raised questions. Gordon had no doubt that it was right 'that Germany's influence in the East should be properly rooted out' and to settle 'who is going to be boss in the East'.[18] But he did start to wonder whether 'Belgium has been overdone'.[19]

Once he reached England to recover from his wound, Gordon was glad to be 'home'; but he raised questions. He described as 'unedifying' the contrast between the mass of the population turning out shells and filling the trenches with men while the politicians blundered and failed to deal with situations. He criticised the censorship and secrecy in the country and felt that Britons tended to 'muddle through' crises. Such responses did not lead to a major questioning of the war's aims. Indeed part of his anger was the legal protection offered to German companies. He fulminated at 'this tenderness towards the enemy' and was amazed that the House of Commons included men of German birth, 'naturalized of course, but how much is a German ever naturalized'.[20] When he returned to fight in the Sinai desert Gordon expressed disillusionment with some of the English forces. He

---

17 See ed. Phillips, *Brothers*, 28-29
18 Gordon Harper to mother, 29 April, 1915 in ed. Phillips, *Brothers*, 52.
19 ed. Phillips, *Brothers*, 54.
20 ed. Phillips, *Brothers*, 104.

reports coming across the bodies of some English yeomanry 'who were living like lords and paying more attention to golf and luxurious camps than their duty'. He concludes, 'The whole way things are run are scandalous.'[21] He even decides that Johnny Turk 'fights square too, which can hardly be said of some of the forces which have been sent against him. I am afraid the old name which Britain had in the past will not be so strong after this. We have descended to telling lies and found the Mohammedan sticking to the truth.'[22] In other words while Gordon was brought up with an exceptionally strong belief in the values and honour of the British Empire this came under some question by 1916. His belief in the cause helped carry him through Gallipoli but does not explain his bravery at Bir el Abd in August 1916.

The second common explanation for endurance and bravery in war is the support of 'the primary group' – the group of friends with whom the soldier fought and before whom he dare not show cowardice. S.L.A. Marshall wrote, it was a man's fear of losing 'what he holds more dear than life itself, his reputation as a man among other men'.[23] This was undoubtedly a strong influence in the case of the Harper brothers. The Canterbury Mounted Rifles had grown out of the territorial force, the CYC; and many members would have been known to the brothers from their shared territorial service. Even if they had not been in the territorials the Mounteds required men to be good horsemen and provide their own horses. So they were likely to be Canterbury farmers, whom the Harpers would have met in rural society. Gordon's letters home to his mother frequently refer to fellow soldiers killed who were known even to his parents: 'I hope you will have seen Jack Petre's parents as he was a great friend of mine. He died most bravely in a bayonet charge'.[24] The most intense circle of friends was those with whom Gordon had gone to school, of whom Jack Petre was one. When the Main Body got to Cairo they brought together the old boys of Christchurch Boys High School and had them photographed to show their collective commitment to the British Empire.

---

21 Gordon Harper to mother, 1 May 1916 in ed. Phillips, *Brothers*, 146.
22 Gordon Harper to Leonard Tripp, 14 June 1916 in ed. Phillips, *Brothers*, 153.
23 Quoted in John Keegan and Richard Holmes, *Soldiers: a history of men in battle* (London: H. Hamilton, 1985), 18. See also Alexander Watson, *Enduring the Great War: Combat Morale and Collapse in the German and British Armies, 1914-1918* (Cambridge: Cambridge University Press, 2008); and his chapter on 'Morale' in *Cambridge History of the First World War, vol II*, ed. Jay Winter (Cambridge: Cambridge University Press: 2014), 174-196; J. Glenn Gray, *The Warriors: reflections on men in battle* (New York: Harcourt, Brace and Company, 1959).
24 Gordon Harper to mother, 23 May 1915 in ed. Phillips, *Brothers*, 67.

Fig. 11.5: Stephen Archer and Gordon Harper at No. 1 outpost

Within two weeks of his landing at Gallipoli Gordon wrote back, 'It was rather sad meeting only two out of a batch of 14 of our Old School boys who were left. They all seemed a bit down about the whole business but they have made a name for themselves.'[25] While on Gallipoli Gordon wrote to Annie Bevan-Brown, the wife of the school headmaster, describing what had happened to every old boy. He then discovered that the letter had gone down in a lighter, so after receiving a gift from her at Christmas 1915 including a piece of school ribbon which he pinned to his tent door, he wrote once again with details of their deaths. Once more he lists those of his 'band of 14 mates' who were killed. He concludes, 'I can only say that the great bond of sentiment which unites us all in times of peace has proved itself by the times we have been through, to be a never failing source of help when help is most needed'.[26] There were two particular mates who had not gone to the Boys High School but to Christ's College where they developed close friendships with Robin. One was Tony Hanmer, the boys' cousin whom they had known all their lives, and the second was Stephen Archer. The two were in the machine gun section of the Canterbury Mounteds and in the earliest photograph of that section were positioned each side of Robin. They frequently appeared in the snaps sent back – one showed Robin and

---

25 ed., Phillips, *Brothers*, 67.
26 Gordon Harper to Mrs Bevan-Brown, 1 March, 1916 in ed. Phillips, *Brothers*, 136-138.

Fig. 11.6: Tony Hanmer firing the Maxim machine gun with Gordon Harper as observer. The gun is now in the family's possession.

Stephen playing affectionate fisticuffs. At Gallipoli the two men worked extraordinarily closely with Gordon. Stephen shared a dug-out at No 1 outpost in June with him and when he died Gordon had photographs taken (or took them himself) of Stephen's grave and headstone.

Tony Hanmer was the No. 1 gunner for the machine gun operated by Gordon and there is a famous photo of Tony firing the gun during the attack on Chunuk Bair in early August, one hour before he was killed. Gordon is standing beside him as the observer. There can be no question that the support of these mates was extraordinarily important, as Gordon himself acknowledged.

Yet of the 14 school mates, every single one, except Gordon himself, lost their lives at Gallipoli. So too did the special mates, Tony Hanmer and Stephen Archer. When Gordon returned to the Mounteds in January 1916 he discovered 'only a sprinkling of the old faces is left but it … just makes life bearable after so many have gone'.[27] Even they did not last. By March he was moaning that many of his wounded mates had been transferred to the infantry or artillery and sent to Europe. They had lost many men this way, taken 'much against their will' – 'Sorry one feels leaving the mates he has

---

27   Gordon Harper to mother, 17 January 1916, in ed. Phillips, *Brothers*, 127.

fought with for so long'.²⁸ By the time of the Sinai battles Gordon and Robin had few old mates left; so this cannot be a full explanation for their bravery in those battles. To be fair new relationships were built up, and indeed when Gordon died another Old Boy wrote back to the school magazine, 'The men of his own gun-section wept like children when they heard the bad news'.²⁹

The writer goes on, 'I feel very much for Robin Harper. The two brothers meant so much to each other'. This is getting to the heart of it. Important as were the relationships with former school friends, old acquaintances from the CYC, and mates with whom the brothers had shared the torment of battle, what really explains the brothers' unusual bravery is their relationship with each other and their wider circle of brothers. As already noted there were seven Harper boys, with Gordon and Robin the two youngest. They grew up among a sea of brothers. They apparently had a reputation around Christchurch as 'those Harper boys' known for carrying out pranks, including on one occasion getting a train to stop by faking a murder on the railway tracks.³⁰

Once war broke out the brothers' relationships became hugely important. Gordon and Robin, who had farmed together, joined up together on the same day and in the same force. They both became machine gunners in the Mounteds. There was also an older brother Philip in the Army Service Corps. He too travelled with the Main Body, and Gordon and Robin made every effort to see him in Cairo. The brothers agreed that each would carry a whistle, presumably a dog whistle from their days on their Canterbury farm, and if they ever needed help from the others they would whistle. Twice this worked – once when they first landed at Anzac Cove, they whistled and the older brother, Philip, came running. Once when Gordon had been injured and he whistled to summon Robin so they could have a final confession together.³¹ Barely a letter goes by when Gordon does not talk about Robin. They fought together in those fierce actions in early August 1915 and then in the attack on Hill 60. When he was injured Gordon's first concern was that Robin was still in the firing line – 'What worried me more than the pain is having to leave Robin behind still in a very dangerous place... But I

---

28 Gordon Harper to mother, 17 March 1916, in ed. Phillips, *Brothers*, 139.
29 *Boys High School Magazine*, 1917.
30 Dola Derham, oral history with Philip Harper, 1991; Katrine Brown, oral history with Philip Harper, 1991.
31 Gordon Harper to mother, 15 May 1915, 23 August 1915, in ed. Phillips, *Brothers*, 64, 93.

am going to hurry back as soon as possible if Robin is still there'.[32] Brotherly love once again came to the fore in the third action at Bir el Abd in the Sinai Desert in August 1916. When Gordon was hit, Robin was about a mile away. He heard the news, galloped across the sand exposed to heavy fire, put Gordon across his horse and carried him to a safe shaded place. After Gordon's death, Robin wrote to his parents, 'You can understand my feelings during this last awful week which has been much worse than the same week of last August when Tony [Hanmer] and many were killed and Gordon wounded.... Gordon has always been more than a brother, if that is possible, especially during the last two years when we have fought side by side all the time'.[33]

This was not the end of the brotherly feelings. Eric, the third brother, had been medically examined for military service in July 1916 but rejected for varicose veins. When he heard of Gordon's death, he decided that he needed to replace him. He had an operation for the veins and despite being 37, married and having a child and a second on the way, he volunteered again and was accepted. He did indeed replace Gordon joining the brother's old unit, the Canterbury Mounteds in Palestine. There while quietening horses one night he was blown up by a shell in the Jordan Valley. Nor was this all. When in September 1939 the radio news announced that the empire was once again at war with Germany, the family recalls that Robin stood up, tightened his belt and said, 'I'm off. They got Gordon and I'd like another go at them'.[34] He was 52. There can be no doubt that the relationship of brother to brother was a strong bond which goes a long way to explain their courage in the heat of battle.

One aspect of the brothers' relationship leads to yet another possible explanation which also appears in the historiography – the effect of culture.[35] The brothers formed for the two youngest an initiation into male culture – pranks and humour, but far more importantly sports and war. At the turn of the century a powerful set of expectations about the central place of male culture emerged in New Zealand. The outbreak of the South African War led observers, especially premier Richard Seddon, to trumpet about the superior ability of New Zealand soldiers, who, because they were allegedly brought up on farms and the outdoor life, were said to perform better than

---

32   Gordon Harper to mother, 23 August 1915, in ed. Phillips, *Brothers*, 92.
33   Robin Harper to mother and father, August 1916, in ed. Phillips, *Brothers*, 163.
34   ed. Phillips, *Brothers*, 172, 174.
35   e.g. Michael C.C. Adams, *The Great Adventure: Male Desire and the Coming of World War 1* (Bloomington: Indiana University Press, 1990).

the urban-bred English. Then in 1905/6 the New Zealand All Black rugby team toured England and Wales achieving astounding results. This came soon after the British had set up a special committee to investigate the physical deterioration of the race as shown by the poor quality of recruits to the South African War.[36] Observers in Britain saw the All Blacks as evidence that although weedy urban Englishmen were imperilling the long-term strength of the British Empire, New Zealand could offer strong men able to perform as well on the battlefield as on the rugby pitch. New Zealanders accepted that rugby was an important training ground for war – Tom Ellison the inventor of the All Black uniform described it as a 'The good, manly and soldier-making game'.[37] So through rugby and the boys' performance in South Africa, New Zealand conceived a special national role as providers of strong men, territorials of the empire. This expectation was well expressed in mainstream media and institutionalised in the secondary school system. It was imposed with particular strength on the younger Harper boys because of the example of their brothers. The Harpers were known as good sportsmen. The third brother, Eric, represented Canterbury at athletics, cricket and rugby and had indeed been a member of the famous 1905/6 All Black rugby team. The fourth brother Cuthbert played rugby for Canterbury.

The influence of the brothers was intensified at school where Gordon played in the 1st XV rugby team and captained the 2nd XI cricket team; while Robin reached the Christ's College 1st XV. The brothers also provided a model as imperial warriors. Three of them served in the South African War; while the father had been active in the volunteer movement captaining the Christ's College Rifles. It was not surprising that when he reached high school Gordon immediately displayed his interest in things military. School cadets at this stage was voluntary, but in his first year Gordon volunteered to be the bugler in the cadet force. He was active for the next seven years, eventually becoming captain of the force. He was usually in charge of one side in their regular sham fights in the environs around Christchurch, such as 'the second battle of Waimakiriri'.[38] Yet the brothers' military tradition was not unsullied. While serving in South Africa, Edmund, the second

---

36   John Springhall, *Youth, Empire and Society* (London: Artchon Books, 1977) 53-64; Jock Phillips, *A Man's Country: The image of the Pakeha male – a history* (Auckland: Penguin Books, 1987), 152-153.

37   Thomas Ellison, *The Art of Rugby Football* (Wellington: Geddis and Blomfield, 1902), 80.

38   ed. Phillips, *Brothers*, 21, 28.

brother, had caught syphilis; and during the time the boys were at Gallipoli and Sinai, Edmund was suffering the later stages of the disease and died in 1918. Gordon constantly asked his mother about Edmund's progress. One can but speculate about the impact of this, but arguably it might have reinforced the intense desire to serve honourably in case the family name and brothers' reputation be further sullied. What is clear is that New Zealand male expectations reinforced by the brother's example helps explain the younger boys' bravery at Gallipoli and the Sinai.

Another factor that is often cited as providing the basis for both soldier's endurance and courage in battle is defence of the family.[39] Men fought because they wished to defend the family home. It is hard to accept this for New Zealand soldiers whose homes were half a globe away and which they did not see again once they had left for war. Yet in the case of the Harper brothers there is no doubt that family relationships are important, leaving aside those with their brothers. Gordon writes almost exclusively to his mother, not his father, and it is obvious that the two had an intense and loving relationship. There are two aspects of the family that may be important here. One is that the family had suffered a notorious scandal in the 1890s. The boys' father, George, was a lawyer and he joined forces in a law firm with his older brother Leonard. Leonard ran an investment operation attracting large sums from overseas investors and the local landed elite for investment in mortgages at a promised high rate of return. But New Zealand suffered an acute depression in the late 1880s and Leonard was only able to pay the interest by taking in more funds. Eventually the deck of cards collapsed, the law firm was declared bankrupt, Leonard and George were disbarred, and Leonard was brought back from England to face charges of embezzlement. Leonard was acquitted but the 'Harper crash' as it was known hurt many people locally and was widely remembered in Canterbury society.[40] It is at least possible that the Harper brothers saw their performance in war as a way of re-establishing the family name.

The second aspect of the family story is that although the boy's father, George, was the son of the Anglican Bishop, their mother, Agnes, was a devout Roman Catholic. This was not only a cause of discussion among respectable Christchurch Anglicans but created some family dissension. When Edmund was born, Agnes insisted on baptising him into the Catholic

---

39 See Watson, 76-84.

40 ed. Robin Cooke, *Portrait of a Profession: The centennial book of the New Zealand Law Society* (Wellington: Reed, 1969), 259-262; Geoffrey W. Rice, *Christchurch crimes and scandals, 1876-99* (Christchurch: Christchurch University Press, 2013), 193-211.

faith; but George with the Bishop's support then scurried him off to be received into the Anglican Church.[41] In the end Agnes' faith won, for all the boys were brought up as devout Roman Catholics and are buried with her in the Catholic plot of the Barbadoes St cemetery, across the road from their father who is beside the Anglican bishop. Catholicism was clearly important to Gordon and Robin. Barely a letter to their mother does not include some mention of attending mass. On Gallipoli Father Dore regularly held prayers every Sunday amid 'the continuous roar of shells and cracking of rifles'.[42] On one Sunday 25 July 1915 Gordon wrote to his mother:

> Father Dore said Mass on a bomb proof altar and we knelt in the open and strange to say not a single shell burst near us, only a few stray bullets whistling over us. We went to Communion (everyone who is there does) and sang hymns. Some of the Maoris were there too and sang with great vigour and said their prayers aloud in Maori, while a little way off some pious Indians, Mohammedans, were flattening themselves out towards the sun and invoking the same 'Allah' as the Turks. Altogether it was a strange setting for Mass and it had a distinct spirit of its own pervading it throughout, as it always does when everyone is on the edge of things. You need have no fear of our needs in this direction, being well looked after.[43]

There is no doubt that religious faith provided comfort and reassurance. One Sunday Gordon wrote to his mother, 'We all realise what we are going through by whatever fate may be selected for us it must be a most happy and most glorious one'.[44] And when Gordon died Robin wrote home, 'Dearest Mother and Father, it is the will of God and we are only suffering what thousands of others are doing every day in this terrible war. Only we have far more consolation than many of them'.[45] Obviously for many soldiers religion provided no consolation; it was merely seen as time-wasting propaganda. But for the Harpers, brought up in a deep religious faith by their mother, it provided comfort and a reassurance that death was no defeat. While Niall Ferguson has argued that many soldiers held on to an optimistic belief that

---

41   Richard L.N. Greenaway, *Barbadoes Street Cemetery Tour* (Christchurch: Barbadoes Street Cemetery, 2007), 15.
42   Gordon Harper to mother, 23 May 1915 in ed. Phillips, *Brothers*, 67.
43   Gordon Harper to mother, 25 July 1915 in ed. Phillips, *Brothers*, 80.
44   Gordon Harper to mother, 13 June 1915 in ed. Phillips, *Brothers*, 73.
45   Robin Harper to mother and father, August 1916, in ed. Phillips, *Brothers*, 163.

they would escape death, this was not the case for Gordon.[46] He repeatedly implies that he is fully expecting death, but has little fear of it because his religious faith promised eternal life.

Fig. 11.7: Mass in the Sinai Desert

There are several other factors which have been suggested by historians to explain the endurance of other soldiers in the Great War but which clearly do not apply in this case – the idea that British infantry were able to survive the trenches of the western front because that experience replicated the boredom and discomfort of industrial work.[47] But the Harpers were self-employed farmers and to the extent that their prior occupational life helped, their experience riding horses and shooting animals on farms is probably of more pertinence. Similarly the argument put forward persuasively by J.G. Fuller that working class leisure activities such as football and music hall entertainments greatly helped in building morale is convincing with respect to British infantry on the Western front, but has little relevance here.[48] There is no mention of such pursuits in the Harper letters and although there

---

46   Niall Ferguson, *The Pity of War* (New York: Basic Books, 1999), 357-366.

47   John Bourne, 'The British Working Man in arms' in *Facing Armageddon: the First World War Experienced*, ed. Hugh Cecil and Peter Liddle (London: Cooper, 1996), 336-352.

48   J.G. Fuller, *Troop Morale and Popular Culture in the British and Dominion Armies 1914-1918* (Oxford: Clarendon, 1990).

are some photos of sports at Zeitoun, there clearly was no opportunity for such activities at Gallipoli or even the Sinai desert.

Yet some of the factors that have been used to explain the endurance of other soldiers in the Great War are undoubtedly relevant to the Harper brothers – their belief in the larger purposes for which the war was fought, the signifance of the support given by the primary group such as friends and unit colleagues, the sense that family values were being maintained. But if we want to explain, not simply men's ability to endure the travail of war, but to carry out fearsome acts of courage, such as those exemplified by the actions of the Harper brothers on Gallipoli and the Sinai, then we need to look for elements which made them different from others and intensifed their ability to overcome pain and fear. Explaining excessive bravery is a harder question than accounting for endurance. To a limited extent Gordon's unusual enthusiasm for the imperial cause is one aspect, but it did not last. More important was the unusually strong relationship between the brothers. This ensured that in any action they were determined not to let the other brother down, or to disgrace their common name. They continually looked to meet up and give the other support. The fraternal relationship was also important in establishing for the boys a model of masculinity in which sporting and warrior achievement were central. That culture, mediated through the brothers, was obviously a powerful factor. Religion was also a strong influence. It was a comfort to the Harpers boys, and took away fears of death in a way not shared by many others. Finally one wonders how far the embarrassments that the family had suffered – the 'Harper crash' and Edmund's syphilis – acted to create a desire that the family name needed to be restored.

We must conclude that it is difficult to generalise about the origins of unusual bravery. Unusually brave men are by definition different from their fellows; so we need to look for explanations that are particular to their own situation. What made them different becomes the central question. For the Harper boys, it was their intense fraternal relationship, their religion and their deep-suited desire to uplift and restore the family name.

Part 5

Grounding Memory – Encounters with Landscape

Chapter 12

THE CARIBOU TRAIL

Commemorating the Royal Newfoundland Regiment in the First World War[1]

Raynald Harvey Lemelin

Introduction

Before I begin this chapter, I feel it is important to disclose who I am and why I wanted to write on this topic. I am French-Canadian; my ancestors have been in North America since 1670, not quite as long as when the colony of Newfoundland was established in 1583. The First and Second World Wars are difficult topics for French-Canadians to discuss, and when we do discuss the two World Wars, we often focus on the 'grand narrative' that French-Canadians largely opposed conscription and opted not to enlist. Sadly, very little voice is given to all those French-Canadians who actually enlisted and fought in the First and Second World Wars.[2] The reason I point this out is that when I first heard of the exploits of the Royal Newfoundland Regiment in the First and Second World Wars, I would often state 'that no one cares what Newfoundland and Labrador did, since they weren't part of Canada when they accomplished these feats'. Apart from being incredibly insensitive, this statement also overlooked the tremendous contributions of

---

1   A similar version of this article was published as: Raynald Lemelin, 'Newfoundland: Commemorating the Royal Newfoundland Regiment in Gallipoli', *History Australia* Vol 12, No. 3 (2015): 183-191. Reprinted with permission.
2   Pierre Vennat, *Les 'poilus' québécois de 1914-1918 : histoire des militaires canadiens-français de la Première Guerre mondiale* (Montréal : Éditions du Méridien, 1999).

the Royal Newfoundland Regiment (RNR) in the First and Second World Wars.

The greatest transformation in my understanding came when I traveled to Northern Labrador for research and first heard the story of Lance Corporal John Shiwak. Shiwak was one of many Labradorian Inuit who enlisted and was killed in combat in 1917 and was buried in Masnieres, France.[3] A few years later, when visiting the city of St. John's, the capital of Newfoundland and Labrador, I became aware of the bravery of the Newfoundland Regiment at the Somme (i.e. Beaumont-Hamel) on July 1, 1916. Although July 1 would always be known as Canada Day for me, I also now recognise it as a day of memorial for Newfoundland and Labrador.

Through my travels and research opportunities, I gained a greater appreciation of other narratives associated with the Great War for in 2014 I meet Arlene King, the Senior Manager, Commemorative Sites, European Operations for Veterans Affairs Canada. During one of our conversations, Arlene King explained how Newfoundland and Labrador had commemorated the achievements of the RNR by establishing the Trail of the Caribou. Although six bronze caribous have been erected in Europe and Canada, she explained that no caribou or any other marker for that matter commemorate 'the only troops from North America involved in this theatre of war'.[4] King was referring to a little known fact that the RNR was the only North American detachment to fight in Gallipoli. Intrigued by this, and concerned by Canada's moderate commemorative activities pertaining to the First World War,[5] I decided to consult various literature and social media outlets on the issue with the hopes of clarifying why no commemorative markers recognising the contributions of the RNR at Gallipoli have been erected. In

---

3   'Lance Corporal John Shiwak Died: November 20, 1917', Canadiangreatwarproject.com, accessed March 19 2015. http://www.canadiangreatwarproject.com/searches/soldierDetail.asp?ID=41221; Earl Pilgrim, *Freddy Frieda Goes to War: A Labrador Native's Story* (St. John, NL: DRC Publishing, 2012).

4   Michael Winter, *Into the Blizzard: Walking the Fields of the Newfoundland Dead* (Toronto, ON: Doubleday Canada, 2014), 80.

5   See Jack Lawrence Granatstein, 'Why is Canada botching the Great War centenary?' *The Globe and Mail*, 21 April 2014, accessed 21 July 2015, http://www.theglobeandmail.com/globe-debate/why-is-canada-botching-the-great-war-centenary/article18056398/; Anne Pélouas, 'Au Canada, un devoir de mémoire pour chaque centenaire' *Le Monde*, 16 Mai, 2014, accessed 20 July 2015, http://www.lemonde.fr/vu-d-ailleurs/article/2014/05/16/au-canada-un-devoir-de-memoire-pour-chaque-centenaire_4415166_4366902.html; Jonathan Weier, *History Matters*, 'What is the 'right way' to commemorate the First World War?' (blog), posted 7 April 2014, accessed 21 July 2015, http://activehistory.ca/2014/04/what-is-the-right-way-to-commemorate-the-first-world-war/.

the summer of 2015, I also had the opportunity to visit Gallipoli and acquire further information on the subject.

A number of authors have discussed the role and commemoration of the RNR during the Gallipoli campaign[6]; more recent articles include Lemelin[7], MacGregor[8], and Winter.[9] Few of these authors with the exception of Gough[10], Lemelin[11], McGaughey[12], MacGregor[13] and Parsons[14] have discussed the absence of any memorial honouring the RNR in Gallipoli.

The Rooms' (i.e. the provincial museum of Newfoundland and Labrador) webpage on the Great War indicates that the 'five military actions involving the Royal Newfoundland Regiment' along the Western Front are commemorated by the presence of a bronze caribou.[15] The absence of any mention of Gallipoli does suggest that the role of the RNR at Gallipoli was until quite recently, perceived as less significant when compared to what transpired in Belgium and France. McGaughey[16] states that the

---

6   Sean Cadigan, *Death on Two Fronts: National Tragedies and the Fate of Democracy in Newfoundland, 1914-43* (Toronto, ON: Allen Lane, 2013); Patrick O'Flaherty, *Lost Country: The Rise and Fall of Newfoundland 1843-1933* (St. John's, NL: Long Beach Press, 2005); Whitney Lackenbauer, 'War, Memory and the Newfoundland Regiment at Gallipoli', *Newfoundland Studies* 15, no. 2 (1999): 176-214; Kevin Major, *As Near to Heaven by Sea: A History of Newfoundland and Labrador* (Toronto, ON: Penguin Books, 2001); Jane McGaughey, 'Stalking the Warrior Tuktu,' (blog), posted on 8 October 2011, accessed March 19, 2015. http://midatlanticmusings.wordpress.com/2011/10/08/stalking-the-warrior-tuktu/; Gerald Nicholson, *The Fighting Newfoundlander: A History of The Royal Newfoundland Regiment* (Montreal & Kingston: McGill-Queen's University Press, 2006); W. David Parsons, *Pilgrimage: A Guide to the Royal Newfoundland Regiment in World War One.* (St. John's NL: DRC Publishing, 1994); Frederick W. Rowe, *A History of Newfoundland and Labrador* (Toronto, ON:.McGraw-Hill Ryerson Limited, 1980); Winter.

7   Raynald Lemelin, 'Newfoundland: Commemorating the Royal Newfoundland Regiment in Gallipoli', *History Australia* 12:3 (2015): 183-191.

8   Tom MacGregor, 'Pilgrimage to Turkey: Going back to Gallipoli,' *Legion Magazine* (January/February 2016): 22-33.

9   Winter.

10 Paul Gough, 'Sites in the imagination: The Beaumont Hamel Newfoundland Memorial on the Somme', *Cultural Geographies* 11, no. 3 (2004): 235-258, doi: 10.1191/1474474003eu306oa

11 Lemelin.

12 McGaughey.

13 MacGregor.

14 Parsons.

15 'Acknowledgements.' Rnr.therooms.ca, 2010. http://www.rnr.therooms.ca/acknowledgements.asp.

16 McGaughey.

replacement of the typical marker (i.e. the bronze caribou) for a granite cross was particularly problematic considering that Turkey is a Muslim State, and therefore both ideas were rejected, and no marker was installed. Perhaps it was simply that the funding ran out as Newfoundland attempted to deal with a crushing debt during the Depression and would later join the Canadian confederation in 1949.[17] Last, since the Canadian Expeditionary Force was not involved in Gallipoli, it has never been an interest of the Canadian Government to recognise the role of the RNR at Gallipoli. In an attempt to answer this question this chapter provides an overview of the Dominion of Newfoundland at the beginning of the First World War, examines the various theatres of war that the RNR engaged in during the Great War, then describes the quest for commemoration (i.e. the establishment of the Trail of the Caribou) and the post-Great War repercussions on the economy of Newfoundland and Labrador. The various notions associated with the lack of commemoration of the RNR at Gallipoli until recently, are examined in the discussion.

Newfoundland and Labrador and the Great War

The Dominion of Newfoundland and Labrador

'Consisting of the island of Newfoundland and the coastal territory of Labrador[18] bordering Canada on the North American mainland, Newfoundland (established in 1583), was one of the British empire's oldest colonies'.[19] With a population of 224,921 citizens, Newfoundland and Labrador in 1901 could be best described as rural with some urban pockets (e.g. St. John's). Although members of the Micmac and Innu First Nations, Inuit, Germans (Moravians), French, Chinese, Lebanese, and Jewish migrants could be found in Newfoundland and Labrador, the majority of residents (97.5%) were born in Newfoundland and Labrador.[20] Despite efforts to diversify the local economy through developments in forestry,

---

17   Cadigan, *Death on Two Fronts*.

18   Although the term Newfoundland is used throughout the text, it is recognised that Labrador was an important component of the dominion. It also recognises that the 2001 amendment to the Canadian Constitution officially changed the province's name to Newfoundland and Labrador. Canadian Broadcasting Corporation, 'Newfoundland's name change now official', accessed 24 August 2015. http://www.cbc.ca/news/canada/newfoundland-s-name-change-now-official-1.279040.

19   Lemelin, 184.

20   O'Flaherty.

mining, railway, and industry, nearly three-quarters (70.6%) of the working population in 1901 was employed in the fishing industry (e.g. catching and curing fish).[21] Other occupations included farming, sealing, the trades, the service industry, and civil servants.[22] This overwhelming dependence on primary industries created challenges in literacy and education.[23]

The Royal Newfoundland Regiment in the First World War

After the declaration of war in August 1914, Newfoundland and Labrador quickly mobilised, and by early September 1914, the First Five Hundred (there were actually 537 of them) also known as the 'Blue Puttees' enlisted.[24] As the last regiment to enter the conflict in Turkey, and the only troops from North America involved in Gallipoli, the Newfoundland Regiment (as it was known then) consisting of 1,076 men, landed at Kangaroo Beach on September 20 to join the 88th Brigade of the 29th Division.[25] 'Gallipoli proved a rough baptism. Thirty men were lost to Turkish gunfire, another ten to disease carried by the hordes of flies'.[26]

The Newfoundland Regiment's engagement with the Turkish Army was limited. However, on November 4, Captain Donnelly, Sergeant Greene, Private Hynes, and three other men from the Newfoundland Regiment, occupied a knoll near the front of the Newfoundland line, that had been used a sniping outpost by Turkish sharp-shooters. Every attempt by the Turkish army to reclaim the position was repulsed and the location was never used again by Turkish snipers.[27] The knoll became known as Caribou Hill and 'Captain Donnelly was awarded the Military Cross, Sgt. W. M. Greene and Pte. E. Hynes received the Distinguished Conduct Medal'[28] for their efforts. During the withdrawal from Gallipoli, the Newfoundland Regiment was part of the last rearguard to leave Turkey in 1916.[29] Following this engagement, the Newfoundland Regiment would see extensive combat along the Western Front of Europe.

---

21 O'Flaherty.
22 O'Flaherty.
23 O'Flaherty.
24 Nicholson.
25 Winter.
26 Major, 328.
27 Parsons.
28 Parsons, 11.
29 Parsons.

On July 1st 1916, the Newfoundland Regiment was 'assigned to the second wave of the British attack on the German trenches in the Beaumont-Hamel sector of the line. The attack failed and the Battalion was cut to pieces – of the 801 Newfoundlanders who took part in the assault, 710 were killed, wounded or missing by day's end. This event, explains Major, 'is the single greatest tragedy in the history of Newfoundland and Labrador'.[30] Although, the Newfoundland Regiment, as highlighted next, would go on to fight in numerous other battles, July 1st would become so firmly embedded in Newfoundland and Labrador lore that it would become a national day of commemoration for the dominion.[31]

After July 1916 'the Newfoundland Regiment fought successfully in a number of battles during the final two years of First World War. The battalion achieved a stunning victory at Gueudecourt in October 1916, experienced further, but costly, successes at Sailly-Saillisel, Monchy-le-Preux, and Cambrai in 1917'.[32] Renamed the Royal Newfoundland Regiment in 1918, the RNR was crucial to the Hundred Days Offensive by the allies, which brought an end to the war.[33]

Although the numbers pertaining to the enlistment and casualties differ, it is estimated that over 6,200 men served in the RNR, the Royal Naval Reserve Forces, and in the Forestry Corps.[34] Considering the population of Newfoundland and Labrador was only 224,921 at the beginning of the century, the total casualties of 3,733 (1,419 dead, 2,314 wounded) are believed to be some of the highest casualty rates for the British Forces.[35] It should also be noted that these figures do not include the 3,268 Newfoundlanders and Labradorians who enrolled in the Canadian Expeditionary Force, nor the nearly 175 Newfoundland and Labrador women who 'served overseas as military nurses, motor ambulance drivers, and V.A.Ds'.[36] Calls to commemorate the lost and sacrifices were made soon after the conclusion of the Great War.

---

30 Major, 329.
31 Gough; Robert J. Harding, 'Glorious Tragedy: Newfoundland's Cultural Memory of the Attack at Beaumont Hamel, 1916-1925', *Newfoundland and Labrador Studies* 21, Vol. 1 (2006).http://ir.lib.uwo.ca/cgi/viewcontent.cgi?article=1049&context=mem2h ist&sei-redir=1&referer=http%3A%2F%2Fscholar.google.ca%2Fscholar%3Fhl%3De n%26q%3Droyal%2Bnewfoundland%2Bregiment%252C%2Bgallipoli%26btnG%3D %26as_sdt%3D1%252C5%26as_sdtp%3D#search=%22royal%20newfoundland%20 regiment%2C%20gallipoli%22
32 McGaughey.
33 McGaughey.
34 O'Flaherty.
35 Rowe.
36 O'Flaherty, 290.

The Trail of the Caribou

Following the conclusion of the First World War, numerous memorials were established throughout Newfoundland and Labrador (Grand Fall, Grand Banks-Windsor), however, the responsibility of developing a national and international commemorative strategy fell to the Patriotic Association, the Great War Veterans' Association, and Lieutenant-Colonel Father Thomas Nangle, the former Roman Catholic Padre of the regiment and Newfoundland's representative on the Imperial War Graves Commission.[37] As the Director of War Graves, Registration, Enquiries and Memorials, Nangle viewed the memorials as everlasting tributes 'to the men who gave their all so that the land may live'.[38]

Two national memorials commemorating the First World War were established in the capital of St. John's; the National War Memorial was established in 1924,[39] while the Memorial University College was created the following year.[40] Nangle and the committee also sought to establish a commemorative strategy across Europe.[41] The Trail of the Caribou as it came to be known was designed to trace the path of the RNR through its engagements in the First World War. Differing from the commemorative obelisks, arches and crosses 'appearing all along the Western Front',[42] Nangle and the committee opted for the establishment of bronze caribous representing the RNR's defiance and bravery in battle (see Table 12.1 below). Devised by the British sculptor Captain Basil Cotto, the bronze caribou design was selected because it was distinctive, artistic, and at £1,000 (C$3,000), relatively inexpensive.[43] The first bronze caribou to be erected was at Beaumont Hamel in 1925.[44] Five others, including one in Bowring Park in St. John's Newfoundland and Labrador would soon follow.[45]

---

37 'Newfoundland and Labrador Heritage Web Site: Commemorations Overseas', Heritage.nf.ca, accessed March 19, 2015. http://www.heritage.nf.ca/greatwar/articles/com_overseas.html.
38 Heritage.nf.ca, 'Commemorations Overseas'.
39 'Newfoundland and Labrador Heritage Web Site: Commemorations', Heritage.nf.ca, accessed March 19, 2015. http://www.heritage.nf.ca/first-world-war/articles/commemorations-at-home.php; 'Remembering the war', Rnr.therooms.ca, 2010. http://www.rnr.therooms.ca/part4_remembering_the_war.asp.
40 Rnr.therooms.ca, 'Remembering the war'.
41 Nicholson.
42 Nicholson, 516.
43 Heritage.nf.ca, 'Commemorations Overseas'.
44 Nicholson.
45 McGaughey.

Table 12.1 – The Trail of the Caribou in Europe

Name	Location	Battle	Battle Date
Beaumont-Hamel Newfoundland Memorial	France	Commemorates the RNR's participation in the Battle of the Somme	1916
Gueudecourt Memorial	France	Dedicated to the Newfoundlanders who fought during the Battle of Le Transloy	1916
Masnières Newfoundland Memorial	France	Commemorates the actions of the RNR during the First Battle of Cambrai	1917
Monchy-le-Preux Memorial	France	Commemorates the RNR's participation in the Battle of Arras	1917
Courtrai/Kortrijk Newfoundland Memorial	Belgium	Commemorates the actions of the RNR during the 100th Day Offensive – Battle of Courtrai	1918

Although there are prominent memorials to the Australian, British, French, New Zealander, and most recently, the memorial to the 10th Irish Division at Gallipoli,[46] there is, apart from the graves found at the Hill 10 and Lancashire Landing Commonwealth Cemeteries, no memorial recognising the role of the RNR in Gallipoli.[47] This omission is somewhat surprising considering that Nangle reportedly included Caribou Hill in Gallipoli in the Trail of the Caribou.[48] The lack of any formal commemoration for the Newfoundlander Royal Regiment at Gallipoli, argues McGaughey, is a serious oversight and 'an enduring mystery in the historiography of the Great War's commemoration.'[49] The following section examines some of the factors both abroad and at home, that could have led to this omission.

The missing Caribou of Gallipoli

Following the establishment of the Turkish Republic in 1923 largely destroyed and abandoned settlements along the European side of the Dardanelles (Çanakkale Boğazı/ Çanakkale Straight) in the province of Çanakkale were repopulated and rebuilt. In 1973, the Gelibolu (Gallipoli) Peninsula Historical National Park covering 33.000 hectares (330 km2) of the southern

---

46 *Royal Munster Fusiliers Association*, '10th Irish Division at Gallipoli', (blog), posted 24 March 2010, http://www.rmfa92.org/10th-irish-division-at-gallipoli/.
47 McGaughey; MacGregor; Parsons.
48 Parsons.
49 McGaughey.

end of the Gallipoli Peninsula was established.⁵⁰ Protecting one of the largest naval and land battlefields in Europe the Park holds an extensive range of sunken ships, guns, trenches, forts, bastions, and the graves and memorials of approximately 250,000 Turkish soldiers as well as 250,000 from Australia, New Zealand, England and France.⁵¹ In addition, there are outdoor exhibits, reconstructed trenches, forts and museums.⁵² With visitations exceeding 230,249 visitors in 2004, the park is quite popular with local, national and international visitors.⁵³ Most recently, the entire peninsula has been included on the tentative list for World Heritage Site designation.⁵⁴ Although the failure to erect a memorial in honour of the RNR in Gallipoli has been attributed as an inability to overcome religious and cultural sensitivities in Turkey, the reality is that 47 Turkish memorials and 33 Commonwealth and French memorials and cemeteries, including one of the newest memorials established in 2010, and dedicated to the 10th Irish Division at Gallipoli⁵⁵ are found throughout the Gallipoli peninsula.⁵⁶

By borrowing heavily to finance its war effort, the leaders of Newfoundland and Labrador 'had done its own people a disservice'.⁵⁷ The results were that by the 1920s Newfoundland and Labrador was overwhelmed with a debt exceeding 34 million dollars.⁵⁸ By 1934, 'interest on the public debt had multiplied to an astounding 63 per cent of revenues',⁵⁹ and the Dominion was on the verge of bankruptcy.⁶⁰ Dismay over this economic uncertainty and political turmoil led individuals to conclude that the future of Newfoundland and Labrador was indecisive because 'the best and the brightest' of her sons had been lost in the Great War.⁶¹ The problem with the myth of the 'lost generation', explains Cadigan, is that this notion demeans

---

50 'Çanakkale (Dardanelles) and Gelibolu (Gallipoli) Battles Zones in the First World War', whc.UNESCO.org (15 April 2014). http://whc.unesco.org/en/tentativelists/5911/.
51 Whc.unesco.org, 'Çanakkale and Gelibolu'.
52 Abdullah Kelkit, Sezgin Celik, and Hayriye Eşbah, 'Ecotourism potential of Gallipoli Peninsula Historical National Park', *Journal of Coastal Research* 26, no. 3 (2010): 562-568.
53 Kelkit et al.
54 Whc.unesco.org, 'Çanakkale and Gelibolu'.
55 *Royal Munster Fusiliers Association*, '10th Irish Division at Gallipoli'.
56 Whc.unesco.org, 'Çanakkale and Gelibolu'.
57 Major, 333.
58 Major.
59 Major, 333.
60 Major.
61 Cadigan.

'intentionally or not, the people who survived the war and, though often damaged in some way, nevertheless went on building their futures'.[62] Nor does it recognise that most Newfoundlanders and Labradorians 'had lost faith in liberal democracy and were, in fact, open to the idea of government by an appointed commission'[63] from Britain, and later became a member of the Canadian Confederation. In 1926, one of the Trail of Caribou's most dedicated and ardent champions, Nangle, departed for Rhodesia, where he married, raised children and joined politics.[64]

When Newfoundland became the newest member of the Canadian confederation in 1949, certain activities pertaining to the military and commemoration came within the jurisdiction of various federal agencies. So, although 'Canada manages a number of First World War battlefields located along the Western Front (including the Beaumont-Hamel National Historic Site),[65] it has been surmised that since the Canadian Expeditionary Force was not involved in the Gallipoli campaign, it has never been of much interest to the Canadian government to recognise the role of the RNR in Turkey. But recent national coverage in Canada of the re-enactment of the Blue Puttees March in St. John's,[66] the celebration of Anzac Day in Newfoundland,[67] and the recent participation of the Canadian minister of state for foreign affairs, Lynne Yelich, along with members of the RNR, in the Anzac centennial ceremonies in Turkey this past April,[68] suggest that there is an increasing awareness of the Gallipoli campaign in the Canadian consciousness. These media events were further supported by a field visit at the Hill 10 cemetery in May 2015, where it was noticed that both the

---

62 Cadigan, xv.
63 Cadigan xvi.
64 Rnr.therooms.ca, 'Acknowledgements'.
65 Gough.
66 Canadian Broadcasting Corporation, 'March of the Blue Puttees to be re-enacted in St. John's', 4 October 2014, accessed 20 July 2015, http://www.cbc.ca/news/canada/newfoundland-labrador/march-of-the-blue-puttees-to-be-re-enacted-in-st-john-s-1.2787849.
67 Jason Kenney, 'Defence Minister Jason Kenney honours ANZAC Day and the Centennial of the First World War Gallipoli Campaign', 25 April 2015, accessed 20 July 2015, http://www.jasonkenney.ca/news/defence-minister-jason-kenney-honours-anzac-day-and-the-centennial-of-the-first-world-war-gallipoli-campaign/.
68 Canadian Broadcasting Corporation, 'Canadians at Gallipoli: Royal Newfoundland Regiment honoured. Newfoundland troops were only North American soldiers at the bloody First World War Battle', 24 April 2015, accessed 20 July 2015, http://www.cbc.ca/news/canada/canadians-at-gallipoli-royal-newfoundland-regiment-honoured-1.3046197.

Canadian flag and the provincial flag of Newfoundland[69] were present on the graves of the soldiers from the RNR.[70]

'The greatest challenge facing the completion of the Trail of the Caribou may not be Canadian apathy so much as Canada's First World Centenary Strategy which, according to Laurent Veyssière, a member of 'conseil scientifique de la Mission du centenaire' plans to do very little between 2014 and 2016, and will rather focus most of its energy on the 150th anniversary of Confederation and the centenary of the Battle of Vimy Ridge in 2017.'[71] Indeed, no new funding will be allocated to the Canadian First World Centenary. Instead, government departments, agencies and crown corporations 'have been ordered to finance the commemoration costs out of existing budgets'.[72] With this type of strategy currently in place, it seems unlikely that any Canadian funding will be dedicated to completing the Trail of the Caribou in the near future.

Conclusion

As stated earlier, various theories have been provided to explain the absence of a marker commemorating the role of the RNR in Gallipoli, including the idea that the role of the RNR at Gallipoli was deemed less significant when compared to what transpired along the Western Front.[73] Others like McGaughey[74] have stated that the replacement of the bronze caribou for granite cross was particularly problematic considering that Turkey is a Muslim State, and therefore both ideas were rejected. Bearing in mind that caribou engravings are present on the graves of Newfoundland and Labrador soldiers throughout Commonwealth Cemeteries, the notion that the caribou or the cross for that matter cannot be displayed on Turkish soil is somewhat inconsistent. Another explanation suggests that the funding simply ran out as Newfoundland and Labrador struggled through the Depression, when

---

69 Note this is the new flag for the province of Newfoundland and Labrador which was officially adopted in 1980. Government of Newfoundland and Labrador, 'Provincial Flag', 2 April 2013, accessed 24 August 2015. http://www.gov.nl.ca/aboutnl/flag.html.
70 Lemelin, 189.
71 Pélouas, 'Au Canada, un devoir de mémoire'.
72 Granatstein, 'Why is Canada botching the Great War centenary?' See also Weier, 'What is the 'right way' To Commemorate The First World War?'
73 McGaughey; Parsons.
74 McGaughey.

they entered the Second World War, and when they joined the Canadian Confederation in 1949.[75]

What this chapter, along with more recent works by Lemelin[76] and MacGregor[77] suggests, is that it was most likely a combination of many factors at home (the debt, Nangle's departure for Rhodesia, the Second World War, and joining the Canadian Confederation) and abroad (i.e. the establishment of protected areas in Turkey) which resulted in the Trail of the Caribou remaining incomplete. The challenge today, is that completing the Trail of the Caribou would require not only provincial support from Newfoundland and Labrador, but also federal support from the Governments of Canada and Turkey. Although seeking the approval from the Turkish Government to complete the Trail of the Caribou in Gallipoli would be complicated especially with the peninsula being recently listed on the tentative list of World Heritage Sites, the reality is that is that there are already a number of cemeteries, memorials and sunken ships near and in Suvla Bay. Thus it may be easier to acquire the approval of the Turkish Government, provided the monument would be respectful of local customs, than to acquire the support of the Canadian Government who appears to have little to no interest in commemorating the first few years of the First World War Centenary.

Completing the original Trail of the Caribou would require provincial support from the provincial government of Newfoundland and Labrador, support from the governments of Canada and Turkey, and discussions with the Commonwealth War Graves Commission, as the potential site manager. Although federal First World War Centenary plans do not include a re-evaluation of the Trail of Caribou, the upcoming centennial of Beaumont-Hamel in 2016, and the Canada 150 funding program, developed to celebrate 150 years of Confederation in 2017, might present a new avenue for pursuing a much needed acknowledgement of the role of the RNR at Gallipoli. There has been a modest recent increase of interest in this aspect of Canada's military history and if some of this momentum can be maintained, it is conceivable that one last bronze caribou will soon stand 'on guard' at Gallipoli.[78]

---

75   Major; Cadigan.
76   Lemelin.
77   MacGregor.
78   Lemelin, 189.

Chapter 13

ARCHAEOLOGICAL LANDSCAPES AT GALLIPOLI

The Anzac Area at Arıburnu

Jessie Birkett-Rees[1]

Battlefield archaeology

Historical photos of the Gallipoli peninsula taken during the First World War show a landscape bustling with activity, a city of tents beside the shore, terraced dugouts excavated into the hillsides, herds of animals and groups of soldiers making their way through the wartime settlements that developed on either side of the front line. The activity and the stagnation experienced in the entrenched front lines is also captured in these images; it must be emphasised that during the Gallipoli campaign, and indeed in many theatres of the First World War, soldiers spent more of their time digging than fighting. Above

---

1 Centre for Ancient Cultures, Monash University. Many people and institutions contributed to the broader project to which this paper relates. My thanks firstly go to my colleagues from Turkey, Australia and New Zealand on the Joint Historical and Archaeological Survey of the Gallipoli battlefields (JHAS), especially the project director Mithat Atabay and field director Antonio Sagona. I am indebted to the Australian Government Department of Veterans' Affairs who funded the JHAS fieldwork and to the Ministry for Culture and Heritage, New Zealand, for their support for the project. Thanks are owed to the Turkish authorities in Ankara, including the T. C. Kültür ve Turizm Bakanlığı and the T. C. Çevre ve Orman Bakanlığı, for granting permission to work on the Gallipoli battlefields. I am grateful to representatives from the Australian Embassy in Ankara and the Australian Consulate in Çanakkale for their interest and assistance throughout the project, and thank Monash University, La Trobe University and The University of Melbourne for their support of this research project.

the battlefield, aerial photos lay bare the complex terrain of Gallipoli and reveal the networks of trenches and tunnels, military encampments and stores, cemeteries and hospitals that spread across the countryside during the conflict. Maps too, some traced from those early aerial photographs, record the complexity of the wartime landscape. But what of this landscape today? Gallipoli today is a site for the cultivation of national narratives and collective commemoration, centred on memorials and cemeteries constructed after the war. With the commemorative landscape as the focus of attention, the remains of the battlefields themselves are largely unobserved and, until now, unrecorded. The first investigation of the archaeological landscapes of the Gallipoli battlefields has allowed us to examine what remains of the wartime landscape and consider it within the context of the broader human history of the Gallipoli peninsula.

Given that we have such a wealth of archival material from the Gallipoli campaign one might wonder what an archaeological approach could possibly add to a site so comprehensively recorded. The answer is context and perspective, as well as insight into the preservation of the century-old earthworks and artefacts from this major industrialised conflict. Archaeologists approach and interpret landscapes in different ways than do military historians, whose accounts have dominated our understanding of the First World War. Rather than examining the battlefield as a scene of victory or defeat, tactics or strategy, heroism or tragedy, archaeologists seek to understand the development of these landscapes over time. This encompasses the formation and preservation of war-era features and the articulation of relationships between the battlefield features, the pre-war record and the post-war commemorative landscape. Here I present some of the results of the Joint Historical and Archaeological Survey[2] and consider the roles of archaeology on the battlefields of Gallipoli and the significance of encounters with the physical record of the past.

This chapter addresses the archaeology of a battlefield and participates in a broader sub-discipline addressing sites and landscapes of conflict. The investigation of landscapes has become increasingly important in

---

[2] Antonio Sagona, Mithat Atabay, Chris Mackie, Ian McGibbon and Richard Reid (eds.), *Anzac Battlefield: Gallipoli landscape of war and memory* (Australia: Cambridge University Press, 2016); Antonio Sagona, Mithat Atabay, Richard Reid, Ian McGibbon, Chris Mackie, Muhammet Erat and Jessie Birkett-Rees, 'The ANZAC (Arıburnu) Battlefield: new perspectives and methodologies in history and archaeology', *Australian Historical Studies* 42 (2011): 313–337.

anthropological archaeology,[3] and the investigation of the new physical and symbolic landscapes constructed during and after the First World War presents very interesting terrain.[4] Battlefields and landscapes of conflict have unique aspects related to their function and offer a unique perspective on the behavioural aspects of a culture, or cultures, in conflict.[5] The study of war has occupied historians for centuries, but archaeologists have begun the study of the physical evidence and anthropological theory of conflict comparatively recently.[6] The necessary methodologies and theoretical approaches continue to develop and have, in the last decade, been united with rapidly developing remote sensing and spatial technologies. These non-invasive techniques broaden the capabilities of archaeology and are resulting in new contributions to the contextual study of past human conflict.[7] 'Conflict archaeology' began as an area concentrating on military strategy and frontline tactics but has developed into an area concerned with the broader anthropology of conflict. Excavations have taken place at many sites of conflict relating to standing structures, such as forts and castles, but this is not typically the case for battlefields for reasons that I will outline below. It is

---

3   Wendy Ashmore and A. Bernard Knapp (eds.), *Archaeologies of Landscape: Contemporary Perspectives* (Oxford: Blackwell, 1999); Barbara Bender, *Landscape: Politics and Perspectives* (Providence: Berg, 1993); James McGlade, 'Archaeology and the evolution of cultural landscapes: towards an interdisciplinary research agenda', in *The Archaeology and Anthropology of Landscape: shaping your landscape*, ed. Peter J. Ucko and R. Layton (London and New York: Routledge, 1999), 458–82; Nicholas Saunders, 'Anthropology and archaeology of the First World War', *Revista Cadernos do Ceom* 26, no. 38 (2013): 17–31; Peter J. Ucko (ed.), *The Archaeology and Anthropology of Landscape: Shaping Your Landscape* (London and New York: Routledge, 1999).

4   Nicholas Saunders, 'Excavating memories: archaeology and the Great War, 1914 – 2001', *Antiquity* 76 (2002): 101–108.

5   Martin Van Creveld, *Technology and War: from 2000 BC to the Present* (New York: The Free Press, 1989).

6   Douglas D. Scott and Andrew P. McFeaters, 'The archaeology of historic battlefields: a history and theoretical development in conflict archaeology', *Journal of Archaeological Research* 19 (2011): 103–32.

7   Jessie Birkett-Rees, 'Geospatial Science and the archaeology of the First World War: context for conflict', *Proceedings of the Geospatial Science Research Symposium GSR2*, (Melbourne: RMIT University, 2012); Jessie Birkett-Rees, 'Capturing the Battlefield: the story of mapping and air photography at Gallipoli, in *Anzac Battlefield: a Gallipoli landscape of war and memory*, ed. A. Sagona et al (Australia: Cambridge University Press, 2016), 59–82; Mark D. McCoy and Thegn N. Ladefoged, 'New developments in the use of spatial technology in archaeology', *Journal of Archaeological Research* 17 (2009): 263–95; Birger Stichelbaut, Jean Bourgeois, Nicholas Saunders and Piet Chielens (eds.), *Images of Conflict: Military Aerial Photography and Archaeology* (Newcastle-upon-Tyne: Cambridge Scholars Publishing, 2009).

only with enhanced non-invasive methods that these sites and this aspect of military history have begun to be explored using archaeological techniques.

Concurrent with the development of archaeological approaches to battlefields is the rising public interest in the history and commemoration of conflict. This interest is clear from the increasing numbers of visitors to historical battlefields and memorials, and in the public appetite for news, exhibitions and publications on the topic. Academic interest in recent conflicts has always been relatively high too, with the substantial historical scholarship on Gallipoli as a key example. Yet engagement with the material remains of recent battlefields was largely an arena for amateur archaeologists and enthusiasts. 'Battlefield archaeology' of the type conducted by relic hunters with an eye for military memorabilia[8] proliferated alongside rising public interest in the First World War and received surprisingly little critique from professional archaeologists.[9] This attitude has since changed, with increasing numbers of professional archaeologists engaged in this area of research, raising awareness of appropriate investigative techniques and ethical practices. Their contributions have seen the archaeological investigation of World War battlefields develop into a legitimate field of research.[10]

The archaeology of the First World War that has since developed is historical archaeology, informed by a wealth of documents, but it is also landscape archaeology with a significant spatial component, industrial archaeology, anthropological archaeology and ultimately public archaeology. The basis of conflict archaeology, at its most fundamental, is the fact that people fight in ways which reflect their training and they live in ways which reflect their cultural and social context, and such behaviour leaves behind physical remains that can be interpreted.[11] As a partner to history, the independent line of evidence offered by archaeological research has the ability to enhance the documentary record and build a more complete understanding of past events. The First World War recently passed out of living memory and has

---

8   John Laffin, *Battlefield Archaeology* (London: Allan, 1987).
9   Nicholas Saunders, 2002.
10 Yves Desfossés, Alain Jacques and Gilles Prilaux, *L'archeologie de la Grande Guerre* (Rennes: Editions Ouest-France, 2008); Nicholas Saunders, 2002; Nicholas Saunders, *Killing Time: Archaeology and the First World War* (Stroud, UK: The History Press, 2011); John Schofield, *Combat Archaeology: Material Culture and Modern Conflict* (London: Duckworth, 2005); John Schofield, Axel Klausneier and Louise Purbrick (eds.), *Re-mapping the Field: new approaches in conflict archaeology* (Berlin: Werlag, 2006).
11 Douglas D. Scott and Andrew P. McFeaters, 2011.

been examined by historians for many years; it is archaeology which is now positioned to produce new information on the material culture of the first global, industrialised conflict.

The joint historical and archaeological survey

The Joint Historical and Archaeological Survey (JHAS) was an interdisciplinary project involving Turkish, Australian and New Zealand historians and archaeologists. The project resulted from a Senate Committee Report on *Matters Relating to the Gallipoli Peninsula* (2005), recommending a survey of the heritage features in the northern battlefields of Gallipoli, the area known as Anzac or Arıburnu, in which the major battles between the ANZAC and Ottoman Turkish troops took place during 1915. The postwar investigation of the battlefield by the Australian Historical Mission in 1919 recommended that this 'Anzac Area' area be reserved as a memorial landscape. In preparation for the peace talks that year, the Imperial War Graves Commission (IWGC) produced a map that defined the 'Old Anzac' position, the area held from April 25 until the August offensive. This map was included as Map 3 in the Treaty of Sevres and the Treaty of Lausanne, which formalised the Anzac Area (Plate 13.1). This treaty also provided for IWGC control of cemeteries built outside the area, fifteen in all, at Cape Helles, Suvla and north of the Anzac Area.

The Gallipoli battlefields remain restricted to archaeological excavation, due to their status as an open cemetery and a national park, and the JHAS is the first project to receive permission to conduct fieldwork this area. The last collaborative survey of these battlefields was the Australian Historical Mission in 1919, led by Charles Bean who had served as a war correspondent at Gallipoli and would later become Australia's official war historian.[12] Bean spent eleven days in the northern battlefields of Gallipoli, assisted in his research by several Gallipoli veterans.[13] These included cartographer Herbert Buchanan, photographer Hubert Wilkins, artist George Lambert and Turkish officer Major Zeki Bey. It was Bean's conviction that the landscape of Gallipoli played a significant role in the conflict and he sought to record and understand certain events in relation to the battlefield terrain. Bean collected 'relics' from Gallipoli and, together with the wartime earth-

---

12 Charles Bean, *Official History of Australia in the War of 1914–1918*, volume 2, 'The Story of ANZAC from 4 May, 1915, to the evacuation of the Gallipoli Peninsula', 11th edition (Sydney: Angus and Robertson, 1941).

13 Charles Bean, *Gallipoli Mission* (Canberra: Australian War Memorial, 1948).

works, drew these artefacts into a historical narrative of the campaign. Bean's method, in which he sought to identify specific trenches and sectors of the battlefield in the post-war landscape, is quite different to the JHAS team's efforts to record what remains of the battlefield without preference for specific positions or historical events. Yet in seeking to add context and meaning to historical events by linking them with the landscape the Australian Historical Mission and the JHAS share some common goals.

The geography of Gallipoli is a dramatic combination of rugged ridges and plateaus, deeply incised by seasonal waterways, giving onto the coasts of the Aegean and Dardanelles. Broad plains exist only near Cape Helles, Eceabat and Suvla Bay. The popular understanding of Gallipoli focusses on the beaches, but it is the northeast-southwest trending ridgelines which define the Anzac Area. These ridges were named by the Allies as the First, Second and Third Ridge inland from the coastal landing places. The Third Ridge was set as the objective for many of the Anzac troops landing at Gallipoli on April 25, but this was never achieved. By the first week of May the front lines had become established along the Second Ridge.[14]

Within the Anzac Area, the JHAS has concentrated on the Second Ridge as a microcosm of the conflict. Some of the more legendary struggles on both sides of the campaign took place here, providing the opportunity to investigate Ottoman and Allied front line positions. The Second Ridge exemplifies the development of trench warfare at Gallipoli, including extensive tunnelling which took place beneath the front lines. In the first few days of the 1915 conflict, the soldiers had to excavate and attempt to consolidate their positions, a process which evolved into offensive and defensive tunnelling and the formation of subterranean positions. The areas behind the front lines are equally significant for our archaeological investigation, as it is here that tens of thousands of people lived for months. The JHAS goal was to record the physical remains of the 1915 battle, along the front lines and behind them, in addition to recording the features of the modern commemorative landscape and the more fugitive pre-war record.

Landscapes of Gallipoli

Today much of the landscape is covered in dense garrigue vegetation, native to the Mediterranean. In the years immediately before the conflict the Gallipoli peninsula was agricultural but the Anzac area grew with 'wild

---

14   Bean 1948, 47.

scrub',[15] cultivated only in the more easterly valleys that give onto the open plain. During the campaign General Sir John Monash commented on the 'prickly scrub, with which these hills are covered, and which has inflicted many an unkind scratch on hands, arms and bare knees'.[16] This wild and unforgiving scrub was much denuded as the conflict progressed and the landscape of war, familiar from historical photos, developed. Sergeant Cyril Lawrence of the 2nd Field Company Engineers vividly described this change after the battle for Lone Pine: 'The undergrowth has been cut down, like mown hay, simply stalks left standing, by the rifle fire, whilst the earth itself appears just as though one had taken a huge rake and scratched it all over'.[17]

After the evacuation and reservation of the Anzac Area, scrub rapidly returned to the gullies and ridges. In 1973 the 33,000 hectare Gallipoli Peninsula Historical National Park was established. With clearance of vegetation forbidden and reduced intervention in the area, the scrub has grown thickly over the former battlefields. Bushfires swept across the Anzac Area in the 1970s and again in the 1990s, for a time laying bare the topography of the battlefield, but the natural vegetation returned even more thickly.[18] This has been added to by stands of pine trees planted by the park authorities in several locations, including along the Second Ridge road. Although this vegetation obscures the remnant earthworks from 1915, the JHAS noted that the scrub has helped to preserve the features in the silt and sandy soils, with the *Arbutus andrachne* (called 'rhododendron' by the Anzacs) having a particular preference for the former trench lines.[19]

The landscape and vegetation of the Gallipoli battlefields have played an important role in the memorialisation of the conflict. This is expertly expressed in art produced after the war, such as George Lambert's *The Landing at Gallipoli*, in which the men blend into the scrub beneath the rugged ridgelines; the small, faceless figures are dwarfed by the detailed character

---

15 Bean 1948, 325.
16 General Sir J. Monash, *Typed War letters of General Monash*, vol. 1, 24 December 1914 – 4 March 1917 (Australian War Memorial collections AWM 3DRL/2316, 1915), 133.
17 Cyril Lawrence, *The Gallipoli Diary of Sergeant Lawrence of the Australian Engineers*, ed. R. East (Melbourne: Melbourne University Press, 1981), 68.
18 Oliver Millman, 'Gallipoli bushfire threat: historian says peninsula is at risk of damaging blaze', *The Guardian* (Monday 6 October 2014, viewed 21 March 2016).
19 Antonio Sagona and Jessie Birkett-Rees, 'Battlefield archaeology: Gallipoli', pp. 83–97 in *Anzac Battlefield: a Gallipoli landscape of war and memory*, ed. A. Sagona et al (Australia: Cambridge University Press, 2016), 92.

of the landscape which rises against them (Plate 8.1). The relationships established between the Anzacs and the terrain in which they found themselves are as complex as Lambert's painting, and emphasise the processes of memory making and the production of cultural landscapes at Gallipoli during the conflict. This can be traced in several media, the first being the spread of place names across the battlefields during the war. The provision of place names to the topography of the peninsula was a military necessity, with tactical concerns highlighted by toponyms such as the 400 Plateau, Baby 700, Shell Green and Shrapnel Valley, but also reveals the sentiments and individuals associated with the newly formed battlefield landscape. Surprise Gully and Korku Dere (Valley of Horror) highlight the emotional responses to experience on the battlefield whilst locations such as Monash Valley and the Kemalyeri memorialise the leaders of the day. There were of course two sides to the conflict and therefore two overlays of wartime place names were produced by the Allied and Ottoman forces (Plate 13.2., see also AWM collections RCDIG1011575). These new names reconfigured the geography of Gallipoli, memorialising the events and personalities of the 1915 war. For pragmatic and sentimental reasons many of the place names created during the war were retained in the post-war landscape; the two geographies coexist today.

A second medium of landscape memorialisation was the collection of battlefield souvenirs, common amongst the Anzac troops. Beyond the collection of personal items or military memorabilia, several chose to keep or send home pieces of the foreign landscape itself.[20] The beauty and terror of Gallipoli evidently appealed to many of the men; the landscape both threatened and protected them and they developed complex feelings for the place. As Sergeant Lawrence explains, 'It has grown upon one: we took it, and tamed it and somehow its very wildness and ruggedness grips you'.[21] Monash sent several holly-oak acorns home and others did likewise, including Captain William Lempriere Winter-Cooke MC who provided the seeds planted at Geelong Grammar. *Quercus calliprinos*, the Gallipoli holly-oak, was also planted in the public contexts of the Royal Botanic Gardens and the Shrine of Remembrance reserve, Melbourne. In addition to the distinctive holly-oak, soldiers Benjamin Smith and Keith McDowell sent home pine cones from the tree which grew on 400 Plateau ('Lone Pine').

---

20   General Sir J. Monash 1915.
21   Richard Reid, *Gallipoli 1915* (Sydney: ABC Books for the Australian Broadcasting Corporation, 2002), 117.

Seedlings were propagated and planted in Australia in the decades following the war.[22]

During the war, the Anzacs attempted to familiarise the landscape of the Anzac Area, with some going so far as to obtain wattle seeds from home to scatter on the graves of fallen friends.[23] A desire to plant the Anzac Area with suitable trees from the Dominions whose armies fought there was entertained after the war, but the seedlings failed to thrive in the different climatic conditions and the plan was abandoned.[24] Interestingly, this process of identification with the rugged landscape and the exchange of flora continues today, with the presence of small eucalyptus trees near Johnston's Jolly evidence of continuing attempts to integrate the distant landscapes of Australia and Gallipoli.

The numerous reasons for identification with the landscape are beyond the scope of this paper, but it is worth noting the enduring and widespread appeal of the peninsula. At one point or another almost all the diarists from Gallipoli reflect on the striking beauty of the landscape.[25] Lawrence likened the Gallipoli coast to a future Nice or Cannes, 'the sunset was simply glorious; jingo it was fine',[26] and the evenings just as flawless, 'at night as the moon rises to the full, the picture is perfect'.[27] The serenity of the landscape of Gallipoli even during the bitter conflict was something of a paradox to the soldiers and remains so to visitors today. Physical beauty is bound with the name of the place, 'kallipolis' meaning the beautiful city in ancient Greek,[28] and has been commented on for centuries, just as the geography of the peninsula and Dardanelles has ensured that Gallipoli has been a desirable and strategic landscape for much of human history. Reading popular histories of Gallipoli one might think that this pivotal geography and conflict over the peninsula began and ended in 1915, but Gallipoli has

---

22   The Shrine of Remembrance, *Shrine of Remembrance Education Program: Background Information*, viewed 21 March 2016.

23   Ken Inglis, *Sacred Places: War Memorials in the Australian Landscape* (Melbourne: Melbourne University Press, 2008), 86; Chaplain William Dexter, 'Diary', 16 December 1915, Australian War Memorial collections, PR00248.

24   Heaton Rhodes to James Allen, 29 May 1916, and reply dated 14 Jun 1916, Army Department records (AD)1, 65/65, ANZ.

25   Christopher Mackie, 'Long Read: Gallipoli, the beautiful city', *The Conversation* 1 August 2014, viewed 21 March 2016, http://theconversation.com/long-read-gallipoli-the-beautiful-city-29581.

26   Cyril Lawrence, 1981.

27   John G. Gillam, *Gallipoli Diary*, (London: Allen and Unwin, 1918, 1989).

28   Chris Mackie, 2014.

been a cultural threshold and a contested landscape for millennia.[29] The broader human history of the peninsula provides thought-provoking context for the conflict which occurred in 1915 and the material remains of previous peoples presented the soldiers of the 1915 war with interesting encounters with antiquity.

Encounters with antiquity

The Gallipoli peninsula has been a corridor for human movement between Asia and Europe for millennia and has been contested by successive empires.[30] It is war which defined Gallipoli and the Dardanelles in antiquity, from the siege of Troy to the Greco-Persian wars, which saw Xerxes and his Persians cross the Hellespont (Dardanelles) and Alexander the Great's reciprocal crossing from Cape Helles into Asia.[31] The Peloponnesian war between Athenians and Spartans also saw early naval battles in the Dardanelles (Xenophon *Hellenica* 2.2.1). The association with conflict is evident in the earliest written histories of the area, whether you take these to be the regional treaties of the Hittites or the later literary histories of Homer, Herodotus and Thucydides. The meeting of eastern and western empires at the Dardanelles in 1915 was the most recent in a series of struggles for control of this strategic region.

Archaeology and war have an enduring relationship and the two are surprisingly entwined during the First World War.[32] The spatial technologies which I, and many archaeologists, now routinely use were for the most part developed for the military, and several came directly from the First World War. The archaeology of the Gallipoli peninsula is also significant to the experience of the soldiers in 1915, whose encounters with antiquity gave them a brief glimpse of the broader human history of the area they were living and fighting in.[33] Various chance meetings between soldiers and the material remains of former inhabitants of the peninsula provide us with rare

---

29   Mehmet Özdoğan, 'Prehistoric Sites in the Gelibolu Peninsula', *Anadolu Araştırmaları* 10 (1986): 54–58.

30   Onur Özbek, 'Sea level changes and prehistoric sites on the coasts of Southern Turkish Thrace, 12,000–6000 BP', *Quaternary International 261* (2012): 162-175; Mehmet Özdoğan, 1986.

31   Chris Mackie, 'Archaeology at Gallipoli in 1915', in *Philathenaios. Studies in Honour of Michael J. Osborne*, ed. Anastasios Tamis, Chris Mackie, and Sean G. Byrne (2010), 213–25.

32   Nicholas Saunders, 2002.

33   Peter Londey, 'A Possession for Ever: Charles Bean, the Ancient Greeks, and Military Commemoration in Australia', *Australian Journal of Politics and History* 53, no. 3

information on the pre-war archaeology of the battlefields and information on the role of archaeology during the battle.[34]

Interest in the ancient record of Gallipoli was not limited to the few classicists and archaeologists in the ranks. The diary entries of Sergeant Cyril Lawrence and others reveal the soldiers' awareness of antiquity within the Anzac Area. Lawrence was tunnelling near Lone Pine on the 400 Plateau and noted that 'in places we run through great deposits of pottery buried as low as twenty feet. This is very fine stuff and in an excellent state of preservation'.[35] The ceramics that Lawrence describes, 'red and of a very fine texture', suggest Roman material. It seems quite likely that a Roman outpost or small settlement once existed on the strategic site of the 400 Plateau; the JHAS fieldwork also located Roman ceramics and tiles in this area.

The remains of the pre-war history of the Gallipoli battlefields were experienced first-hand by the soldiers of 1915, contributing to our understanding of the human record on the peninsula and also contributing to the soldiers' experience of Gallipoli. For some, the location already carried with it the resonance of Classical history and mythology, but the instances in which the creation of the wartime landscape revealed the physical record of past people gave soldiers such as Sergeant Lawrence pause for thought. The strategic geography of Gallipoli and soldiers' responses to its striking landscape and deep history provide a valuable substrate to the material record of World War I.

Surveying Gallipoli

Archaeology is most closely associated with excavation, which is by nature a destructive process. But excavation is not the only method available to the archaeologist. This is fortunate because excavation is not permitted in

---

(2007): 344–59; Chris Mackie, 2010; Sarah Midford, 'Constructing the 'Australian Iliad': ancient heroes and Anzac diggers in the Dardanelles', *Melbourne Historical Journal* 2 (2011): 59–79.

34 Fernand Courby, Joseph Chamonard and Edouard Dhorme, 'Corps expéditionnaire d'Orient. Fouilles archéologiques sur l'emplacement de la nécropole d'Éléonte de Thrace', *Bulletin de Correspondance Hellénique* 39, no. 1 (1915): 135–240; David Gill, 'Excavating Under Gunfire: Archaeologists in the Aegean during the First World War', *Public Archaeology* 10, no. 4 (2011): 187–199; C. A. Hutton, 'Two Sepulchral Inscriptions from Suvla Bay', *The Annual of the British School at Athens* 21 (1914/1916,): 166–168; Edmond Pottier, 'Fouilles archéologiques sur l'emplacement de la nécropole d'Éléonte, en Thrace. Note sur le rapport présenté au nom de l'État-major du corps expéditionnaire d'Orient à l'Académie des Inscriptions', *Comptes rendus de l'Académie des Inscriptions et Belles-Lettres* 60 (1916): 40–47.

35 Cyril Lawrence 1989, 33.

the Anzac Area, which is reserved as a memorial landscape for the many missing. For this reason, the JHAS research was completely non-invasive, using established archaeological survey and remote sensing techniques.[36] The dense scrub which now covers the Anzac Area, together with the unusually rough terrain, meant that conventional grid-based archaeological survey was not effective. The JHAS instead operated a feature-based survey, following trench lines to delineate their full extent and recording all associated artefacts and features within the transect.[37] The only subsurface investigation consisted of remote sensing, using ground penetrating radar (GPR) to identify potential tunnel locations along the Second Ridge Road between Quinn's Post and Lone Pine.

The position of earthworks and artefacts were recorded with precision using differential GPS (DGPS). The spatial data recorded during the survey allows us to integrate the record of material remains on the battlefield with historical documents from the war era, including military maps and aerial photographs. The goals of the survey were to record what visibly remains within the former battlefield and for this reason the spatial data from the project were recorded against a blank background and associated with historical maps, plans and photographs after fieldwork. This prevented the survey team from following historical maps in the field and mitigated any tendency to infer features where there were not distinctly visible remains. Using a Geographic Information System (GIS), the assembled archaeological record has been linked with features recorded in Ottoman and Allied historical documents. The layered structure of GIS, which incorporates qualitative and quantitative information and relates different layers through the use of a shared coordinate system, lends itself to the integrated analysis of this range of spatial data. Within the project GIS we are able to move between the different scales of artefact, site and landscape, to study different temporal layers of information in isolation or in unison, examine earthworks and artefact distributions, investigate rates of preservation, and analyse the relationships between the pre-war, wartime and modern commemorative features.

Core concepts in archaeological research are context and integrity; these principles are central to our methodology and interpretation. In archaeological terms, context is the relationship that features and artefacts have to each other and the situation in which they are found. For archaeologists,

---

36 Chris Gaffney, 'Detecting trends in the prediction of the buried past: A review of geophysical techniques in archaeology', *Archaeometry*, *50*, no. 2 (2008): 313–336; McCoy and Ladefoged, 2009.
37 Antonio Sagona et al, 2011; Antonio Sagona and Jessie Birkett-Rees, 2016.

this context allows for meaningful analyses, reconstruction of site formation processes and interpretation of behaviour. By recording artefacts in context at Gallipoli we are able to understand the formation and preservation of the battlefield site. The archaeological integrity of the site is also important here. The integrity of a feature or site relates to disturbance and post-depositional processes. For a site to have integrity means that the site must be relatively undisturbed, with its patterns and layers of artefacts and other archaeological evidence relatively intact. The multidisciplinary approach of the JHAS, which links geospatial science with historical and archaeological analyses, allows us to examine the system of features and artefacts that evolved as a unit over nine months in 1915 and make some useful and unique observations about the Anzac area.

Several key categories of features recorded during the five seasons of the JHAS fieldwork include trenches, tunnels and dugouts. The earthworks situated beyond the principal memorial sites are weathered but remain relatively untouched and retain their integrity. The JHAS recorded 16.5 kilometres of trench lines, a substantial sample of the battlefield, extending along the Second Ridge from Chatham's Post in the south to Baby 700 in the north and from No.3 Outpost on North Beach along the coast to Hell Spit (Plate 13.3). The trenches, which were once around 2 metres deep, are now preserved to a height of 80–90 centimetres on average, including the accumulation of leaf litter. In exposed areas such as Courtney's Post depths can be as shallow as 30 centimetres and, depending on the degree of slope and erosion, widths vary from 60 centimetres to close to 3 metres. Tunnels once connected to the trench system and formed an important subterranean feature of the battlefield. The underground landscape of Gallipoli is fascinating and well documented in the field notebooks and diaries of the sappers and engineers, though little of this landscape is visible on the surface today. Tunnelling took place in front line areas and the JHAS recorded slumped tunnels and tunnel openings still visible at No.2 Post in the north of the Anzac area, and along the Second Ridge at Quinn's Post, Johnston's Jolly, Lone Pine, Silt Spur and Holly Ridge. Dugouts were also an important part of the battlefield earthworks, and are often located near the remnant trench lines, as roughly circular depressions of 50 centimetres depth on average. Single dugouts were common but often groups of two or three were located and, in areas behind the front lines, semi-subterranean spaces of several meters were found. Dugouts served multiple purposes in the battlefield and the remains of ordnance and cooking and eating equipment were frequently found within.

The categories of artefact on the battlefield are numerous and include ordnance, ceramics and bricks, metal containers, wire, and personal items such as buttons, buckles and boot heels. Given the industrial scale of the conflict it is unsurprising that ordnance pieces were collectively the most common artefact recorded in our survey. Fragments of shrapnel, shells, bullets, cartridge casings and magazine clips are scattered throughout the survey area. Unexploded bullets with Mauser cases and Ottoman head stamps denoting their type, date and place of manufacture provide valuable contextual information, as do bullets and cases stamped with Latin letters and Roman numerals. Shrapnel fragments are also common finds on the battlefield, found as irregular fragments and curved pieces of heavy metal from medium or large calibre shells. Small, spherical bullets or shrapnel balls from inside shells were also scattered over the battlefield.[38]

In addition to the ordnance that is found in all areas of the battlefield, certain types and distributions of artefacts provide important information on the integrity of the site. Barbed wire, of British and German manufacture, was found almost exclusively along the former front lines of the Second Ridge where entanglements of wire would have been arranged in no-man's land. When the survey results are plotted against an Ottoman map of the battlefield produced in 1916 (AWM RC03163, Plate 13.2) from a survey conducted under Brigadier General Mehmet Şevki Pasha directly after the Allied evacuation, the distribution of barbed wire aligns almost perfectly with the instance of barbed wire recorded in 1916 (Plate 13.4). This suggests that there has been little disturbance to parts of the front lines.

Bricks also provide interesting material evidence, often stamped with Greek or Ottoman letters indicating their production house in Madytos (Eceabat) or Çanakkale. The complex networks of trenches which developed at Gallipoli are substantial feats of engineering which integrated wood and metal supports. In addition to these materials, the Turkish army used bricks to reinforce their earthworks. When the survey results are plotted against war-era maps of the trench lines, it is clear that the bricks are located solely along Turkish defensive lines. This strategy and material is absent from the Anzac trench systems and therefore highlights both a different battlefield practice of the Turks and the different accessibility of resources between the coastal positions of the Allies and the Ottoman Army positions, with an

---

38 Antonio Sagona, Jessie Birkett-Rees, Michelle Negus Cleary, Simon Harrington, Mithat Atabay, Reyhan Körpe and Muhammet Erat, 'Artefacts from the Battlefield', in *Anzac Battlefield: a Gallipoli landscape of war and memory*, ed. A. Sagona et al (Australia: Cambridge University Press, 2016), 159–191.

expanse of productive country behind them. The pre-1915 bricks found on the battlefield vary in form and origin, suggesting that they were repurposed from local supplies or produced in numerous batches, rather than produced specifically for the reinforcement of trench lines.

In areas of unstable ground in the southern section of the Anzac Area, particularly along Holly Ridge and Knife Edge, we found evidence of substantial walls and buttresses. A photograph published in Charles Bean's *The Story of Anzac* shows a brick wall up to 12 courses high along parts of Knife Edge (see AWM collections G02095), and it is likely the bricks we located were part of this structure. The location of the bricks in roughly the position they were recorded in 1919 suggests that the structures of the battlefield are well preserved in this area. On Holly Ridge there has been considerable erosion of the Turkish front line trenches by water flowing down a modern fire trail, but the bricks used to support the trench remain and reveal the trench line despite the substantial erosion of the earthworks. This is encouraging as it indicates that the pattern of particular types of surface artefacts on the battlefield can be used to detect features in areas where the earthworks have eroded.

The instance of food and drink containers from the war era, mainly found in trenches, dugouts and in areas which correlate with no-man's land on historical maps, remind us of the daily experiences of living in this landscape. The artefacts relating to food and drink on either side of the lines provide information about the types of food eaten, where this took place and where rubbish was disposed of. The coastal (Anzac) side of the battlefield and no-man's land revealed higher numbers of food tins and ceramic SRD jars, whereas the Turkish trenches revealed two cooking stones, a brick oven and numerous glass bottle shards. On the Anzac side, the decreasing appetite for the pre-packaged food eaten by the troops is recorded by Bean and expressed in colourful terms in several soldiers' war diaries. After months of canned corned beef, hard biscuits and tea, we read of soldiers making porridge from the biscuits or a stew of bully beef and biscuit in attempts to make the food palatable. By December, Lieutenant Ronald McInnis wrote, 'It will be a treat to get my Christmas parcel from home – it would be hard for anyone away from here to imagine the intensity of our feelings regarding anything to eat'.[39]

---

39 Ronald A. McInnis, *War diary of Ronald McInnis* (Australian War Memorial collections, AWM PRO097, 1915), entry 4 December 1915.

The remains of the detested bully beef tins, distinctive rectangular tins with rounded edges, are the most common metal container found by the survey, followed by circular tins. It must be remembered that materials were in short supply on the Anzac lines and containers such as jam tins and jars were often repurposed as makeshift grenades ('jam tin bombs', see also AWM G00267),[40] which might make their presence in the trenches and dugouts less likely. In contrast to the Anzac rations, historical sources indicate that Turkish soldiers were served cooked meals of vegetables, beans, chickpeas and lentils, and each soldier had an allowance of fresh meat.[41] The archaeological record of cooking facilities and the lack of tins from pre-packaged foods generally supports this description of a higher instance of fresh produce. It does not follow that the Turkish soldiers were without hardships but the distribution of food and drink containers provides an interesting point of difference between the archaeological record within Ottoman and Allied areas.

Water was also scarce on the Allied lines. Each soldier was issued with a standard Pattern 1903 Mark VI royal blue canteen, of which the JHAS found four. But many different containers were used for the transport and storage of water, from the large water tanks still visible at The Nek to empty kerosene tins and ceramic SRD jars (see AWM A01818). Thus the finds of ceramic SRD jars, which originally held rum rations, or bottle glass from various breweries and juice producers, such as Bomonti and Nectar in Constantinople,[42] may also be indicative of water storage and reuse of vessels. SRD fragments are found almost exclusively in Allied activity areas whereas bottle glass is common in Ottoman lines. These artefacts still present on the surface, though weathered or fragmentary, provide different and arguably more valuable information than the many hundreds of war-era 'relics' removed from the battlefield for museum display. When interpretation of the artefacts is able to be made with the benefit of their archaeological context these finds inform us on the integrity of the battlefield and enhance interpretations of daily life during the 1915 conflict.

The JHAS has pieced together the remaining record of some important sectors of the battlefield earthworks, including sections of the front lines, communication trenches, dugouts and support areas, including Malone's

---

40 Ronald J. Austin, *Gallipoli: Encyclopedia of the Dardanelles Campaign*, (Victoria: Slouch Hat Publications, 2005).

41 Antonio Sagona et al, 'Artefacts from the Battlefield', 2016.

42 E. Eren, 'Bira İmalathanelerinden Bira Fabrikalarına – Bomonti ve Olimpos,' *Toplumsal Tarih* 144 (2005): 84–93.

Terraces and the Maori Pah. The visible earthworks are recorded in three dimensions, meaning that we can quantify their length, width and depth. We can add a fourth dimension to the landscape by examining the record that was mapped in this same area in 1916. We can also go back further and consider the record as it was being created by referring to aerial photographs produced in October 1915. Comparing the length of trenches and tunnels recorded in 1915 and 1916 with the record of the survey made in 2010-14 allows us to quantify the preservation of the battlefield earthworks. For example, in a 100 metre square immediately south of the Lone Pine memorial 36% of the original trench lines recorded in 1916 remained in 2014. The results vary according to the slope and soils of the battlefield, but we can confidently say that the Anzac Area presents one of the best preserved WWI battlefield landscapes in the world.

On the Western Front, the record of the First World War was variously destroyed, modified or symbolically buried beneath newer layers from the Second World War.[43] This was not the experience at Gallipoli; several concrete bunkers were installed along the coastline during the 1940s but no entrenched warfare took place on the peninsula again. For this reason, the First World War features at Gallipoli are in a unique state of preservation, disturbed only by commemorative structures, memorials, cemeteries and the infrastructure of the Park. The relationship between these commemorative features and the battlefield beneath is complex. Several parts of the Anzac Area were substantially modified in the 1920s in order to create monuments such as Lone Pine, and modification of the landscape has continued with sites such as the 57th Infantry Regiment Memorial (est. 1992) and the Anzac Commemorative Site (est. 2000). Landscapes of conflict exist in the present and change in appearance and interpretation is part of the human legacy of sites of conflict. Just as the war-era earthworks intersect with Roman remains at Lone Pine, the commemorative structures overlay and intersect with the battlefield features excavated by those who they memorialise.

The battlefields of Gallipoli are cultural artefacts, subject to changing social attitudes and actions toward war and memory. Through the destructive process of industrialised warfare, new landscapes steeped in new meanings were created at Gallipoli. The incision of trenches and tunnels revealed evidence of earlier layers of human history, engaging the soldiers during the war and informing us in the aftermath. The landscapes of Gallipoli –

---

43   Nicholas Saunders, 2002.

beautiful, dramatic, multi-vocal and always contested – present us with a palimpsest of human history, conflict and material remains.

Academic and public interest in the legacy of the Great War conflict is reaching new heights in the centenary years of the conflict. Whilst the Western Front saw much higher casualties than the Gallipoli campaign, the conflict over the Peninsula holds a unique position in the national histories of Turkey, Australia and New Zealand. The military history of the Gallipoli campaign has generated abundant literature, but until recently we knew very little about the archaeological record of the Gallipoli battlefields. There is a considerable archaeological record in this strategic and contested landscape. In several cases the more ancient remains have literally been buried by commemorative features for more recent conflict, including the Lone Pine memorial which sits on ground once occupied by a Roman camp and the Abide monument which overlays the ancient Greek city of Elaious. Over these more ancient and elusive remains, the expansive network of trenches, tunnels and terraces conspicuously changed the landscape of the peninsula and, to a large extent, remains to be seen today. Together with the record of smaller artefacts across the battlefield this archaeological assemblage provides context for our understanding of behaviour and daily life in the Anzac area. Where other First World War sites were reclaimed for settlement and agriculture after the war, Gallipoli, and specifically the Anzac Area, was reserved, resulting in a uniquely well-preserved landscape from the first global, industrialised conflict.

Part 6

Anzac's Early Days

Chapter 14

ANZAC DAY'S EARLY RITUALS

Bill Gammage

To commemorate the Great War, Turkey, Australia and New Zealand focus on Gallipoli. This is striking, since militarily Gallipoli was their least significant front, and compared to what came after, though not before, the Anzac countries suffered few casualties there. Instead the three nations feel the symbolic importance of the campaign.

There a common focus ends. Although each country built a national memorial in solid classical style, Ankara's memorial centres on a leader, Wellington's and Canberra's on a democratic army. The Anzac countries mark 25 April, the day of the Landing; Turkey marks 18 March, the day its defences defeated a combined British and French fleet – one of history's great victories. But 18 March is not nearly so widely or deeply remembered as 25 April. 18 March was the occasion of the first conference I attended in Turkey, in Ankara in 1990, but nothing in particular marked the day. It has never been a holiday, and apart from that conference there seemed little interest in it.

Turkey's most important national day is probably Republic Day, 29 October, the day Ataturk proclaimed the republic in 1923. Both national memorial and national day pivot on him. Remembering leaders rather than followers may be a heritage of Empire, and perhaps is why in 1990 the few Turks interested were puzzled at the fuss Australia and New Zealand made of the Anzac battlefields and of 25 April. They saw 25 April as a distinctly Anzac occasion, and I believe only 1990's big and publicly funded Anzac ceremonies began to spark Turkish interest in the day.

Çanakkale Province has much more interest than elsewhere in 18 March. The hillside monuments above Kilitbahir thank the victors of both 18 March and the Gallipoli campaign, and Çanakkale's university is named 18 March. True, the Ankara conference venues put the Turkish, Australian and New Zealand flags in pride of place in comparison to the flags of Britain, France, Germany and the other conference participants, but I attribute this to Prof Dr Mete Tuncoku. He was very familiar with Çanakkale and 1915, and he organised the conference with great insight and empathy. I take this chance to pay tribute to Mete for his outstanding contribution to Turkey's Gallipoli history and to Turkish – Anzac relations, then and since.

In several countries, parallels to 18 March can be found – Waterloo, Gettysburg, Amritsar, Pearl Harbor, D Day – days not forgotten but not national. But I know of no parallel to Anzac Day's spontaneity, variety and centrality, and henceforth I discuss it.

Even in Australia and New Zealand most national holidays – Australia Day, Waitangi Day, Empire Day, King's Birthday, Labour or 8 Hour Day – were first promoted by a sectional interest, and only later moved into a national pantheon. Anzac Day began by spontaneous combustion, so it has always mirrored what Australians and New Zealanders think about their country, by celebrating or not celebrating, and if they celebrate, how this differs from place to place and year to year.

Since 1916 places large and small have searched earnestly but haphazardly for the right way to mark the day. The search was unprecedented. No other national day marks so much loss for so little triumph, yet so quickly became a people's day. Almost everyone feels able to say what Anzac Day rituals should or should not be: solemn or serious, run by clergy or civic officials or the RSL or RSA, a holiday and if so what kind, who should participate, should differences between Protestants and Roman Catholics be allowed for and if so how, which hymns if any, what order of march, what should happen afterwards. Countless values, emotions and assumptions contest, and countless home-grown balances are struck.

Some elements of the day reflect what the AIF and NZEF did: a march to a church service, words of sacrifice and achievement, sports, dinner, drink, two-up – a day both to remember and to enjoy. From Egypt in 1916 Tom Carroll, a veteran of the Landing, told his father,

> we had a great day here … All the troops had a holiday and it was well appreciated. The band marching around the camp and playing aroused the camp at 5 o'clock … A mass was given in commemoration of our fallen comrades, and to commemorate the landing at Anzac … it brought Sad memories to me and also made tear[s] come to my eyes …

There was ... a water carnoval [sic] down on the Canal in the afternoon ... [with dummy boats, a high dive platform, and a greasy pole] ... a Steam launch ... [had] a lady on board her, and when the soldiers seen her they yelled out ... 'Smoother up!' This is a warning to those who are naked... There was a scatter every where for their clothes ... three officers [were] paddling a canoe across the canal. A soldier spots them ... got hold of [the canoe] and made it capsized. The officers with all their clothes on were soon struggling in the water, every body roaring a treat at them. Any how they managed to reach the shore ... [two men were paddling] ... 'S.S. Suddenjerk' ... [under] 'Admiral Smashemup'. Printed on its sides was, 'Washing taken in', 'Are we down hearted? No!', 'We have plenty of time for sport and [to] beat the Germans too' ... that ended my Sorrowful & enjoyable day.[1]

Carroll was in John Monash's Fourth Brigade, and Monash too attended a solemn morning service, the afternoon 'screamingly funny' Canal festivities including a skit on the Landing, and a night concert in the YMCA Hut.[2] For the rest of the war, 'Sorrowful & enjoyable' typified soldiers' Anzac Days. A march to and from morning services led to an afternoon 'Sports Carnival' with competitions, prizes and comic events, and dinner and drink at night. 25 April was a chance to be free for a moment from the toil and tension of war.[3]

In London on Anzac Day 1916, 1300 Australians and 700 New Zealanders, mostly convalescents brought by train from camps on Salisbury Plain, marched from Waterloo to a service in Westminster Abbey. The New Zealanders then dispersed, while the Australians marched via Buckingham Palace to lunch at the Hotel Cecil, then through Trafalgar Square to a free picture show. 'No other body of troops', Michael McKernan observes, 'British, Colonial or Allied, was to be so honoured during the war.' Since April 1915 the British press had fulsomely praised the Anzacs, including in terms some now attribute to Charles Bean, but this day's events probably stemmed more from the British establishment's enthusiasm for Prime Minister Billy Hughes, then stumping the UK demanding a more aggressive prosecution of the war. The King, Queen, Kitchener and other dignitaries

---

1   Pte T Carroll, 4 Bde HQ, Farm labourer, of Ballarat, Vic. RTA 12/4/19, aged 31. L 28/4/16, Australian War Memorial (AWM) 3 DRL/7685.
2   KS Inglis (J Lack ed), *Anzac Remembered* (Melbourne: University of Melbourne, 1998), 14-15.
3   AWM Souvenirs 1, 1/2/1, 2/1/1, 3/1/1.

were at the Abbey, the King sent an Anzac Day message to his two most distant possessions, and the press baron Lord Beaverbrook took a shine to Billy and had one of his papers hail the Anzacs 'The Knights of Gallipoli'.⁴

One of those knights, Norman Bethune, took part in the march, and told his sister:

> We got a wonderful reception and talking to people afterwards, they said it was one of the biggest things that ever took place in London, and certainly since the war ... I noticed a lot of women crying and they called out all sorts of things to us. I heard one old lady say 'Oh you darlings' and other things I heard 'The Cream of the Empire' [and] 'You didn't have to be fetched'. We had to march to attention and the people couldn't quite understand why we looked so serious, and kept calling to us to smile. Flowers were showered on us and handkerchiefs. One girl kissed hers and held it out to me. I didn't notice in time and it dropped behind me. Just as we turned into the Strand, I think it was, the band struck up 'Australia will be here' and it was fine ... The service in the Abbey was most impressive, especially when at the end the 'Last Post' was blown in the church ... we had a very good lunch... [Then] went down to the theatre, but unfortunately it could not accommodate us all and I missed it. Those of us and there were hundreds of us who did not get in, were given leave until midnight ... There was one 'Arriety' looking girl at Waterloo who was heard to say 'aren't they a bit of alright not 'arf'.⁵

For some at home this light-heartedness was shockingly irreverent, but Norman's brother Douglas was killed at the Nek seven months before, and now he told his sister, 'I wouldn't have missed it for worlds, though it hurt dear too.' What soldiers thought was not what civic leaders thought, sometimes not even what their own leaders thought: on Anzac Day 1919 the AIF marched in farewell through London, and many marchers refused to turn 'eyes right' to the King.⁶

---

4   E Andrews, '25 April 1916', *JAWM* 23, Oct 1993, 16-18; M McKernan, *The Australian People and the Great War* (Melbourne: Thomas Nelson, 1980), 120; Bruce Scates, Frank Bongiorno, Laura James and Rebecca Wheatley, "Such a great space of water between us': Anzac Day in Britain, 1916-39', *Australian Historical Studies* 45, No. 2 (2014): 220-241.

5   Tpr NM Bethune, 8 LH, Farmer, of Swan Hill, Vic. DOW 19/4/17, aged 31. L 27/4/16 courtesy Nicky Tichener, Adelaide.

6   E Andrews, *The Anzac Illusion* (Cambridge: Cambridge University Press, 1993), 186; P Payton, *Regional Australia and the Great War* (Exeter: University of Exeter Press, 2012), 197.

Home in Australia, and I think in New Zealand, perhaps half those men never marched again. 'I had enough of following officers around during the war', a returned man told me in 1968. Bill Harney found his memories too painful, never applied for his medals, and never attended an Anzac Day ceremony, though he never forgot his AIF mates. Ken Inglis reminds us that over half of Australia's returned men did not join the RSL, for reasons varying from battling the nightmares of war, too much boozing on the day, the day run by officers, and objecting to speakers saying what men died for.[7] Certainly it is arrogant of any speaker to pronounce on that last, but most do.

Australia's first 'Anzac Day' was in Adelaide on 13 October 1915, Eight Hours Day, an Adelaide holiday. A 'spectacular procession' of soldiers, patriotic tableaux, concert parties and trade union displays went from the Trades Hall to Adelaide Oval to watch comic events, a balloon ascent, kite flying, and two old trams on specially built rails rushing headlong at each other to crash with an almighty bang and flying timber. The churches held services, and everywhere were appeals for volunteers and funds for wounded soldiers. Over £2500 was raised.[8]

The day both had a union flavour, and echoed how the AIF overseas celebrated. By April 1916 this kind of day was disputed in Australia. Few questioned the march, though that word did not become popular until World War 2. Instead the civilian word 'procession' was generally used, or if not, 'pageant' or 'parade' – words taken from joyous processions before the war. But who should process? Returned men certainly, bands of course, veterans of earlier wars sometimes, anyone in uniform usually – AIF in training, defence personnel, navy and army cadets. Civic groups might be in or out: Scouts, Guides, school children, fire brigades, ambulances, friendly societies, unions, rejected volunteers. 'Who should process' shuffled back and forth across the Anzac countries, and across the years.

Where should a procession end? Often it was at a church, for a 'service', a word quickly entrenched in Anzac Day ritual. In 1916 that may have been encouraged because Anzac Day was also Easter Tuesday, but in later years too churches were popular places to stop, as in the AIF and NZEF. But if a church, which one? From 1916 many Protestants opted for what they called a 'united service', meaning that clergy of each available denomination took part, and over the years took turns to host and lead. That reflected

---

7   *Bill Harney's War*, Sydney 1983 (originally J Thompson, *Harney's War*, ABC Radio, 1965?); KS Inglis, *Sacred Places* (Melbourne: Melbourne University Press, 1998), 243–4.

8   JG Pavils, *Anzac Day: The Undying Debt* (Adelaide: Lythrum Press, 2007), 2-3; Anon, *The Emergence of Anzac Day*, web posted 23 April 2011, 2.

army practice, but it didn't suit Protestants in some places, and it didn't suit Roman Catholics anywhere: they went to mass on their own, and at first not even to that, as the Pope didn't allow it until 1923.[9]

Doctrinal differences were a constant headache for an RSL or RSA wanting unity among returned soldiers, and for ecumenical clergy troubling over what hymns to sing, who should lead them, what prayers, what blessing if any. One solution was that participating clergy be returned men wherever possible, but that worked only sometimes. Some RSL spokesmen lost patience with doctrinal dispute. 'Anzac Day is bigger than any of the churches', the RSL's William Yeo stated bluntly about 1965. Melbourne dropped its united service in 1938; Sydney tried that in 1956 but was obliged to reinstate it next year. In 1953 Darwin's RSL president 'mentioned the denominational problem that the proposed programme had caused. It was resolved that the Administrator be approached with a view to amicable settlement.' Darwin's RSL secretary recalled,

> The Catholics ... would not attend an Anzac Day service officially ... I remember asking old [Bishop] John O'Loughlin – wouldn't have a bar of it: didn't want to be involved with the RSL; didn't want to be involved in Anzac Day.
>
> [Interviewer] *Why was that?*
>
> Don't know. Military I suppose ... So usually either the Methodists or the Anglicans gave [a] short address there. The Anzac service itself did have hymns and things. It was pseudo-religious, but there was no minister to come and take the service. But there was at the dawn service. It was rather strange that. So part of our job was building up these particular ceremonies, and creating dances. That was a big thing. 'Cause you could hold a dance there, which meant that you got whatever girls were available – coming in. Apart from the beer.

Darwin first made the service after the march non-religious, then in 1992 dropped it.[10]

---

9 Inglis, *Sacred Places*, 67, 210-12, 429.

10 For this paragraph, KS Inglis (C Wilcox ed), *Observing Australia 1959 to 1999* (Melbourne: Melbourne University Press, 1999), 67-9, 78, 127-9; talk with Ron Bibby, Darwin RSL, 26 Sep 2012; NTRS 1715, Darwin RSL Minutes, Box 1, 30 Mar 1953; NTRS 226, TS 663, Peter Spillet interviewed by Francis Good, Darwin 1991, tape 2, 15-16, 6 Feb, & tape 6, 8, 25 Feb, both courtesy of Francoise Barr, NT Archives Service.

In 1916 the organisers most concerned to find a way to resolve such divisions were in Brisbane, where the chairman of the State Recruiting Committee, AJ Thynne, prompted Premier Tommy Ryan, a Catholic, to ask the mayor to call a meeting to plan Anzac Day. On 10 January a pleasingly wide cross-section of citizens turned up, including Thynne, the governor, the premier, the mayor, General James McKay back from Anzac, prominent businessmen, and several clergy including a rabbi, Catholic Archbishop James Duhig, and Chaplain Lt-Colonel David Garland, an Anglican. The meeting formed an Anzac Day Commemoration Committee, and elected Garland secretary.

The Committee formed definite ideas about what should happen on Anzac Day. Recognising intractable differences between Protestant and Catholic and Christian and Jew, it settled for separate morning services on the theme of sacrifice, followed (not preceded) by a march and lunch 'for the men', then a combined evening service with hymns but no theology, a short address by a local dignitary, appeals for recruits, light entertainment with a military flavour, and at 9pm two minutes silence, the Last Post and the National Anthem. During the day school children would be targeted, with a special Anzac issue of *The School Paper* and school assemblies to tell Anzac's story. Civic leaders were to keep the day solemn: hotels, theatres and racecourses should close and there should be no sports or fund raising. This was known as a 'closed' day.

Garland got Ryan to write to the other state premiers, while he wrote to civic leaders across the country:

> It will be noted that so far as Queensland is concerned, the day is to be kept with solemnity and with avoidance of anything approaching jubilation or carnival. For this reason, no attempt is being made to raise funds for any purpose... Of course, Queensland does not presume to impose its views on any other State, but, at the same time, it is felt the observance should be, as far as practicable, Australasian; therefore we venture to acquaint you with the steps we have taken.[11]

Far be it from us, he was saying, to tell you how to mark the day, but copy us.[12]

---

11 Garland to Perth City Council, 23 March 1916, in Anon, 3.
12 Brisbane 1916: NAA MP472/1, item 1/16/3062; Andrews, *JAWM*, 13-20; Anon; *Brisbane Courier*, 10 January 1916; JA Moses, 'The struggle for Anzac Day 1916-1930',

In 1916 there was no chance that any state could impose a format on 25 April, not even in Queensland. Garland really meant Brisbane, and even there the Committee's provisions were not exactly followed, let alone elsewhere in Queensland or further afield. In Townsville, wounded Anzacs, AIF men on leave, and men called up for compulsory training marched then dispersed, some to separate church services. That afternoon a Salvation Army band offered an entertainment, and at night three picture theatres opened and the mayor called 'a monster patriotic meeting' where civic officials and clergy spoke, and a returned 9 Battalion man gave a 'racy speech'. Rockhampton held church services but no march, and an evening 'torchlight procession' led by navy cadets, twenty 'Anzac heroes', army cadets, eight friendly societies one after the other, the Australian Natives Association, the fire brigade burning coloured flares, and the ambulance brigade, all flanked by badge sellers and fund raisers and ending with a patriotic concert in the theatre.[13]

Adelaide, Perth and Darwin all got Garland's letter, and all ignored it and each other. In Darwin the *Northern Territory Times* merely quoted from the Anglican *Parish Paper*, which acknowledged Garland's letter and to a degree endorsed his emphasis on sacrifice, but was hardly ecumenical. Under the heading 'St Mark's Day', it wrote,

> Anzac Day will always stand out in the minds of the Australian people as the day on which our new nation came of age. It has been said that a people does not become a nation until it has passed through the baptism of blood. On St Mark's Day, 1915, Australia was baptized as a nation.

About 40 men, most not returned, marched to the Anglican Cathedral for a 10am Anzac Memorial Service and the national anthem. If anyone else did anything in Darwin on the day, 'apart from the beer', the *Times* did not report it.[14]

Adelaide's day was a government-led recruiting and fund raising effort. The governor declared 25 April 1915 'a red letter day' which had ensured that Australia's glory would never fade. Public servants were told to take leave to attend a recruiting rally, trains and trams were told to stop for two minutes at 9am while crews led passengers in three cheers each for the King, the 'Anzac Heroes' and the Empire, and the Chamber of Manufacturers

---

Journal of the Royal Australian Historical Society, 88: 2 (June 2002), 54-74; JA Moses, *Anzac Day as Australia's All Souls' Day...*, Australian Association for Mission Studies address, Oct 2008.

13   Townsville *Daily Bulletin* 24, 25 April 16; Rockhampton *Morning Bulletin* 26 April 16.
14   *NT Times*, 20, 26, 27 April 1916.

asked for similar demonstrations in work places across the state. A morning procession of cars took wounded Anzacs to speeches and lunch in the Cheer-Up Hut, but there was no march, and men in camp kept training, their commandant telling them that this was the best way to honour the Anzacs, and the men sang 'Australia will be there'. There was a service in the Town Hall, and an evening voluntary church parade at the Anglican Cathedral. No speech said much about sacrifice; most spoke of duty and the need for conscription.[15]

In Perth 25 April was declared a holiday. There was no newspaper, but 'places of entertainment' were open. The Anglican and Catholic cathedrals held services, and the Wesley Church a united service before a 'procession' and review of troops and returned men, then a Town Hall lunch attended by clergy including the Catholic archbishop, at which the mayor declared that on this day in 1915 'the Australian nation was born'.[16]

Melbourne, and therefore the Commonwealth seated there in 1916, chose, as the Minister for Defence put it, to hold only 'informal' celebrations 'in a small way'. The government was waiting to see, he explained, if 25 April or the day the war ended proved a better day to celebrate. That was a mistake. The King got to hear of it, and on 22 April icily telegraphed the Governor-General: 'Tell my people of Australia and New Zealand that to-day I am joining them in their solemn tribute to the memory of their heroes who died in Gallipoli.' Panic in Melbourne. There was nothing official there, so the Governor-General and the Governor of Victoria sprinted north to join Sydney's celebrations. They were neither expected nor much accommodated, but allotted a second saluting stand, and amid a crowd of 50-60,000 people largely ignored. Spontaneous combustion had burnt a few fingers. Never again would officials be so badly wrong-footed, and the King did not send another Anzac Day message until 1920.[17]

Hobart too officially did nothing on 25 April, deferring activities to Friday 28 April, because 'the promoters' judged Friday more suitable for the day's 'greatest purpose': raising funds for wounded soldiers' club rooms. Methodists held a morning 'united service', though apparently without Anglican, Catholic or Salvation Army participation. That afternoon the 40 Bn marched from Claremont camp to a 'parade' of returned soldiers, veterans of other wars, and senior cadets arrayed before a temporary cenotaph in the

---

15   Adelaide 1916: Pavils, 10-11; MJ Reardon, 'Anzac Day in Adelaide, 1916 to 1922', (Adelaide University History Honours thesis 1979), 2-7.
16   Perth 1916: *Mercury* 26 April 1916; *West Australian* 26 April 1916.
17   Melbourne 1916: Andrews, *Journal of the Australian War Memorial*, 13-14

Domain, where the Chief Justice spoke. Then all government offices and many businesses closed from 2.40-3.15pm while the parade marched to afternoon tea and a concert in the Town Hall. The city was decorated like 'a huge bazaar', with bunting, flags, stalls, badge sellers and cars selling fruit, mostly apples. 'Indeed', a reporter wrote, 'the streets were a regular Paddy's market. One could buy almost anything.' Next day there was a 'voluntary general church parade' – one way to encourage an ecumenical service without imposing it. Swansea also marked Anzac Day on 28 April, also to raise funds; Ulverstone held a united church service on the 25th; Launceston compromised by closing the shops for late afternoon church services and a dinner and smoke social for wounded soldiers on the 25th, and fund raising on the 28th.[18]

In Sydney Premier WA Holman was also President of the Anzac Day Executive. He announced that 25 April would be 'a big recruiting effort', and handed its arrangements to the showman JC Williamson. Williamson organised a 'procession' led by cars carrying invalid soldiers, a drum-head memorial service in the Domain, 'special services in nearly all churches' which Catholics were told not to attend, recruiting meetings, and 'lady collectors' for an Anzac Memorial.[19] In ways like this and the Red Cross, the war gave women a public prominence rare until 1914.

Spontaneous combustion sparked equally varied Anzac Days in country towns. A procession led Newcastle wounded to separate church services. Kapunda did nothing on 25 April, but on 30 April the brass band led a 'procession' of councillors, the Progress Association, various church choirs, senior cadets, returned soldiers, adults and children to a united memorial service. Mittagong, Bowral and Robertson each held a 'united' service, Bowral in the 'beautifully decorated' Church of England, the others in the School of Arts, though it's not clear that Catholics came, and returned men certainly didn't – they went on free rail passes to Sydney. In Wagga a band led police, two returned men, two volunteers, cadets, the mayor, a few aldermen and many recruiters down the main street to the Town Hall, then to a church service. The Narrandera Council granted a holiday, held a procession, fund raising, and a patriotic concert 'reminiscent of Empire Day'. The mayor said the day was not to remember the brave men who died but to celebrate the landing in 1915, while another speaker asserted that the

---

18   Hobart 1916: *Mercury* 25-29 April 1916.
19   Sydney 1916: *SMH* 24, 26 April 1916; *Mercury* 26 April 1916; Andrews, *JAWM*, 15; Moses, 2002, 64.

day would become 'Australia's National Festival Day'. In Albany the mayor hosted a united service in the Town Hall, but eleven returned men accepted a free trip to Perth instead, while the remaining eight, all convalescent, were given dinner at the London Hotel.[20]

Garland's prescriptions for Anzac Day also found few parallels in New Zealand. Prime Minister William Massey thought the day should be one of solemn remembrance, then promptly allowed Auckland a half-holiday 'with a view', he said, 'to assisting the recruiting campaign'. Auckland held a recruiting meeting that night, but otherwise its remembrance was 'widespread but largely unofficial'. Wellington's public buildings and business houses were covered with flags, and ships in the harbour with bunting. In the Town Hall that afternoon clergy and military leaders, but no returned soldiers, spoke at a 'National Memorial Service'. That night the Town Hall saw a 'great patriotic meeting', where returned soldiers paraded to repeated cheering, and Massey and other ministers, the leader of the opposition, and the mayor all praised the achievement of the Anzacs. Masterton held a united service 'in reverent and grateful remembrance of what brave men have done, and have given, for our nation and for humanity', with four hymns, two prayers, a psalm, and addresses by a minister and an adjutant.[21]

Fun or funeral, it seemed clear that Anzac Day should be a public holiday, to let more people turn up. But what sort of public holiday? On the day or the nearest Sunday; a full or half day or just time off for a procession or recruiting meeting; shops, hotels, theatres, racecourses and sports grounds open or closed; something between. Behind these puzzles lay a deeper question: who should decide what happens on 25 April? Who should take charge of the legacy of Anzac?

New Zealand was first to tackle the holiday question, first to enforce a closed holiday, and decades later last to relax it. In 1916 Wanganui and Dunedin declared a full holiday and Auckland and Rotorua a half holiday, but most places had none, and the RSA wasted no time in campaigning for one. Massey stalled: most employers and some churches wanted to commemorate on the nearest Sunday. The RSA would not have it, and on Armistice Day 1920 parliament declared 25 April a closed public holiday.

---

20 For this paragraph, *Albany Advertiser* 29 April 1916; P Donovan, *Storm: An Australian Country Town and World War 1* (Adelaide: Donovan & Associates, 2011), 94; B Gammage, *Narrandera Shire* (Adelaide: Narrandera Shire Council, 1986), 204-5; Inglis, *Sacred Places*; S Morris, *Anzac Days*, ms Wagga nd c/- Ian Hodges.

21 NZ 1916: *Dominion*, 26 April 1916; Masterton Anzac Day Program, 25 April 1916; M Henry, 'Making New Zealanders through commemoration: Assembling Anzac Day in Auckland, 1916-1939', *NZ Geographer* 61:1 (April 2006), 5 (online 1-16).

The draft bill proposed that the day be treated as a Sunday, but Massey got that deleted, allowing shops, theatres and sports grounds to open. The RSA was outraged, and in February 1922 the Act was amended to treat 25 April as a Sunday. In New Zealand that mattered. There were no Sunday papers, sports or races, and no hotels or theatres and very few shops open.[22]

In Australia most RSL branches found such solemnity awkward. They wanted a holiday but not a 'closed' holiday. They wanted their mates remembered but 25 April made Australia's national day. They wanted solemn services in the morning but afternoon sports, races, and reunions with two-up and beer. They opposed moving services to the nearest Sunday but wanted the solemnity that clergy provided. Slowly they worked towards a solution. Under RSL pressure, the 1922 Premiers' Conference agreed that the holiday be observed on the day. The 1923 conference agreed 'That Anzac Day shall be observed throughout the Commonwealth as Australia's national day', and that the morning be set aside for religious and memorial services and the afternoon for 'instilling into the minds of the children of Australia the significance of Anzac Day'. In the afternoon adults could play healthy sports only, and there would be no race meetings. West Australia had declared a holiday in 1919 and Queensland in 1921; the Commonwealth and South Australia followed in 1922, NSW in 1924, Victoria in 1925 and Tasmania in 1927. The holiday was the first component of Anzac Day systematically imposed from above.

But it was not systematic. In no two states was it alike. In varying degrees Queensland, Victoria and Tasmania decreed a closed day; Western Australia, South Australia, and New South Wales an open day. In 1929 the RSL Federal Executive urged the prime minister to make 25 April a closed day. This was a state matter, but in its territories the Commonwealth announced a largely closed holiday, though with post and telegraph offices open for business from 9-10am. In Darwin this was exactly the time the march was held, Darwin being hot. There were other problems, and not until 1964 in Queensland and 1967 in New Zealand was the closed holiday frittered away.[23]

---

22   NZ holiday: *Dominion*, 26/4/16; Henry, 5, 10; JO Melling, 'The New Zealand Returned Soldiers' Association 1916-1923,(Victoria University of Wellington MA Thesis, 1952), 123-5; Moses, 2002, 65; NP Webber, *The First Fifty Years of the NZ RSA 1916 to 1966*, Wellington 1966?

23   Australia holiday: Premier's Conferences 1921-3, NAA A457, 520/1/58 & A461, 13/1/10 Part 1; Inglis (Lack ed), 15-16; Inglis (Wilcox ed), 63-9; Moses, 2002, 54-74; Pavils, 42-4.

What if Anzac Day was a Sunday, as in 1920 and 1926? This was a problem, especially since in New Zealand and some states Sunday was closed. Churches wanted services on Sunday and anything secular on Monday, including the march; employers opposed a Monday holiday; civic and RSL leaders divided; in New Zealand the RSA bristled at what its 1919 conference called 'Mondayising' Anzac Day, but many sub-branches moved there. In 1920 the day was commemorated sometimes on Sunday, sometimes on Monday, sometimes on both. By 1926 New South Wales, Queensland, South Australia and the Commonwealth had shifted the march to a Monday holiday, but other states kept to Sunday. For decades a Monday holiday was debated and haphazard. For example 25 April was a Sunday in 1954, but less than three weeks before the Darwin RSL was still asking the Administrator if the Monday would be a holiday. Among other concerns, it wanted to know how many 'free eats' to cater for after the march.[24]

Fiddling with rituals many saw as sacred may have provoked one more instance of spontaneous combustion on Anzac Day: the dawn service, which arose so spontaneously that we debate where it began. The word 'service' implies a religious origin, but the Australian War Memorial claims that the dawn service 'has its origins in a military routine ... stand to'. In fact no-one has been able to link the origins of the dawn service to either church or military.

In Australia an unofficial 'first dawn service' competition has three claimants. The earliest is Toowoomba, where at 4am on Anzac Day 1919 a small group of returned men laid flowers on war graves and memorials, then toasted their mates with rum. In 1920 and 1921 a bugler joined them to sound the Last Post and Reveille. This was not strictly a 'service', but it was certainly dawn.

Sydney laid claim. Near dawn on Anzac Day 1927 some carousing Anzacs were coming home from the Gallipoli Club. Passing the Cenotaph, they saw an old lady laying flowers. Somewhat shame-faced they helped her, and in 1928 organised Sydney's first dawn service. The *Sydney Morning Herald* reported that the organisers, not the RSL but the Association of Returned Soldiers and Sailors Clubs, 'expressed their satisfaction at the unexpected success of the innovation. 'Such a gathering', [the secretary] said ... 'shows that the public is still very far from forgetting what the occasion means." The *Herald* wrote, 'About 100 men and 30 women and children gathered

---

24 *NT Times* 24 April 1920, 23 April 1921; Darwin RSL Minutes, NTRS 1715, box 1, 31/3 & 7/4/54; NAA A461, 13/1/10 Part 1; Webber, 13.

at the Cenotaph at 4.30am, and heads bowed in silence.' Wreaths were laid, but there was no bugle, no speeches, no prayers. 'One old lady, partly crippled with age and obvious long distress, haltingly walked to the foot of the Cenotaph, where ... she hid modestly her token of long remembering – a tiny bunch of white daisies, picked from some suburban garden, and held together with a piece of cord. She could not have given more.' Messages on those wreaths share with newspaper *In Memoriam* notices the most moving moments of Anzac Day: 'To my dear daddy', one said in 1928, another 'To Jack, for all at home in England, 1914-18. From Mother', and a third, 'Here I am darling.'

The third 'first dawn service' claimant is Albany, from where the first AIF – NZEF convoy left in 1914. Nothing known supports claims for an Albany dawn service in 1916, 1923 or 1929, but in 1930 the rector of St Johns wrote in his church register, 'Anzac Day, 6am. Holy Communion – 30 (attended)', adding much later, 'Procession to Memorial – Wreaths laid – Collection for distressed soldiers' fund – First dawn service in Australia'. The *Albany Advertiser* reported this ceremony, and in 1931 two additions to it, when the congregation filing up to take communion passed the coffin of the mother of an Anzac, and when the rector led some of his flock up Mt Clarence. But in 1929, two years before, the same paper reported a dawn service in Perth. The *West Australian* too reported an early morning 'march' to a service at the State War Memorial in 1929, run by the RSL, with no clergy reported.

Even Perth was not first. In 1916 Rockhampton held a 6.30am service in the town centre, conducted by Protestant clergy, with hymns, prayers, and addresses. Despite heavy rain 800 people came, but no returned men, though 20 marched later that day. The service was not repeated in 1917, 18 or 19.[25] And time zones let Tinui on New Zealand's north island shade Rockhampton and probably other Australian towns. After early church, though later than dawn, the vicar led his congregation up a steep hill overlooking the village, including Scouts lugging the pieces of a large metal cross, which they erected on top. If there is a first dawn service this might be it, though I haven't checked Fiji or Tonga!

---

25 Dawn Services. Sydney: John Hayes to Lucas Jordan, 28 Sep 2012; *SMH* 26 April 1926, 25 April 1927, 26 April 1928. Albany, Perth: *Albany Advertiser* 25 April 1929, 24 April 1930, 27 April 1931; *West Australian* 26 April 1929; J Bartlett, *Built to Last* (Albany: 1998), 122. Toowoomba, Sydney, Albany: G Seal, '... 'and in the morning...': adapting and adopting the dawn service', *Journal of Australian Studies* 35, No. 1 (March 2011): 49-63. Rockhampton: *Morning Bulletin* 26 April 1916-19.

The dawn service spread quite slowly: to Unley in 1930, Brisbane 1931, Hobart 1932, Melbourne 1933, Hindmarsh 1934, Adelaide and London 1935, Auckland 1939, Canberra 1943, Alice Springs 1948, Narrandera 1950, Darwin by 1955, Moruya 2012. As it spread its simplicity eroded. Today it is commonly thought the appropriate service to mark grief and honour sacrifice, and wreath messages can still tug the heart, like one in Darwin in 1966: 'To my Son whom I shall never see again on this earth.'[26] But bugles and clergy and officials are now common, and spontaneity rare.[27] Yet today 'dawn' might be 4.30am as at Anzac Cove, or anywhere between 4 and 6am local time.

What is Anzac Day's future? Supposedly it is a returned services' day, but the reunions and two-up are fewer and less boisterous now, and the sports once dominated by returned men now make only token reference to them. Is it the national day? Waitangi Day reconciles more than divides, so has more power than Australia Day. Outside New South Wales especially, 26 January can cause dissent, even hostility, and Anzac Day challenges it. Yet 25 April looks back, neither warning nor inspiring the future towards ideals useful to peace.

In other ways too the Day has been shepherded towards conformity, yet retains some of its early diversity. What services should be held, by whom, and where? Each place finds its own answer, but in general an RSL or RSA branch decides, sometimes and sometimes not allowing clergy to declare the meaning of sacrifice or the importance of memory. Many churches still hold special services on 25 April and on the nearest Sunday, but only for their congregations, not as voices of national commemoration. Should the silence be one minute or two, and should silence or the Ode fall between the Last Post and Reveille (or Rouse, as it has become in some places)? There is no common answer. When should the march be? Afternoon and evening processions have moved to various times in the morning. Where should it finish? Town hall, church, oval and Boer War monument were soon supplanted by that widening spread of Great War memorials which so changed the landscape of the Anzac countries, but not all marches end there – Adelaide's doesn't for example. Who should march? Former enemies, as Turks did in 1953 and in some places have since? Defence Force contingents

---

26 NTRS 1268/P1, Darwin RSL Correspondence Files 1952-71, Box 7: *Wots Doin* News Sheet 5, June 1966, NT Archives.

27 Dawn service spreads: Adelaide *Advertiser* 26 April 1930, 26 April 1935, 27 April 1936; Hobart *Mercury* 29 April 35; *Northern Standard* 30 April 1948; Gammage, 213; Henry, 11; Inglis, *Sacred Places*, 330-1, 422-4; Pavils, 123-5; Seal, 49-63.

not comprising returned men or women? They march now, and they help march organisers, but so do police and council workers, who don't march. Only the Defence Force marches as an occupation. Next of kin? Most villages and small towns say yes, reflecting community spirit. Bigger places either say no, or confront straggling next of kin groups which now out-lengthen any other. They will keep lengthening until almost everyone is eligible to march: what then? Might the march become just a procession? Already it is as much about ancestor worship as memory. Is this better than no march at all? Perhaps, yet what an Anzac Day it would be, to see the last veteran marching alone, band playing, crowd applauding, symbolically announcing for how long Australia and New Zealand have been at peace.

Chapter 15

THE ABC OF WAR

Early Children's Histories of Anzac

Frank Bongiorno

The story is a heroic one, and every boy and girl should read it, not only for the enthralling interest of it, but because ... there is aroused in the mind a more glowing pride in this land that can produce such men as the Anzacs, men who stand unrivalled in the art of warfare, in initiative, resource, and all that makes for a good soldier as well as for good citizenship.[1]

Books for young people can provide a vivid picture of the values prevailing in a society, yet they have so far received limited attention from scholars writing about the Anzac legend and the history of the First World War. There has been an explosion of First World War-themed stories in Australian young people's literature and history in recent years, as well as continuing debate about how Anzac and war should be taught in schools.[2] Historians have also explored the manner in which Australia's education system prepared its pupils for war and, once conflict had broken out in 1914, how individual

---

1   Alfred G. Waterworth, *The Story of Anzac Day: Told for Boys and Girls* (Launceston: Returned Sailors and Soldiers Imperial League Launceston Sub-Branch/Tasmanian Education Department, 1920), 50.

2   Anna Clark, *History's Children: History Wars in the Classroom* (Sydney: NewSouth, 2008), 43-63; Marilyn Lake, 'How do schoolchildren learn about the spirit of Anzac?', in Marilyn Lake and Henry Reynolds with Mark McKenna and Joy Damousi, *What's Wrong with Anzac?: The Militarisation of Australian History* (Sydney: NewSouth, 2010), 135-56.

schools, teachers and education systems responded to the crisis.³ There has also been a recent study of the controversies of the mid-1920s over who should be authorised to speak of the war in Australian schools on Anzac Day.⁴ But historical attention to early efforts to produce Australian war histories for children and youths remains limited.

In his study of what he calls 'the heroic theme in Australian war writing', Robin Gerster briefly considers a few books written for children about Australia's role in the war; they provide additional support for his argument concerning the prominence of the notion that 'Australians excel, even revel, in battle' and that their performance in war was both a measure of their supposed racial vigour and a reinforcement of it. The Australian soldier is represented 'as a twentieth-century embodiment of classical heroic virtue'.⁵ The war trilogies of the two best known Australian children's authors of the era, Ethel Turner and Mary Grant Bruce, have figured in more detail in a study by Brenda Niall, who argues that from these books there emerges a 'composite portrait of the Australian soldier' that accords largely with the image found in Charles Bean's writings on war and its role in displaying and adapting national character.⁶

While it will give some attention to fiction, this chapter will mainly focus on avowedly 'historical' writing about the war designed for children during the war and early post-war years. There is a sense in which this immediately sets up a false distinction. The themes to be discovered in supposedly non-fictional writing – histories, if you will – are so similar to those found in novels that there really seems very little point in making a hard and fast distinction between fictional and non-fictional modes. Some fiction in any case claimed for itself a share of the authority and authenticity that

---

3   S.G. Firth, 'Social Values in the New South Wales Primary School 1880-1914: An Analysis of School Texts', in *Melbourne Studies in Education 1970*, ed. R.J.W. Selleck (Melbourne: Melbourne University Press, 1970), 123-59; Michael McKernan, *The Australian People and the Great War* (Melbourne: Nelson, 1980, 43-64); Rosalie Triolo, *Our Schools and the War* (Melbourne: Australian Scholarly Publishing, 2012); Maxwell N. Waugh, *Soldier Boys: the Militarisation of Australian and New Zealand Schools for World War I* (Melbourne: Melbourne Books, 2014).

4   Phillip Deery and Frank Bongiorno, 'Labor, Loyalty and Peace: Two Anzac Controversies of the 1920s', in *Labour and the Great War: the Australian Working Class and the Making of Anzac*, a special issue of *Labour History*, ed. Frank Bongiorno, Raelene Frances and Bruce Scates, no. 106 (May 2014): 205-28.

5   Robin Gerster, *Big-Noting: The Heroic Theme in Australian War Writing* (Melbourne: Melbourne University Press, 1987), 2, 5.

6   Brenda Niall, *Seven Little Billabongs: The World of Ethel Turner and Mary Grant Bruce* (Melbourne: Melbourne University Press, 1979), 135.

its authors associated with real history. Joseph Bowes, a Queensland vicar who wrote the *Anzac War Trail* about the Australian Light Horse's desert campaign, explained that his book was 'a story and not a history', but that he had 'striven to place it in historic perspective. Some of the characteristics are imaginary, but not all'. Here was an each-way bet; his accounts might not be 'photographic', he explained, but they were in broad 'agreement with official despatches'.[7]

My approach here is to consider historical and contemporary 'nonfiction' for young people in the larger context of children's war literature. The mass societies that fought the First World War quickly recognised the need to tell war stories suitable for the young. In the Australian case, right from 1915 when State education departments circulated Ellis Ashmead-Bartlett's stirring account of the Australians' landing at Gallipoli,[8] there were private, commercial, semi-official and official efforts to place before Australian children stories of the heroic deeds of Australian soldiers in the theatres of the war where the Anzacs fought. In a recent study of Victorian schools and the war, Rosalie Triolo has emphasised the significant role played by the Victorian *School Paper* in disseminating ideas about and images of the war – and not only among the children who were expected to part with a penny of their pocket-money to buy each issue.[9] The various State-based school magazines must have reached thousands of homes, and are likely to have been read by adults as well as children.[10]

It was a feature of the heroic tradition of war writing that it tended to evade the most brutal aspects of industrialised slaughter, but it is nonetheless the case that young people's histories and novels do not entirely shy away from war's violence and destruction.[11] Mary Grant Bruce's *Jim and Wally*, for instance, has the boys badly injured in a gas attack. It might not be the modernism of Wilfred Owen, but no one who read her account should have been under any illusion concerning the foulness of war and the damage

---

7   Joseph Bowes, *The Anzac War Trail* (London: Humphrey Milford/Oxford University Press, n.d. [1917]), vi.
8   Ellis Ashmead-Bartlett, *Australians in Action: the Story of Gallipoli* (Sydney: W.A. Gullick, Govt. Printer, 1915).
9   Triolo, *'Our Schools and the War'*, xvi.
10 See, for instance, Norma Townsend, 'Moulding Minds: The *School Paper* in Queensland, 1905 to 1920', *Journal of the Royal Australian Historical Society*, 75, part 2 (October 1989): 142-57.
11 Triolo, *'Our Schools and the War'*, 272, shows that the Victorian *School Paper*, in a similar vein, did not entirely avoid matters such as wounding.

inflicted by poisonous gas.[12] In Ethel Turner's *Captain Cub*, Millicent's fiancé Jim returns to Australia having lost an arm and a leg, and with 'innumerable scars ... on his face'; that Millicent evidently intends accepting him despite his disfigurement, and that he is presented with a sum of money by a benefactress that will supposedly set him up for life, cannot entirely mitigate the impact of his hideous injuries.[13] Even books written for very small children drew attention to the suffering created by war. *The Young Australias'* [sic] *ABC of War* predictably tells its readers that 'A' is 'for ANZACS', but it also includes 'R' for 'homeless REFUGEES'; even in this little picture book there is something rather more complex than a mere glorification of war being carried on.[14]

Australian children's histories were preoccupied with explaining why the war had broken out, why Britain had entered it, and why Australia had joined in the slaughter. Such literature was concerned with the political, diplomatic and ideological history of the war in ways that underline one of its key purposes: to justify the conflict to a young audience who might otherwise have wondered why a distant war should matter to them.[15] C.E. Sutton Turner in *Quick March: the story of England's Great War: a book for Australian boys and girls* explained that a seventeen year old had killed a prince and princess, and that Austria had responded by unjustly deciding to punish the entire Serbian people.[16] More commonly, authors blamed Germany for the war. 'There would have been no war if Germany had not meant that there should be war', explained Charles Atkins, an army captain and Melbourne municipal councillor in a book presented to State school children in that city.[17] '[T]he real cause of the war', according to Alfred G. Waterworth, a Tasmanian school-teacher writing a book on behalf of the Returned Sailors' and Soldiers' Imperial League, 'was the desire of Germany for world power and dominion over other nations'. Britain, he indicated, entered the war not so much out of a narrow perception of a threat to its national or imperial interests, but out of a sense of altruism, chivalry and honour:

---

12   Mary Grant Bruce, *Jim and Wally* (London and Melbourne: Ward, Lock), 1916, 27-9.
13   Ethel Turner, *Captain Cub* (London and Melbourne: Ward, Lock, 1917), 194.
14   *Young Australias'* [sic] *ABC of War* ([Australia], Gordon and Gotch, n.d. [c. 1918]), 6.
15   See also Triolo, '*Our Schools and the War*', 16, for the Victorian *School Paper* on these matters.
16   C.E. Sutton Turner, *Quick March: The Story of England's Great War: A Book for Australian Boys and Girls* (Sydney: Turner & Sons, n.d. [c. 1915]).
17   Cr. Captain Charles Atkins, *Australia and the Great War* (Melbourne: Bennie & Pelzer [Printers], n.d.), 3.

When Britain saw Belgium invaded, when she saw France in danger, when she saw solemn promises broken, she could stand aside no longer. She knew that the liberty of the whole world was in danger; she knew that, should Germany win, the rule of the war lords would prevail, the rule of oppression and injustice. She knew that no freedom-loving nation on the face of the earth would be safe. So to save France and Belgium, to save liberty, to save humanity, she declared war on Germany.[18]

Britain had entered the war, another author agreed, because of its commitment to freedom and justice. He thought it unsurprising that Australia should sympathise with the fate of Belgium, another small nation, but it was Australia's membership of the British Empire which had been decisive in her entry into the war.[19] As C.E. Sutton Turner explained, 'You know Australia is part of the great British Empire, so that Britain's enemies are also our enemies, and her friends are our friends'.[20] But another text pointed to Australia's own interest in ensuring the defeat of Germany which, if it were not vanquished, would surely seize Australia and New Zealand, confiscate property, fill the country with German colonists, and impose the German language on the population – and how school-children already struggling with French must have feared such a fate![21]

What kind of empire did these children learn that they were defending? Some Australian historians have seen 'British race patriotism' as the dominant nationalist ideology of Australia in this period.[22] Yet the empire that is evoked in the pages of children's histories is a cosmopolitan one, a global community united not by race but by common identification with a British empire of liberty. The image is of a benevolent empire bringing the benefits of British freedom to people across the world, the Indians being prepared to fight, explained one text, because 'they are as free in their own country as we are in ours, and they know it, and have shown that they know it by their splendid loyalty to Britain from the very beginning of the war'.[23] The British-based Australian expatriate author E.C. Buley, in *A Child's History*

---

18   Waterworth, *Story of Anzac Day*, 13.
19   H.D. McLelland, *The Great War: Written for Young Australians* (Sydney: Government Printer, 1916), 16-17.
20   Turner, *Quick March*, 5.
21   McLelland, *Great War*, 31-2.
22   See, for instance, Neville Meaney, 'Britishness and Australian Identity: The Problem of Nationalism in Australian History and Historiography', *Australian Historical Studies* 32, no. 116 (April 2001): 76-90.
23   McLelland, *Great War*, 14.

of Anzac – a book that the Victorian Education Department said 'should be in every school library'[24] – emphasised that the Australians had found at Gallipoli 'a great variety of nations' that included 'coloured soldiers from the French Colonies in Africa', as well as 'Sikhs, Gurkhas, and Pathans; some of the pick of the Indian army'. The Maori from New Zealand, Buley explained, was 'a born warrior ... No finer coloured race exists in the world'.[25] Egypt, too, according to one author, had benefited from British rule, which had helped to make it 'one of the prosperous nations of the world'.[26]

Turkey often figures in Anzac mythology as a worthy and honourable opponent, but the Victorian *School Paper* of August 1915 deployed a more familiar orientalism when it explained that the sons of the world's youngest Commonwealth were 'fighting against an effete monarchy; it is a new and vigorous Antipodes pitted against the corrupt and truculent armies of the 'Sick Man of Europe"'.[27] After the campaign was over, having ended in the defeat and withdrawal of the allies, the mythologisation of the Anzacs' glorious deeds seemed better served by presenting the Turks in more positive terms, as brave and noble warriors. This admiration did not extend to the Ottoman Empire's political arrangements; Buley's book stresses the Turks' foolishness in being duped into siding with Germany, a condescending attitude that denies the capacity of the Ottoman Empire to make its own diplomatic judgments about how its interests would be best served. 'It would be very hard to say why Turkey had done this', Buley went on, 'for we have always been very good friends with the Turks, and have helped them in trouble, not once, but many times'.[28] Whereas the clash between the British Empire and Germany is understood as a great war of ideas, Buley does not pay the Turks the courtesy of attributing to them a politics comprehensible in conventional diplomatic terms. Yet while he presents them as having ruled their empire badly, their soldiers are presented as brave, if less effective as fighters than the Anzacs. '[H]ad the Anzacs been Turks, and the Turks Anzacs', Buley speculated, 'the invaders would very quickly have been driven from the peninsula of Gallipoli'.[29]

---

24 Triolo, *'Our Schools and the War'*, 260.
25 E.C. Buley, *A Child's History of Anzac* (London, New York and Toronto: Hodder and Stoughton, 1916), 66-7, 164.
26 McLelland, *Great War*, 10.
27 *School Paper for Grades VII and VIII* (Victoria), 2 August 1915, 99. For a discussion of the Victorian *School Paper*'s treatment of the Turks, see Triolo, *'Our Schools and the War'*, 263.
28 Buley, *Child's History*, 34.
29 Buley, *Child's History*, 122.

Buley presents the Anzacs' time on the peninsula as a little like a voyage of discovery in which initial prejudices against the Turks as 'cruel and cowardly' are conquered as the Australasians gain a fuller appreciation of their opponent's humane warrior virtues.[30] The Anzacs, he explains, had become aware of the killing of the Armenians, having heard 'stories of Turkish cruelty that made their blood run cold'. Indeed, so appalled were the Anzacs by what they had heard, and what it seemed to signify the Turks would do to them if they fell into their hands as prisoners, that some committed suicide rather than suffer as the Armenians had. Yet despite the truth of the stories they had heard, the Turk proved 'a merciful and chivalrous foe', and '[t]he same men who would turn old men and little children out of their homes, and beat them till they fell by the way, would risk their lives to take a drink of water to a wounded enemy'.[31]

One purpose of this kind of rhetoric was to hold on to a sense of warfare as still governed by traditional virtues of heroism and gallantry, rather than being industrialised mass butchery. Moreover, the emphasis on Turkish warrior virtues underlined the Anzac achievement, demonstrating that the Australians had held their own against an able and worthy foe. But a further reason for the emphasis on Turkish virtue was that it allowed the author to explain who the true enemy really was: Germany. Whereas there were civil exchanges at Gallipoli between the Turks and the Australians, it was explained, the Germans were said to have remained aloof.[32] In the end, the Ottoman Empire, rather like the British Empire itself, is understood as a victim of Germany and 'it is a great pity there should ever have been a quarrel with the Turks'.[33] Children's histories explained that Germany was the enemy, since, as a booklet by H.D. McLelland, the deputy chief inspector of schools in New South Wales, explained, that nation had 'seemingly gone mad with the idea that its people are a chosen people of God, superior to all others in all things, and destined to bring all other races under their sway'. McLelland's book included a lengthy description of the German political system intended to underline the differences between the free institutions of Britain and her dominions, and the Prussian tyranny that characterised the German state. The Germans, he said, were 'not free as we understand the word'.[34] The children's histories do not dwell on German atrocities; similarly,

---

30   Buley, *Child's History*, 106.
31   Buley, *Child's History*, 107-8.
32   Buley, *Child's History*, 112.
33   Buley, *Child's History*, 116.
34   McLelland, *Great War*, 26, 29-31.

Triolo has suggested that the Victorian *School Paper* was remarkably reticent about discussing the enemy during the war years, possibly reflecting the leadership of the Victorian Education Department's continuing admiration for German pedagogy.[35] In any case, defining the differences between the British and German empires could be a hazardous business in wartime. C.E. Sutton Turner, presumably writing before Britain's introduction of conscription in Britain in early 1916, explained that there was

> one great difference in the armies of Great Britain and Germany. In the British Empire, of which Australia is a part, only those who volunteer become soldiers and go to war. But in Germany and Austria every man is compelled to be a soldier, and forced to go to war, whether he wants to or not.[36]

It is easy to understand why the voluntary ethic would be treated here as the essence of British freedom because service in defence of empire was understood as among the greatest of virtues in children's history, as well as in fiction for young people. The novels of Mary Grant Bruce and Ethel Turner set down the pathways by which both young men and women could achieve such virtue. For the men, military service is the ultimate call to duty in time of war. In Ethel Turner's *The Cub*, after an initial reluctance to join in the fight, by the end of the novel John Calthrop (the Cub) is overwhelmed by the impulse to help the mother country. While the heart's desire of this wealthy young man has been to build cheap homes for the poor, he abandons his philanthropy for the army out of 'the feeling you get for England at the mere thought of her being in danger'.[37] Early in its sequel, *Captain Cub*, it is explained that '[h]e was a man, he had had the fierce, strong joy of being able to do something better than knit when the war broke out'.[38]

The reference to knitting – a common wartime activity of women on the home-front[39] – underlines the distinction between men's and women's service, which can never be equated. In Mary Grant Bruce's *Jim and Wally*, the troubled relationship of women to war is played out in an extended discussion of whether Norah Linton will be allowed to light a beacon that is needed to capture some German submariners active in coastal Ireland,

---

35 Triolo, '*Our Schools and the War*', 24, 28-31.
36 Turner, *Quick March*, 8.
37 Ethel Turner, *The Cub: Six Months in His Life* (London, Melbourne and Toronto: Ward, Lock, 1915), 249.
38 Turner, *Captain Cub*, 18.
39 McKernan, *Australian People and the Great War*, 73-4.

where the family is having a break while the lads recover from their gassing. There is a tension between the image of the independent 'Australian Girl'[40] – a product of a new world pioneering society – and prevailing assumptions concerning the gender order:

> 'I know you couldn't have me where there's shooting,' she said. 'But I can do something, if you'll let me: and in Australia women always did help men when there was need, and they didn't talk about things being 'women's work.' Women had to fight the blacks, too.'[41]

Here is the idea of a new and more vigorous version of white British womanhood, formed by a harsh frontier. Initially, the two young Australian soldiers resist her being in any way involved but on Norah's insistence that their plan has a better chance of success if this task is allocated to her, she goes ahead with it, and with the desired results.

In Turner's *Captain Club*, while the English Brigid is sufficiently spirited to take a ride on a flying fox, her virtue resides in her devotion to fundraising and charity, in contrast with Mrs. Gale, the stepmother of an Anzac, who uses her connection with him to exploit the sympathy of others to ensure that she 'waxed more happy and prosperous' than before the war.[42] The Calthrop girls, too – the Cub's sisters – are by way of contrast with Brigid somewhat frivolous young society women disconnected from the disciplines that should rightly have been imposed by the war. But the war ultimately brings about the reform of all so that they learn to see their duty, rather as it makes real men – vigorous in both their physique and their character – of boys.

For the men, service often leads to death, but the histories for children assured them that there was no more honourable death than in defence of one's country. Gallipoli acquired a special status where Australians, being 'outnumbered by two to one ... flung themselves into the impossible, and earned more by death there than by an easy victory elsewhere'.[43] Following Ashmead-Bartlett – indeed, sometimes merely reproducing his famous account of the landing – the children's histories present the Anzacs as 'cheerful fellows, who looked on the bright side of life even in the face of

---

40 Tanya Dalziell, *Settler Romances and the Australian Girl* (Crawley: University of Western Australia Press, 2004).
41 Bruce, *Jim and Wally*, 236.
42 Turner, *Captain Cub*, 88.
43 *The School Paper, Classes V and VI* (Queensland), April 1916, 38.

death'. For Buley, the charge at the Nek was a triumph of heroism 'because they knew they could not win' but still 'went out cheerfully to their death'.[44]

Yet the novels and histories do not treat the Anzacs only as heroes in the imperial tradition, for they are a particular kind of hero, an Australian hero, whose character has been formed by the conditions of Australian life. So Ethel Turner's The Cub, for all his wealth, joins the army as a private, advances quickly through the ranks to become an officer, and he has a best mate in a working-class lad named Harry Gale (or Galileo) – who also becomes an officer.[45] The Anzacs were in this way presented as classless and egalitarian, and the Australian Imperial Force as a meritocracy in which quality rose naturally to the top.[46] For Buley, the Anzacs were also 'daring and resourceful', 'steady and cool', and with a remarkable courage and endurance in adversity.[47] Like the war correspondent and official historian Charles Bean, Buley identified them with the bush, where they 'had been trained to do naturally things that, maybe, would never have occurred to an ordinary British soldier'.[48] Buley was an Australian working as a journalist in England who had discovered a lucrative trade in churning out popular books on the war, and one can sense his hesitation here in ascribing a superiority to Australian troops when compared with their British cousins.[49] Similarly, in commenting on the Suvla Bay landing, Buley was careful not to question the courage of British troops who failed to advance, instead merely suggesting that they were poorly led, being sent 'into a strange country in the dark'.[50] Unlike Anzacs, whose bush-bred skills meant that they were capable of marching through unknown country, the British could not be expected to go forward so readily. But that there was something special about the Anzacs almost every text could agree. 'Germany did not make very many mistakes', declared one account, 'but the ones that it did make were very big mistakes. The biggest mistake of all was to think that it had nothing to fear from

---

44 Buley, *Child's History*, 18, 160.
45 Turner, *Seven Little Billabongs*, 136, 148.
46 For an exploration of this theme, see Geoffrey Serle, 'The Digger Tradition and Australian Nationalism', *Meanjin Quarterly*, 24, no. 2 (1965): 148-58.
47 Buley, *Child's History*, 100, 104.
48 Buley, *Child's History*, 19.
49 John Lack, 'Buley, Ernest Charles (1869–1933)', Australian Dictionary of Biography, National Centre of Biography, Australian National University, http://adb.anu.edu.au/biography/buley-ernest-charles-12825/text23153, published first in hardcopy 2005, accessed online 26 March 2015. See also E.C. Buley, *Glorious Deeds of Australasians in the Great War* (London: Andrew Melrose, 1915).
50 Buley, *Child's History*, 137.

Australia'. This history then goes on to explain how the Australians led the allies to victory on the Western Front. Where British troops find themselves 'driven out', the Australians – whose 'well-won honour' it was 'to be chosen to lead in all the most difficult and most dangerous attacks' – staunchly and successfully resist the Germans.[51]

Importantly, the Gallipoli campaign was not fought in vain. Children's histories sometimes went to great lengths to set out the benefits that had arisen from a campaign that it was all too easy to see as having been bungled from the jump. Waterworth's history for Tasmanian children, for example, quoted a number of sources, such as Charles Rosenthal, the Australian officer, Arthur Mee, the British journalist and educator best known for his best-selling children's encyclopedia, and John Masefield, the English writer and later poet laureate, who were each able to discern strategic advantages having flowed to the allies from the campaign. Gallipoli had diverted the resources of the Central Powers, weakened the Turks in a manner that assisted the allies in later campaigns in Palestine, even possibly encouraged Italy to enter the war against Austria.[52] If such flights of the imagination were insufficient to persuade the young reader, Waterworth had more in store: he reproduced a poem by the Presbyterian minister, J.L Rentoul, which presented the Anzacs, rather implausibly, as liberators of the oppressed Armenians:

> Pale Armenia–freed at last,
> Outrage, tears, and tortures past,
> Woman's wail and maiden's cry
> Pleading to a ruthless sky! –
> Anzac lads, 'twas not in vain
> All your valour and your pain.[53]

The storming of the cliffs of Gallipoli was presented to the Australian young as an exemplary history – a story 'that must be placed among the imperishable glories of our race' – in a way that joins these early histories of Anzac for children to our own times. Waterworth argued in 1920:

> The Anzacs climbed and fought with dogged perserverance and indomitable courage; they won because they never dreamed of failure

---

51 Atkins, *Australia and the Great War*, 6, 10.
52 Waterworth, *Story of Anzac Day*, 54-5.
53 Waterworth, *Story of Anzac Day*, 63.

or surrender. They had determined to conquer or die. If you face your battle in that spirit you will conquer.[54]

Such sentiments do not belong to a dead past: the notion that the Anzacs exemplified a 'spirit' to be emulated in the present remains the central message in literature, songs and images still designed for Australian children. Indeed, it permeates the Anzac message delivered to the Australian people more generally, via their leading politicians, media and culture industries.[55]

* * *

Anzac children's literature has proliferated in recent years, and scholars interested in the reasons for, and nature of, the Anzac resurgence since the 1980s may well find a rich ore to be mined for this purpose in works designed to be read by young. The disjunctures and continuities with past young people's literature should be a major theme of such studies. Books for children about the war in the period from 1915 were designed to serve a propagandist purpose, but they also disclose with a notable clarity many of the historical meanings that contemporary society attached to the war. Children's histories, as a result of their didactic purpose, are probably more explicit about matters, such as the distinction between German 'liberty' and British liberty, taken for granted in propaganda designed for a general audience. We find many of the same themes in writing for children as in other kinds of wartime literature, history and journalism – including the prominence of the heroic theme, the evil of Imperial Germany, the valour and humanity of Ottoman troops, and perhaps above all, the effort to distinguish a particular distillation of British virtue in Anzac troops as well as in the women they left behind.

---

54   Waterworth, *Story of Anzac Day*, 55-6.
55   Tony Abbott, *Speech at the 2015 Dawn Service, Anzac Cove, Gallipoli* http://parlinfo.aph.gov.au/parlInfo/search/display/display.w3p;query=Id%3A%22media/pressrel/3798640%22

INDEX

@ABCNews1915 65, 71
#freshinourmemories 73–4

25 April (animated film) 62
57th Regiment Memorial 219
400 Plateau (Lone Pine) 210, 213
'1915' (McDonald) 115

Abbott, Tony 25, 30, 31
@ABCNews1915 65, 71
'Abdul' (Bean) 108
Abide monument 220
Adelaide, Anzac Day commemoration 227, 230–1
Afghanistan conflict
  Australian soldiers deployed in 50–1
  contestation and legitimation of 85
agency, historical consciousness and 73–4
Akçam, Taner 33
Albany, first dawn service 236
All Black ruby team, 1905/6 tour of England and Wales 183
Allen, L.H. 110
Alpers, O.T.J. 171, 177
Anafarta Ridge 16, 17
Anderson, Benedict 21
Andrejevic, Mark 72
Anne Frank: a history for today exhibition 164
anthropological archaeology 204
anti-conscription movement 110
Anzac Area
  archaeological survey 213–20
  artefacts 215–18
  dimensions 207, 208
  dugouts 215
  earthworks 215, 218–19
  food and drink containers 217–18
  key features of battlefield 215
  monuments 219
  reserved under treaties 207, 208
  trenches 215, 216–17, 219
  tunnels 215
Anzac BBC radio documentary 38, 39–46
The Anzac Book (Bean) 108
Anzac Centenary 100 Stories project 70–1
Anzac Centenary commemoration period 38
Anzac Commemorative Site 219
Anzac Cove, official naming 29
Anzac Cove and Gallipoli: Then and Now interactive 55

Anzac Day
  75th anniversary delegation to Gallipoli 30
  Adelaide's first procession 227
  dawn services 30, 235–7
  debates over commemorative practices 224–37
  first commemoration 227
  future of 237–8
  as holiday 233–4
  in New Zealand 233–4
  origin 224
  participation in marches 237–8
  Prime Ministers at Anzac Cove services 30
  religious services 227–30
  services in London 225–6
  Turkish representatives at ceremonies 28–9, 31
  Turkish-Australians participation in parades 31
'Anzac Day, Davenport' (Ireland) 115
Anzac Day Media Style Guide 39, 40, 43, 54
Anzac, the Landing 1915 (painting) (Lambert) 121–30, 209
Anzac landing
  Hedley Howe's account 123
  location of 15
  representation in Lambert's painting 123–7
  timing of 14
Anzac legend 25, 148
An Anzac Muster (Baylebridge) 109
Anzac myth 37–8, 108–9
'Anzac' (poem) (Brereton) 110
Anzac revival 28, 30
Anzac War Trail (Bowes) 241
AnzacLive project 66–9, 72, 83–4
archaeology
  anthropological archaeology 204–5
  battlefield archaeology 203–6
  conflict archaeology 205
  context of sites 214–15
  historical archaeology 206
  integrity of sites 215
  methodology 213–14
Archer, Stephen 179–80
Ari Burnu, renamed Anzac Cove 21, 29
Armenian genocide 2, 24, 26, 31–4, 245
Armenian Genocide Centenary National Commemoration Evening 33

– 251 –

Armitage, Simon 52
Army Service Corps 181
Arras, Battle of 198
art
  commemorative paintings 121
  history paintings 125–7
  narrative paintings 120
Ashmead-Bartlett, Ellis 125, 149, 241, 247
Aspinall-Oglander, C. 13
Assmann, Jan 85
Association of Returned Soldier and Sailors Club 235
Asya, Ari Nihat 63
Atatürk, Mustapha Kemal
  association with Turkish national days 223
  as first President of Turkey 25
  at Gallipoli 19, 25, 26, 101, 102
  messages about the Anzacs 27
  'speech' attributed to him 21, 26, 27–8, 30, 102
  in War of Independence 25, 102
Atkins, Charles 242
Auckland Mounted Rifles 173
Australia
  birth of the nation 20, 128
  national days 224
Australian Broadcasting Corporation (ABC) 65
Australian Historical Mission to Gallipoli 121, 123, 207–8
Australian Imperial Force 106
Australian national identity 22, 25, 104–5, 149
Australian soldiers, qualities 106–7, 108, 126
Australian war literature
  characteristics of Australian soliders 106–7, 108
  histories 91
  poetry from non-combatants 110
  representations of the 'enemy' 108–9
  since 1960s 91
  thematic richness 115
  works by veterans 109–10
Australian War Memorial, Canberra 65, 66, 73, 121, 122, 128, 148, 164, 165
Australian War Museum, Melbourne 123, 127, 146
Australian War Records Section 132, 139
authenticity 43
authenticity contract 72–4

Baby 700 210, 215
Bairnsfather, Bruce 137
Balkan alliance, chimerical nature of 17–18

battle iconography 135
Battle of Trafalgar 156–7
battlefield archaeology 203–6
battlefield souvenirs 210
battlescapes
  danger spots 137–8
  Daranelles 134–8
  emptiness of 132–5
  Flanders 136
  'promised land' 138
  responses by artists and photographers 151–2
Baxter, Archibald 90
Baylebridge, William 109
Bean, C.E.W.
  and Anzac myth 13, 108, 125
  on Armenian genocide 34
  and Australian Historical Mission to Gallipoli 121–2, 207
  on war photography 140–1
Beaumont, Joan 128
Beaumont-Hamel 196, 197, 200
Benson, George 151
Bereft (Womersley) 94
Berlant, Lauren 81
Berry, David M. 56
Bethune, Douglas 226
Bethune, Norman 226
Bevan-Brown, Annie 179
Bey, Major Zeki 207
Bir el Abd 174–5, 176, 178, 182
Bishop, Julie 32
Blood Swept Lands and Seas of Red art installation 154–6, 162, 163–4, 164
'Blue Puttees' 195, 200
Bowers, Mike 55
Bowes, Joseph 241
Bowker, Geoff 83, 84
bravery in battle
  and belief in a larger cause 176–8
  and defence of family 184
  explaining 186–7
  and male culture in New Zealand 182–4
  and support of primary group 178–82
Brereton, J. Le Gay 110
Brisbane, Anzac Day commemoration 229–30
Britain
  AIF farewell march, Anzac Day 1919 226
  Anzac Day service 1916 225–6
  commemoration of Gallipoli campaign 154
British forces, at Suvla Bay 16–17
British race patriotism 243

INDEX

The Broken Years: Australian Soldiers in the Great War (Gammage) 106
brotherly love 181–2
Brown, James 38
Bruce, Mary Grant 240, 241, 246
Buchanan, Herbert 207
Buley, E.C. 243–5, 248
Bulgarian army 18
Burton, Ormond 92, 112–13
bushman ideal 107
Butler, Jean Kelly 70

Cambrai, First Battle of 196, 198
Campbell, Alan J. 28
Campbell, Alec 37
Canada
  conscription 191
  First World War Centenary Strategy 201
Canadian Expeditionary Force (CEF) 140, 194, 196, 200
Çanakkale 1915 (film) 64
Çanakkale Martyrs' Memorial 29, 63–4
Canterbury Mounted Rifles 169, 171, 172–3, 174–5, 178, 179, 182
Canterbury Yeomanry Cavalry (CYC) 170, 171, 178
Captain Cub (Turner) 242, 246, 247
Caribou Hill 195, 198
Carroll, Tom 224–5
centenary commemorations, at Gallipoli 31–2
Central Powers 97
Chatham's Post 215
children's war literature
  on Anzacs 248–9
  on British Empire 243–4, 246
  on death; heroism and honour 247–8
  explanations for war 242–3
  on Gallipoli campaign 249–50
  on Germany 245–6, 248–9
  non-fiction versus fiction 240–1
  purpose 250
  on Turks 244–5
  violence and destruction of war 241–2
  on women's service 246–7
A Child's History of Anzac (Buley) 243–5
Christchurch Boys High School 171, 178–9
Christ's College 171, 179, 183
Christ's College Rifles 183
Chunuk Bair 16, 61–2, 91–3, 114–15
Churchill, Winston 13, 17–18, 19
cinematic devices, to create 'reality' 62
Clark, Anna 59, 80
Clendinnen, Inga 33, 70

collaborative story-telling 47
'Collateral Murder' video 49–50
collective memory 82, 85, 128
Colville, Quintin 158–9
Coming Rain (Daisley) 89
commemoration, blockage by commemoration 85
commemorative paintings 121
composite photographs 139, 140–3
conflict archaeology 205
Connelly, Captain 195
conscription
  in Canada 191
  and voluntary ethic 246
Corlett, Peter 78
Cotto, Basil 197
Courtney's Post 215
Courtrai, Battle of 198
Cramer, Janet 40
Crozier, Frank 151
Crusading at Anzac AD 1915 (Silas) 146
The Cub (Turner) 246, 248
cultural memory 128–9
Cummins, Paul 154
Curow, Allen 112

Dağlarca, Fazıl Hüsnü 103
Daisley, Stephen 89
Dardanelles
  failed Allied naval attack 14, 98, 99, 223
  naval battles in antiquity 212
Dart Center for Journalism and Trauma 54
Darwin, Anzac Day commemoration 227, 230
Davutoglu, Ahmet 31
De Groot, Jerome 71
Dead Man's Patch 145
Deleuze, Gilles 136
Dennis, C.J. 107
Department of Veterans Affairs 73
'dialogical memorialization' 29
diplomacy, role of commemoration 22
Distinguished Conduct Medal (DCM)
  recipients 173, 195
Dominion Museum, Wellington 61–2
Donaldson, Mark 51
'Dua'/Prayer (Asya) 63
dugouts 215
Duhig, James 229
DurDe (Say Stop to Racism and Nationalism) 33

editorial control 42–3
Ellison, Tom 183

– 253 –

empathetic connection to the past 61, 69–70, 79
The End of the Great Day (Silas) 143
The Epic of Gallipoli (poetry) (Dağlarca) 103
Erdoğan, Recep Tayyip 26, 32, 63, 64
Erickson, Edward 22
Ersoy, Mehmet Akif 99–100
ethically responsible journalism 54
ethnographic journalism 40, 42
exhibitions 60–1

Facebook 63, 66, 67
Falklands War 84
family history, links to Gallipoli 58
Farrer, Reginald 134
Faulkner, Andrew 46
Ferguson, Niall 185
57th Regiment Memorial 219
Finkel, David 48–50
First Ridge 208
First World War
  emergence of commemoration 84–5
  transnational analysis 22–3
Fitzsimmons, Peter 91
Floridi, Luciano 80
food and drink containers 217–18
Forestry Corps 196
Forgotten Fighters exhibition 158
Forster, E.M. 92
400 Plateau (Lone Pine) 210, 213
Francis, *Pope* 33
#freshinourmemories 73–4
friendly fire 15, 115
Fuller, J.G. 186

Gallipoli: The Scale of Our War exhibition 60–1
Gallipoli campaign
  futility of 19
  purpose 17–19
  symbolic importance 9, 20, 22, 25, 102, 128, 223
Gallipoli Evening (Murphy) 150–1
Gallipoli (film) (Weir) 69, 91
Gallipoli peninsula
  archaeological record 212–13
  historical contestation over 211–12
  landscape 208, 208–11
  war cemeteries 207
  war memorials 199
  see also Anzac Area
Gallipoli Peninsula Historical National Park 198–9, 209
'Gallipoli' (poem) (Allen) 110

'Gallipoli' (poem) (Gilmore) 110
Gallipoli (poetry collection) (Pepeyi) 102–3
Gammage, Bill 69, 106
Garland, David 229–30
Gellert, Leon 109
George V, King 225–6, 231
German army 18, 19
Gerster, Robin 108, 240
Getty Images 55
Ghurkas 16
Gifkins, Michael 89–90
Gillard, Julia 30, 31
Gilmore, Mary 110
Göçek, Fatma Müge 33
The Good Soldiers (Finkel) 49
Gopnik, Adam 156, 164
Great War, centenary of outbreak 153
Great War Exhibition 61–2
Great War Veterans' Association, Newfoundland 197
Greco-Persian Wars 212
Greek army 18
Green, Charles 149
Greene, Sgt W.M. 195
group narration 42
Guattari, Felix 136
Gueudecourt 196

Halbwachs, Maurice 82
Hamilton, General Sir Ian 126, 172
Hamilton, John 38
Hanmer, Tony 179–80, 182
Harney, Bill 227
Harper, Agnes 171, 184–5
Harper, Edmund 183–4
Harper, Eric 182, 183
Harper, George 171, 184
Harper, Gordon 168–87
Harper, Leonard 184
Harper, Philip 181
Harper, Robin 168–87
Hawke, Bob 30
Hawksley, Rozanne 159–60
Hell Spit 215
Hemingway, Ernest 91
Hess, Aaron 75–6
Heyward, Michael 89
Hill 10 198
Hill 10 cemetery 200–1
Hill 60 172–3, 176
Hill 971 16
Hill, Brian 52
Hill Q 15
historical archaeology 206

INDEX

historical avatars 66–9
historical consciousness 59, 71–4
historical distance, collapse of 80
history
  blurring with memory 57
  consumption and production of 58–9
  critical engagement with the past 80–1
  intersection with memory 41–2
  learned history 83
  lived history 82, 83
history paintings 125–7
Hobart, Anzac Day commemoration 231, 231–2
Hockey, Joe 33
Hogue, Oliver 108
Holly Ridge 215, 217
Holocaust 57, 84
Holocaust survivors 164
Home and Away, Anzac Special 77–8
'Honouring the Dead – The Wall' 162, 167
Hoskins, Andrew 57, 58, 63
Howard, John 30
Howe, Hedley 123, 124
Hughes, Billy 128, 225, 226
Hurley, Frank 120, 132, 138–43, 151
Hyde, Robin 90, 113
Hynes, Private E. 195
Hynes, Samuel 127–8

İğdemir, Uluğ 27, 28
immersive journalism 41, 54
imperial allegiance in Australia 105–6
Imperial War Graves Commission (IWGC) 197, 207
Imperial War Museum, London 149, 153, 160
Inglis, Ken 25, 227
Instagram 66, 67
Inuit soldiers 192
Iraq War 85
Ireland, Kevin 115

Jackson, Peter 61–2
Jim and Wally (Bruce) 241, 246
Johnson, David 76
Johnston's Jolly 211, 215
Joint Historical and Archaeological Survey (JHAS) 207–8, 213–20
Jones, David 135
Jones, Jonathan 155, 157, 161, 164
Justice and Development Party (Adalet ve Kalkinma Partisi, AKP) 26

Kabatepe Ari Burnu Beach Memorial 21, 29
Kant, Vedica 26

Kardashian, Kim 33
Kaya, Şükrü 27, 28
Kemalism 26
Kemalyeri 210
Kenderdine, Sarah 60
Kent, David 108
King, Arlene 192
King, John 31
Knife Edge 217
Korean War 28, 29
Korku Dere (Valley of Horror) 210

Lambert, George 121–3, 125, 126–7, 129, 148, 151, 207, 209
Lancashire Landing Commonwealth Cemeteries 198
landscape memorialisation
  battlefield souvenirs 210
  exchange of flora 210–11
  importance 209
  toponyms 210
larrikins 107
Lawrence, Sgt Cyril 209, 210, 211, 213
Lawson, Henry 105, 106–7
Le Transloy, Battle of 198
learned history 83
Lee, John A. 90
Lees, Justin 67
Lewis, Wyndham 134
lieux de mémoire 23–4
literature *see* Australian war literature; New Zealand war literature; Turkish war literature
lived history 82, 83
local history boom 58
Lone Pine 210, 215, 219
The Long Way Home 52
long-form journalism 46, 48, 50, 54
Loughnan, Robert 177
Luxford, J.H. 175

McDevitt, Michael 40
McDonald, Roger 115
McDowell, Keith 210
McInniş, Lt Ronald 217
McKay, James 229
McKenna, Mark 80
McKernan, Michael 165, 167, 225
McLelland, H.D. 245
Macleod, Jenny 24
male culture, in New Zealand 182–3
Malone, Colonel William George 92–3, 115
Malone's Terraces 218
Manne, Robert 24

Maori Pah 218
Maritime Greenwich World Heritage Site
    156
Marshall, S.L.A. 178
Mascall-Dare, Sharon 37, 38, 39–46, 47
Masefield, John 123, 249
Massey, William 233
Masters, Chris 50–1
Matthews, Harvey 109
media, role in commemoration 82–4
media coverage of Anzac Day
    ethical responsibility 38
    ethically responsible journalism 54
    formulaic coverage and clichés 38
    framework for 38–46
media organisations, recreation of Gallipoli
    events 64–5
mediality 83
Mee, Arthur 249
Melbourne, Anzac Day commemoration 227, 231
Melbourne Museum 165–7
memorial diplomacy 22, 28–34
memory
    blurring with history 58
    disruption by ICT 80
    fallibility of 53
    future of 85
    intersection with history 41–2
memory booms 57, 84
Mesopotamian campaign 19
Military Cross recipients 195
military life 51
minesweepers 14
Monash, General Sir John 208–9, 210, 225
Monash University, Anzac Centenary 100
    Stories project 70–1
Monash Valley 210
Monchy-le-Preux 196, 198
The Moods of Ginger Mick (Dennis) 107
Moore-Jones, Horace 148
Mori, Mashahiro 78
Mosse, George 21
Murdoch, Keith 154
Murphy, Idris 150–1
Museum of Australian Democracy 65
museum exhibitions 60–2
Museum of New Zealand Te Papa Tongarewa
    60
museums, representation of war, memory and
    commemoration 156–67
myths of Gallipoli campaign
    actions of British force 16–17
    location of Anzac landing 15

lost opportunities 15–16
naval attack on Dardanelles 14
propagation of 13
purpose of operation 17–19
timing of military campaign 14

Nangle, Lt-Col Father Thomas 197, 198, 200
narrative paintings 120
Nash, Paul 134, 144, 151
nation building, and commemoration of death
    in war 22
National Army Museum, UK 154
National Library of Australia 65
National Maritime Museum, Greenwich
    154, 156
National Museum of American History 162
National War Memorial, St Johns 197
NATO alliance 29
The Nek 218
Nelson, Admiral 156–7
Neuhaus, Susan 46, 47, 48
new memory 82
New South Wales, Anzac Day
    commemoration 232–3
New Zealand
    Anzac Day commemorative practices
        233–4
    colonial history 111
    Imperial allegiance 176–8
    literary nationalism 111–12
    male culture 182–3
    national days 224
    visit by Duke and Duchess of Cornwall
        177
New Zealand Expeditionary Force
    at Chunuk Bair 16, 61–2, 91–3, 114–15
    training in Cairo 171–2
New Zealand soldiers, qualities of 182–3
New Zealand war literature
    Daisley's *Traitor* 89–95
    early silence 111–12
    views of the opponent 113–14
Newfoundland and Labrador
    as British Dominion 194–5
    commemoration of RNR's achievements
        191, 197–8
    involvement in First World World 195–6
    as member of Canadian confederation 200
    public debt following war 199
Newfoundland Regiment *see* Royal
    Newfoundland Regiment (RNR)
News Corp Australia 65, 66, 67, 83
newsworthiness, accuracy and 48

INDEX

Niall, Brenda 240
9/11 Museum and Memorial 164
'1915' (McDonald) 115
No Man's Land 134, 135–6, 137–8
Nolan, Sidney 148–51
Nora, Pierre 23
The Not Dead documentary film (Channel Four, UK) 51–3
Not for Glory (Neuhaus & Mascall-Dare) 46–8

Official War Artists 143
O'Loughlin, Ben 58, 63, 64
On Chunuk Bair (play) (Shadbolt) 91–2, 114–15
The One Day of the Year (Seymour) 115
Önen, Yekta Ragıp 27
ordnance, remains of 216
Otago Mounted Rifles 172–3
Ottoman army 96, 97
Ottoman culture 25
Ottoman Empire 25, 34

Pale Armistice: in Death only are we United (Hawksley) 160
Palestinian campaign 19
Pamuk, Orhan 33
participatory audience 71–2
Pasha, Brigadier General Mehmet Sevki 216
Passport to Hell (Hyde) 113
Patriotic Association, Newfoundland 197
Peloponnesian war 212
Pepeyi, Haluk Nihat 102–3
Perry Miniatures 61
Perth, Anzac Day commemoration 231
Petre, Jack 178
photography *see* war photography
Pierce, Peter 107
Piper, Tom 154, 156
Pooley, Leanne 62
Pope's Hill 143
post-traumatic stress disorder 38, 48, 51–3, 69
postdigital era 56
postdigital world, media, memory and history 57–60
Powerhouse Museum, Sydney 164
Powles, Guy 174
The Price of Freedom: Americans at War exhibition 162
Prior, Robin 126
prosthetic architectures 60

Queensland, Anzac Day commemoration 230
Quercus calliprinos (Gallipoli holly-oak) 210
Quinn's Post 215

'real time' narratives 65
Reality TV 72
reconnaissance photography 133
recreations of Gallipoli
  by media organisations 64–5
  exhibitions in New Zealand 60–2
  filmed reenactments in Turkey 62–4
religious faith 185–6
Remembrance Day 154
Rentoul, J.L. 249
Republic of Turkey *see* Turkey
Returned Services' Association (RSA) 233–4, 237
Returned Services League (RSL), membership 227
Roberts-Smith, Ben 51
Roman ceramics 213
Rosenthal, Charles 249
Royal Australian Army Medical Corps, women's contributions to 46–8
Royal Botanic Gardens, Melbourne 210
Royal Museums Greenwich (RMG) 154, 156
Royal Naval Reserve Forces 196
Royal Navy Museum, Portsmouth 153, 154
Royal Newfoundland Regiment (RNR)
  actions at Gallipoli 192, 195–6
  actions on Western Front 196
  commemoration of Western Front actions 193, 196, 197–8
  contributions to war efforts 191–2
  First Five Hundred 195
  lack of memorial honouring Gallipoli service 193–4, 198–201
  need for acknowledgement of Gallipoli service 202
Rumania 19
Rumanian army 18
Runia, Eelco 84
Rüsen, Jörn 59
Russell, Andrew 172
Ryan, Tommy 229

Sailly-Saillisel 196
Sandakan Death Marches 78
Sargsyan, Serzh 32
Sari Bair Ridge 15–16
School Paper (Victoria) 241, 244, 246
Schumann, Adam 48
Second Ridge 208, 215
Seddon, Richard 182
selfies, and social remembering 74–8
Serbian army 18
Seymour, Alan 115
Shadbolt, Maurice 91–2, 114

– 257 –

Shanks, Michael 60
Shiwak, Lance Corporal John 192
Shrapnel Valley 210
Shrine of Remembrance reserve, Melbourne 210
Silas, Ellis 68–9, 143–7, 151–2
silence, history and 24, 34
The Silent Division (Burton) 112–13
Silt Spur 215
Sinai campaign 174–6
Sing, Billy 43
Sivan, Emmanuel 41
sketching for reconnaissance purposes 137
smartphones 75, 77
Smith, Benjamin 210
social contracts 72–4
social media
  authenticity contract 72–4
  and historical avatars 66
  infiltration by mainstream media 64–5
  logics of personalization and spreadability 64
  in Turkey 62–4
social memory 128
social remembering, selfies and 74–8
sociotechnical commemoration 84
Somme, Battle of the 198
'The Song of the Dardanelles' (Lawson) 106
Songs of a Campaign (Gellert) 109
South African War 182, 183
souvenirs, from battlefield 210
State Library of NSW 66
Stephens, Tony 37
Stopford, General 16–17
The Story of Anzac (Bean) 217
subjectivity 42
suicide by veterans 48, 49
Surprise Gully 210
Sutton Turner, C.E. 242, 246
Suvla Bay 16–17
Sydney, Anzac Day commemoration 227, 231, 232, 235–6
syphilis 184

Tasmania, Anzac Day commemoration 231–2
Taylor, Richard 61
Templar, D. 173
10th Irish Division memorial 199
Thank You for Your Service (Finkel) 48–50
'then and now' montages 55–6
Third Ridge 208
Thynne, A.J. 229
Toowoomba, first dawn service 235
toponyms 133, 210

Tout-Smith, Deborah 166
Tower of London, art installation 154–6
Trail of the Caribou 192, 197–8, 201
Traitor (Daisley) 89–95
Treaty of Lausanne 207
Treaty of Sèvres 25, 207
trench warfare 135–6, 208
Triolo, Rosalie 241, 246
Trooper Bluegum at the Dardanelles (Hogue) 108–9
Troy 148, 212
Tuncoku, Prof Dr Mete 224
Turkey
  birth of nation 19, 25, 102
  celebration of victory over Allied fleet in Dardanelles 223–4
  commemoration of Great War 223
  denial of Armenian genocide 24, 26, 31–2, 33, 34
  distancing from Ottoman heritage 101
  founding tenets of republic 101
  history of republic 25–6
  memory of Gallipoli in public life 30
  Republic Day 223
Turkish government, attitude to social media 62–3
Turkish Historical Society 25–6, 27–8
Turkish Human Rights Association IHD 33
Turkish national identity 22, 25, 97–101
Turkish nationalist movement 101
Turkish war literature
  absence of voice of combatants 104, 116
  patriotic poetry 98–101, 104
  perceptions about Australians 100, 102–3, 104, 105, 106, 116
  representations of the enemy 98–101, 102–4, 108, 116
Turner, Ethel 240, 242, 246, 247
25 April (animated film) 62
Twitter 62–3, 64, 65, 67
'Two Brothers' (Matthews) 109–10

Ülken, Hilmi Ziya 103
'uncanny valley' 78–9, 82
Uncommon Soldier (Masters) 50–1
Üngör, Uğur 33
United States, veterans of wars in Iraq and Afghanistan 48–50
Uyar, Mesut 22

Veyssière, Laurent 201
Victoria Cross recipients 51
video re-enactment of Çanakkale battles, produced by Turkish government 63–4

Vietnam Veterans Memorial, Washington 162–3
Vietnam War 69, 84
Vimy Ridge, Battle of 201
Voices of Gallipoli (Shadbolt) 91–2
Volkmer, Ingrid 83

Waite, Fred 172
Walker, Arthur 46
War + Memory art installation 159–60, 162, 165
War Artists at Sea exhibition 158
war cemeteries, Gallipoli peninsula 207
war commemoration, changing character in postdigital age 56–7
war ecology 85
War of Independence 25, 102
war memorials, on Gallipoli peninsula 199
war photography
  challenges of 131–2, 140
  composite photographs 139, 140–3
  and emptiness of battlescapes 132–3
  as misleading or fake 120
  reconnaissance photography 133
war reporting, advice for journalists 54
Waterworth, Alfred G. 242–3, 249–50
Webster, Laura 149
Weir, Becca 133
Weir, Peter 91
Western Front 19
  photographs by Hurley 139–43
Westminster Abbey 154
Weta Workshop 60–1
White, Patrick 94
Whitman, Walt 89
Wilkins, Hubert 121, 122, 139, 207
Wilkins, Lola 148
Wilkinson, Frank 70–1
Williamson, J.C. 232
Winter, Caroline 128
Winter, Jay 24, 41, 57, 84, 119
Winter-Cooke, Capt. William Lempriere 210
witnessing 70
Womersley, Chris 94
Woolworths 73–4
WW1: Love & sorrow exhibition 165–7

Yelich, Lynne 200
Yeo, William 228
The Young Australias' ABC of War 242
YouTube 63
Yurdakul, Mehmet Emin 99